THE SUBJECT
OF
TRAGEDY

Identity and difference
in Renaissance drama

Catherine Belsey

METHUEN: London and New York

First published in 1985 by
Methuen & Co. Ltd
11 New Fetter Lane, London EC4P 4EE

Published in the USA by
Methuen & Co.
in association with Methuen, Inc.
29 West 35th Street, New York, NY 10001

© 1985 Catherine Belsey

Filmset by Northumberland Press Ltd
Gateshead, Tyne and Wear
Printed in Great Britain by
Richard Clay (The Chaucer Press) Ltd
Bungay, Suffolk

British Library Cataloguing in Publication Data
Belsey, Catherine
The subject of tragedy.
1. English drama – Early modern and Elizabethan,
1500–1600 – History and criticism   2. English
drama – 17th century – History and criticism
I. Title
822'.3'09   PR651

ISBN 0 416 32700 1
0 416 32710 9 Pbk

Library of Congress Cataloging in Publication Data
Belsey, Catherine.
The subject of tragedy.
Bibliography: p.
Includes index.
1. English drama – Early modern and Elizabethan,
1500–1600 – History and criticism.   2. Sex role in
literature.   3. English drama – 17th century – History
and criticism.   4. English drama (Tragedy) – History
and criticism.   I. Title.
PR658.S42B45   1985   822'.009'355   85–15230

ISBN 0 416 32700 1
0 416 32710 9 (pbk.)

To Andrew,
who has lived through the whole of this
and is inscribed in all of it

CONTENTS

PREFACE

This book has three main aims. The first is to contribute to the construction of a history of the subject in the sixteenth and seventeenth centuries. The human subject, the self, is the central figure in the drama which is liberal humanism, the consensual orthodoxy of the west. The subject is to be found at the heart of our political institutions, the economic system and the family, voting, exercising rights, working, consuming, falling in love, marrying and becoming a parent. And yet the subject has conventionally no history, perhaps because liberal humanism depends on the belief that in its essence the subject does not change, that liberal humanism itself expresses a human nature which, despite its diversity, is always at the most basic, the most intimate level, the same. I do not share this belief or the conservatism it implies.

The second aim is to demonstrate, by placing woman side by side with man, that at the moment when the modern subject was in the process of construction, the 'common-gender noun' largely failed to include women in the range of its meanings. Man is the subject of liberal humanism. Woman has meaning in relation to man. And yet the instability which is the result of this asymmetry is the ground of protest, resistance, feminism. The history of women since the seventeenth century has been the history of a struggle to secure for woman the rights and benefits man has awarded himself.

At a more fundamental level it is also the history of an effort to redefine the terms of liberal humanism itself, to challenge the meanings and values which give rise to the asymmetry.

Thirdly, I have tried to bring together history and literature (or fiction, since 'literature' implies a value judgement which is irrelevant to my argument). It is true that historians frequently dip into fiction in quest of evidence, and that literary critics often feel it necessary to take account of the background to the text. But the relationship I propose between fiction and history is not one of foreground and background, text and context. The project is to construct a history of the meanings which delimit at a specific moment what it is possible to say, to understand, and consequently to be. People make history under determinate conditions. One of these conditions is subjectivity itself, and this is in turn an effect of discourse. To be a subject is to be able to speak, to give meaning. But the range of meanings it is possible to give at a particular historical moment is determined outside the subject. The subject is not the origin of meanings, not even the meanings of subjectivity itself. Fiction, especially in the period from the sixteenth century to the present, is about what it is to be a subject – in the process of making decisions, taking action, falling in love, being a parent.... Fictional texts also address themselves to readers or audiences, offering them specific subject-positions from which the texts most readily make sense. In that it both defines subjectivity and addresses the subject, fiction is a primary location of the production of meanings of and for the subject. The fiction of the past, intelligible in its period to the extent that it participates in the meanings in circulation in that period, constitutes, therefore, a starting-point for the construction of a history of the subject.

In quoting texts from the past I have modernized the typography but reproduced the spelling given in my source. Abbreviated references are provided in the text, and full details of the editions cited are supplied in the bibliography. Plays are identified by their titles, and all other works by their authors or editors.

Chapter 5, 'Alice Arden's crime', is a revised version of an essay which first appeared in *Renaissance Drama* 13 in 1982. It is reproduced by permission of Northwestern University Press. I have also drawn on the following earlier publications: 'Shakespeare's "vaulting ambition"', *English Language Notes* 10, 1973:198–201; 'The stage plan of *The Castle of Perseverance*', *Theatre Notebook* 28, 1974:124–32; 'Tragedy, justice and the subject', *1642: Literature and Power in the Seventeenth Century*, ed. Francis Barker *et al.*, Colchester, University of Essex, 1981:166–86; and 'Literature, history, politics', *Literature and History* 9, 1983:17–27.

The wisdom and scholarship of G. K. Hunter first stimulated my interest in the drama of the sixteenth and seventeenth centuries when he supervised my research at the University of Warwick. He is not to blame for the consequences. In the course of writing the book I have incurred debts to Paul Atkinson, Simon Barker, Ying Chang, Martin Coyle, Tom Dawkes, Terry Hawkes, Margot Heinemann, Ludmilla Jordanova, Valerie Lucas, Kate McLuskie and Robin Moffet. I am grateful to them for their help. In addition, I have discussed much of the material with Francis Barker. Antony Easthope made valuable comments on Chapter 2. I owe Felbrigg to Peter Hulme. Andrew Belsey, Jonathan Dollimore, Terry Eagleton and Chris Weedon read the manuscript. Their incisive criticisms have made a world of difference.

I
INTRODUCTION: READING THE PAST

History is always in practice a reading of the past. We make a narrative out of the available 'documents', the written texts (and maps and buildings and suits of armour) we interpret in order to produce a knowledge of a world which is no longer present. And yet it is always from the present that we produce this knowledge: from the present in the sense that it is only from what is still extant, still available, that we make it; and from the present in the sense that we make it out of an understanding formed by the present. We bring what we know now to bear on what remains from the past to produce an intelligible history.

Criticism is always in practice a reading of texts. *Hamlet* does not 'speak for itself'. Dr Johnson's *Hamlet* and Coleridge's, Bradley's and Ernest Jones's, are all different, produced, like history, by bringing to bear on the extant material the knowledges available at different moments, with the effect of producing a range of interpretations. In the case of *Hamlet* the 'document', the written text, is not one but several, the effects of editorial accretions on the basis of three distinct Jacobean versions, each new edition the result of assumptions about what 'makes sense', historically, as a tragedy, as a play by Shakespeare, as *Hamlet*. But this is only the beginning of the problem. Even if there were a pristine *Hamlet*, an *authorized* version direct from the pen of Shakespeare, we should still have no choice but to read it from the present, to produce for it a meaning intelligible from our own place in history.

To read the past, to read a text from the past, is thus always to make an interpretation which is in a sense an anachronism. Time travel is a fantasy. We cannot reproduce the conditions – the economy, the diseases, the manners, the language and the corresponding subjectivity – of another century. To do so would be, in any case, to eliminate the difference which makes the fantasy pleasurable: it would be to erase the recollection of the present, to cease to be, precisely, a traveller. Reading the past depends on this difference. The real anachronism, then, is of another kind. Here history as time travel gives way to history as costume drama, the reconstruction of the past as the present in fancy dress. The project is to explain away the surface strangeness of another century in order to release its profound continuity with the present. The past is read as – and for – evidence that change is always only superficial, that human nature, what it is to be a person, a man or a woman, a wife or a husband, is palpably unchanging. This history militates against radical commitment by denying the possibility of change.

The visitor to Felbrigg Hall in Norfolk considering the exterior of the house from the south-west is able to identify the articulation of two quite distinct moments. Only fifty years divides the west wing chronologically from the south front, and yet that the two are held physically together seems a triumph of mortar over probability. The west wing, designed in the 1670s and completed during the course of the next decade or so, belongs eminently to the modern world. The facade is of warm red brick, with three symmetrical bays, the middle one projecting very slightly, so that the effect is of a single but differentiated plane. The two storeys, with regularly positioned long, slender windows, are surmounted by a hipped roof with a row of dormer windows. The emphasis is on proportion and elegance, and decoration is modestly confined to the moulded pediments above the two doorways on the ground floor. The west wing is harmonious, familiar, intelligible, a sympathetic object of the twentieth-century gaze. The south end of the facade, however, is joined uneasily to the Jacobean building of the 1620s. The western aspect therefore includes, beyond the symmetry of the mellow brick building, a single bay faced with a mixture of stone, flint and brick. The predominant colour is grey. The windows have small leaded panes. Above the bay is a triple chimney-stack and an extravagant Flemish gable adorned by a stone lion. The south front consists of seven bays, alternately one projecting and two deeply recessed. The porch, a triumphal arch with elaborate Doric columns, heavy, ornate capitals and carved heraldry, lays ostentatious claim to magnificence and to dynasty. Above the south front is a tall parapet, and here in the projecting bays, and thus separated by considerable distances, is carved in large, three-dimensional stone letters, cut out against the sky, the message, GLORIA ... DEO IN ... EXCELSIS.

The south front is neither modern nor sympathetic. The familiar Victorian imitations of Jacobean domestic architecture tended to smooth away such excesses of ornamentation, and such overt assertions of authority, divine and genealogical, with the effect of reducing its strangeness. But Jacobean Felbrigg makes no effort to subdue its own self-display or to bring the details of its decoration into harmony with classical proportion. It does not, in other words, submit to the gaze, and by doing so offer to pacify the spectator. The manner of the south front at Felbrigg is insistent and imperative. It seeks obedience rather than consent.

Not that Felbrigg Hall belongs to the repressive apparatus. There are no traces here of the fortification characteristic of the late middle ages – no vestigial moat, gatehouse or corner turrets. Felbrigg is clearly and decisively domestic. But it is not private. Unlike the country houses of the eighteenth century, the Hall was designed in the 1620s to be seen from

3

the outside. But the meanings it makes visible are hard to read in the twentieth century because they participate in a signifying practice different from our own. Jacobean Felbrigg is strange because it is the signifier of a set of meanings which are now unfamiliar. It indicates an understanding of the family and its social and personal relations which no longer obtains. The south front asks, therefore, to be read in its difference from the west wing. That difference – of signification, meaning, knowledge, and of the corresponding order of subjectivity they produce – a difference of architectural style which is also ultimately a difference at the heart of what it is to be a person, is the material of a history of change.

This book takes as its starting-point not architecture but plays. The project, however, is to identify a similar discontinuity of meanings and knowledges, to chart in the drama of the sixteenth and seventeenth centuries the eventual construction of an order of subjectivity which is recognizably modern. The assumption I make is that fiction, like architecture and painting, is a signifying practice which can be understood in its period to the extent that it shares the meanings then in circulation. This is quite distinct from the claim that fiction reflects the practices of its period. That the plays of the early seventeenth century almost without exception condemn enforced marriage does not imply that in the early seventeenth century no parents compelled their children to marry against their will. But the debates about enforced marriage, both on the stage and off it, reveal the meaning and the contests for the meaning of marriage in the period. And their differential allocations of autonomy to the children correspondingly reveal differences of meaning for masculine and feminine freedom of choice.

The project is not, then, a social history of the period, but a (sketch-) map of a discursive field. Questions concerning the number of couples who married without their parents' consent (or the spread of literacy in the period, or the economic alliances of the 1640s), though important and interesting, are not the primary questions addressed here. Fictional texts do not necessarily mirror the practices prevalent in a social body, but they are a rich repository of the meanings its members understand and contest. And in order to be intelligible at all, fiction necessarily ascribes certain meanings, however plural and contradictory, to subjectivity and to gender. It therefore constitutes a possible place from which to begin an analysis of what it means to be a person, a man or a woman, at a specific historical moment.

That is not to claim, of course, that we can recover from fiction or anywhere else the experience of being a man or a woman in another period. Writing is not the transcription of something anterior to itself, a recoverable presence, 'how it felt'. Meanings are not the record of experience, though they may define the conditions of its possibility. On the assumption that meanings are first learned, rather than experienced or felt, the meanings in circulation at a given moment specify the limits of what can be said and understood. The range of ways of understanding what it is to be a person is given in signifying practice.

Neither social history, nor the history of experience, this book is offered, none the less, as more than a history of ideas. The destination of meaning is the subject. To be a subject is to have access to signifying practice, to identify with the 'I' of utterance and the 'I' who speaks. The subject is held in place in a specific discourse, a specific knowledge, by the meanings available there. In so far as signifying practice always precedes the individual, is always learned, the subject is a subjected being, an effect of the meanings it seems to possess. Subjectivity is discursively produced and is constrained by the range of subject-positions defined by the discourses in which the concrete individual participates. Utterance – and action – outside the range of meanings in circulation in a society is psychotic. In this sense existing discourses determine not only what can be said and understood, but the nature of subjectivity itself, what it is possible to be. Subjects as agents act in accordance with what they are, 'work by themselves' to produce and reproduce the social formation of which they are a product.

Or to challenge it. Signifying practice is never static, and meanings are neither single nor fixed. Meaning is perpetually deferred by its existence as difference within a specific discourse; it is perpetually displaced by the trace of alterity within the identity which is no more than an effect of difference. A specific discourse is always embattled, forever defending the limits of what is admissible, legitimate or intelligible, attempting to arrest the play of meaning as it slides towards plurality. Alternative discourses propose alternative knowledges, alternative meanings. For these reasons, signifying practice is also the location of resistances. Since meaning is plural, to be able to speak is to be able to take part in the contest for meaning which issues in the production of new subject-positions, new determinations of what it is possible to be.

In this sense signifying practice is not outside the material struggles taking place in a social formation. And fiction, as a location of meanings and contests for meaning, is itself a political practice. Fiction defines and redefines the subject, problematizes the areas of subjectivity which seem most natural, most inevitable, most evidently given. It also addresses the subject. A specific text proffers a specific subject-position from which it is most readily intelligible. It offers to pacify or to disrupt, to impel or to enlist, constructing (and naturalizing) a place for the subject in the process.

Despotic regimes have always recognized, though in rather different terms, the close relationship between fiction and politics, and have subjected works of art to detailed censorship. The Tudor monarchs took drama under increasingly central control from the mid-sixteenth century onwards. The elaborate system developed in the period of licensing plays and players is indicative of the government's concern with the political implications of drama. The Stuarts extended royal control by converting the prominent London companies into servants of members of the royal family. Meanwhile, the jurisdiction of the Revels Office gradually increased. By the seventeenth century the Master of the Revels was responsible for ensuring that no seditious matter was presented on the stage. He was empowered to require the alteration of single words, passages or whole scenes, or to suppress plays in their entirety. Texts were changed, and playwrights were imprisoned. Liberal humanism, by contrast, locates drama either above the level of politics (as art) or below it (as mere entertainment). Although sexual censorship continued into the 1960s, liberal democracy tends to refer questions of political censorship to reviewers, who largely 'work by themselves' to protect orthodoxy by condemning what is radical as bad art (or boring), often without mentioning politics at all.

I use the term 'liberal humanism' to denote the ruling assumptions, values and meanings of the modern epoch. Liberal humanism, laying claim to be both natural and universal, was produced in the interests of the bourgeois class which came to power in the second half of the seventeenth century. There are, of course, dangers in collapsing the historical specificities and the ideological differences of three centuries into a single term. Liberal humanism is not an unchanging, homogeneous, unified essence, and the development, often contradictory, of the discourses and institutions which sustain it, deserves detailed analysis. But there are alternative dangers in a specificity which never risks generalization. We may point to large differences as well as small ones, woods as well as trees, epochs as well as decades. To find in Locke, for instance (as we do not, say, in Hooker) a liberalism and a humanism which still recognizably constitute elements of twentieth-century common sense is not to deny the importance of the specific location of Locke's texts in the 1690s on the one hand, or the subsequent and continuing debates and divisions within liberal humanism on the other.

Indeed, the rise of the New Right could be held to obviate the need for a critical analysis of liberal humanism itself. The time may come, it might be argued, when we shall look back with nostalgia to the liberal-humanist present. But liberal humanism, which in another sense of both those plural terms is often neither liberal nor humanist, is a contradictory phenomenon. While it is true that major reforms have been made in its name, it also provides the framework for a market economy, defended by a powerful police force, and a naturalization of inequality both in the state and in the family which is profoundly authoritarian. There is a sense in which John Stuart Mill and F. A. Hayek, at opposite ends of a continuum, share a discourse. It is a discourse which excludes both Marxism and post-structuralism.

The common feature of liberal humanism, justifying the use of the single phrase, is a commitment to *man*, whose essence is *freedom*. Liberal humanism proposes that the subject is the free, unconstrained author of meaning and action, the origin of history. Unified, knowing and autonomous, the human being seeks a political system which guarantees freedom of choice. Western liberal democracy, it claims, freely chosen, and thus evidently the unconstrained expression of human nature, was born in the seventeenth century with the emergence of the individual and the victory of constitutional-ism in the consecutive English revolutions of the 1640s and 1688. But in the century since these views were established as self-evident, doubts have arisen concerning this reading of the past as the triumphant march of progress towards the moment when history levels off into the present. And from the new perspectives which have given rise to these doubts, both liberal humanism and the subject it produces appear to be an effect of a continuing history, rather than its culmination. The individual, it now seems, was not released at last from the heads of people who had waited only for the peace and leisure to cultivate what lay ineluctably within them and within all of us. On the contrary, the liberal-humanist subject, the product of a specific epoch and a specific class, was constructed in conflict and in contradiction – with conflicting and contradictory consequences.

One of these contradictions is the inequality of freedom. While in theory all *men* are equal, men and women are not symmetrically defined. Man, the centre and hero of liberal humanism, was produced in contradistinction to the objects of his knowledge, and in terms of the relations of power in the economy and the state. Woman was produced in contradistinction to man, and in terms of the relations of power in the family. Woman's story in the sixteenth and seventeenth centuries lags behind man's. The field of women's resistance, however, is more sharply defined.

The choice of tragedy as the starting-point for a discussion of the construction of the subject is in one sense an arbitrary one. All signifying practice is the province of such a project. But for precisely this reason any single contribution to the history of the subject has to start somewhere. Fiction, I have already suggested, has a certain specificity in that its topic is above all subjectivity itself – the intimate personal and interpersonal relations which define what it is to be a man or a woman. In addition, while a sermon or a treatise on the same topic relies for its success on the elimination of difficulties, narrative depends for its continuation on obstacles and impediments to the resolution of conflict. Fiction therefore tends to throw into relief the problems and contradictions which are often only implicit in other modes of writing. In the sixteenth and seventeenth centuries the fictional mode which addresses the broadest audience is drama. Performed both at court and in the city, before an audience which was representative of the social range and the social mobility of the capital, the drama of the period before 1642 can be seen as a focus of the contests for the meaning of subjectivity and gender which can also be identified elsewhere. When the theatres reopened in 1660 the stage became a place of affirmation of the common sense, literally the shared meanings, of the new order. And if all narrative foregrounds problems, while comedy moves towards final reconciliation, tragedy is subject to no such imperative. The Renaissance plays I discuss in detail in this book are locations of the intersection of rival discourses, and this rivalry is not resolved.

Tragedy is no more, however, than a point of departure. I make considerable reference to plays not classed as tragedies, and to texts not in the category of fiction. On the assumption that fiction is not outside the meanings in circulation in its period, the specificity of fiction is not to be confused with independence. Claims for the autonomy of art ultimately place it outside signifying practice and outside meaning. In quest of the history of the subject I turn constantly to non-fictional texts. These are not in any sense background material but are primary locations of the meanings and contests for meaning which are my concern. The object of beginning with tragedy is not to privilege these plays but to put them to work for substantial political purposes which replace the mysterious aesthetic and moral pleasures of nineteenth-century criticism.

The Subject of Tragedy is not offered as comprehensive or definitive. It is an attempt to identify a project and to put into practice a way of reading the past. It is also mildly polemical – in the hope that debate may constitute a stimulus to the conditioned production of new knowledges.

Part I: MAN

2
UNITY

2.1 Discontinuity

From a bed at the centre of the world the newly-born Mankind rises unsteadily to his feet. Under the bed is his soul, concealed there ready to rise and play at the inevitable moment in the future when Mankind's death will release it from its temporary alliance with the body. In between, Mankind's destiny is to wander about this earth on which he has been born. He is the site of a constant struggle between good and evil, granted a brief respite in an emblematic castle of virtue which is raised above the level of the earth, but lured back from its harsh asceticism in old age by the promise of worldly comforts. The host of allegorical figures dispersed across the circular stage represent both his human characteristics and the rival forces in the cosmic struggle of which he is the momentary location. Mankind is never wholly sure whether he belongs on earth or elsewhere, never entirely clear how to differentiate between honest virtues and lying vices. If he chooses rightly that is an effect of grace; if he finally achieves salvation it is because he casts himself on the mercy of God. Bullied, cajoled and coerced, uncertain and unstable, the eminently unheroic hero of *The Castle of Perseverance* displays for his fifteenth-century audience the frailty and the vanity of man.

In *The Order of Things*, first published in France in 1966, Michel Foucault proposed that man, 'an invention of recent date', the product of certain 'arrangements of knowledge', was in the process of perishing as those arrangements disappeared. Vain, frail, precarious, dispersed across a range of discourses, the figure of man is threatened by the return of the repressed – language, of which he is no more than an effect. Should the reassertion of language, which currently offers to dislodge the certainties of humanist consciousness, succeed in rearranging our knowledge, 'then one can certainly wager that man would be erased, like a face drawn in sand at the edge of the sea' (Foucault, 1970:387).

Between these two textual identifications, these two historical moments, man, the discursive hero of a specific class, has taken control of human history and human destiny. No longer dispersed but unified, no longer uncertain but knowing, independent of providence and of language, free, man has imperiously claimed those rights which his unity, knowledge and autonomy legitimate. Western liberal society, patriarchal, militaristic, and predicated on economic competition and conflict, is the result of that claim – evidently, since it is so clearly what people want, what they freely, knowingly choose.

This book is a contribution to a history of man, and of his other, woman, who defines him by her difference. That history is not yet complete. We are a product of it and we produce – and reproduce – it. We reproduce it, that is, unless a rearrangement of our knowledge makes possible a future which is different from the present.

The Castle of Perseverance opens with the World on his scaffold above the circular playing area. We may conjecture that he is magnificently dressed. He lists the countries of the known world as the lands he owns and reveals that his glory reaches to heaven (ll.170–95). Only when the Flesh and the Devil on their scaffolds have declared their power and proclaimed Mankind's imminent destruction does the protagonist himself, at ground level, speak to define his own condition. He is faint and feeble, bemused, uncertain whether to go or to stay; he does not know why he was born; he has no power to help himself. He knows only that two Angels have been assigned to him, the Good Angel who comes from Christ and the Bad Angel who is his foe. He is by no means convinced that he will succeed in following the Good Angel, but he prays to Christ for help (ll.275-326).

There follows a debate between the Angels in which Mankind speaks only to say that he is perplexed by the choice he must make ('As wynde in watyr I wave', l.379), and finally to opt hesitantly for the Bad Angel and the World (ll.393–401). This sets the formal pattern for the rest of the play. As the protagonist, Mankind says relatively little. In the playing area all the authority, visually and intellectually, belongs to the figures who tower above him on their scaffolds or discuss him in the third person. His assent is the stake in a contest which takes place around him, outside him, largely beyond his understanding.

To be a subject is to speak, to identify with the 'I' of an utterance, to be the agent of the action inscribed in the verb. In this sense it is hard to identify Mankind as a subject. Agency in the play is distributed among the other forty or so speaking parts. These figures are simultaneously internal and external to the human protagonist: internal in so far as good and evil, asceticism or worldliness represent human propensities; external in so far as their personifications live on when Mankind dies – necessarily, since they are forces engaged in a cosmic struggle between good and evil which can end only at doomsday, when Christ finally triumphs over Satan. Mankind is thus a fragmented and fragmentary figure. His being is dispersed across a battlefield in which his conflicting faculties struggle to possess him, to determine his eternal destiny. At the same time he is the temporary location of a conflict which exists before he is born and continues after his death. Vice and virtue take up residence within him for a time and he is no more than their consenting instrument.

He is, furthermore, an instrument in constant process. In the morality plays of the fifteenth century character is not destiny. Mankind, whose Angels constantly impel him to change, cannot stand still. He is obliged to choose the direction of his earthly pilgrimage. But no choice is ever final. Repentance is perpetually possible; temptation inevitably recurs. Following his initial commitment to worldly values, Mankind makes his way to the World's scaffold, thus turning his back on God, whose scaffold is at the opposite side of the circle. Thereafter he is introduced to the Flesh and the Devil, and in consequence to the Seven Deadly Sins. In the midst of his worldly pleasures, however, Mankind repents. Penitence comes swiftly, apparently unmotivated, as the effect of God's grace (ll.1403–15). Mankind withdraws from the world into the Castle of Perseverance to be instructed and defended by the Virtues. The World, the Flesh and the Devil besiege the Castle in vain, but Mankind, succumbing to the argument of Covetousness that his purse, not asceticism, will be his best friend in old age, returns to the earth and earthly values. At his death he appeals to the World for help. The appeal is in vain. The World rejoices that their bond will soon be broken and his victim will lie in torment. Thus he has served many (ll.2869–81). Casting himself on God's mercy, Mankind dies, and the remainder of the play makes it clear that by his choices he has incurred damnation. His soul is carried off to hell and saved, after a debate in heaven, not by his merits but through the mercy of God.

The Castle of Perseverance dates from the first quarter of the fifteenth century. It is the earliest and the largest complete extant morality play. A hundred years later in *The World and the Child*, although the number of actors required has been reduced to two, the analysis of the nature of human life has not changed radically. The hero submits to the World, and the play presents his life as a conflict between the World and Conscience, Conscience and Folly. The World is supported by seven kings, the deadly sins. In the intervening century a series of morality plays show their protagonists as bewildered, gullible victims of a war in which they must participate but which they do not in any sense initiate. Man – since all the central figures are masculine – is thus a transitory configuration of fragments, of states of being over which he has only the most minimal control. So tenuous, indeed, is this control that in *Wisdom* (*c*.1460), though man is explicitly the stake in the contest between Christ and Lucifer, the human figure is not represented in the play. Instead Anima, the soul, played as a maiden (l.16 S.D.) and her three faculties, Mind, Will and Understanding, are alternately corrupted and redeemed, while Lucifer employs all the subtlety at his disposal to secure the absent man for hell by defiling 'his' attributes (ll.325–80).

In these circumstances it is possible to see a certain irony in the virtuous instruction to the hero of another play of roughly the same period, 'The temptacyon of the flesch ye must resyst lyke a man' (*Mankind*, l.226). With what strength, on the basis of what resources, does 'a man' resist? How is man as battlefield simultaneously man as soldier? 'Vita hominis est milicia super terram' ('The life of man upon earth is a warfare', Job 7:1), continues Mercy, Mankind's instructor. 'Oppresse yowr gostly enmy and be Crystys own knyght' (ll.228–9). The answer to the riddle is, of course, that the strength and the resources are God's. Virtue is no more than consent to their operation. Christ's own knight is precisely that, led, motivated, fortified by a power which lies elsewhere.

He is therefore necessarily unfixed, in process: the discontinuity is diachronic as well as synchronic. The moral identities of the morality heroes are not given in advance. Each of them is capable equally of sin and of repentance. Man, the central figure of Medwall's *Nature* (*c*.1490–1500) twice falls into sin and twice repents, finally becoming the child of salvation. *The World and the Child* similarly recounts two temptations and two repentances. Everyman moves from worldly insouciance through near-despair to Christian serenity at the moment of death. What the hero is determines what he does only in the sense that what he is is radically discontinuous. Even in *Apius and Virginia*, a play of the 1560s, where Apius's temptation and fall is dramatized allegorically, the hero's wickedness is not an inevitable effect of his disposition. It is on the contrary a state of being which takes hold when he invites the Vice to 'enter' into his judgement (l.413). In consequence 'Conscience and Justice come out of him' (l.428 S.D.). As Apius defines this episode, 'Two states of my life from me are now glided' (l.430). These 'states' of vice or virtue are mobile, interchangeable, defining only while they remain in place, able to be dislodged in response to pressures initiated elsewhere.

In *The World and the Child* the discontinuity is represented in terms of a single hero whose name constantly changes. He is initially identified by the speech prefix as Infans, but he tells the World that his mother called him Dalliance. The World renames him Wanton and instructs him to come back when he is fourteen. When Wanton returns his name is changed to Lust-and-Liking, and at twenty-one he becomes Manhood. Manhood is converted by Conscience but when he succumbs to Folly he is renamed Shame. Finally, as Age, he learns the error of his ways and is named Repentance. In each case the name, always allotted by another figure, never chosen by the hero, signifies a distinct mode of behaviour. Wanton enjoys beating other boys, scrumping and birdsnesting; Lust-and-Liking devotes himself to clothes, love, mirth and melody, but also to revel and riot; Manhood is a knight.

In the fifteenth century the representative human being has no unifying essence. Consisting of 'a body and of a soull, of condycyon contrarye' (*Mankind*, l.195), man *is* neither the one nor the other. The soul is immortal and looks upwards towards its true home; the transient body clings to the earth of which it is composed. But life in the world entails an uneasy, unstable alliance between the two, a division between contraries which cannot be resolved until death. Disunited, discontinuous, the hero of the moralities is not the origin of action; he has no single subjectivity which could constitute such an origin; he is not a subject. History is a preparation for the Day of Judgement, the perpetual re-enacting of the psychomachia, a recurring battle for possession of human beings in which they are simultaneously the stake and the instruments. The agents of history, its subjects, are good and evil, God and the Devil.

2.2 The spectator

The setting of this timeless history is mapped in detail in a stage plan which accompanies the manuscript of *The Castle*

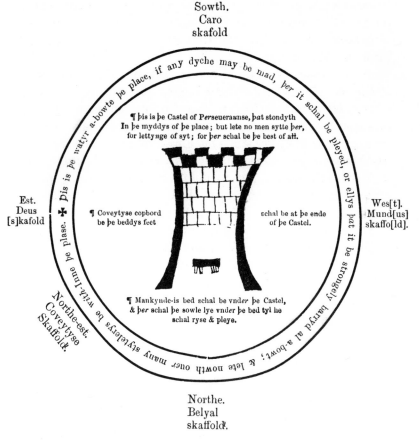

Sowth.
Caro
skafold

¶ þis is þe Castel of *Perseueraunse*, þat stondyth In þe myddys of þe place; but lete no men sytte þer, for lettynge of syt; for þer schal be þe best of all.

Est.
Deus
[s]kafold

¶ Coveytyse copbord be þe beddys feet

schal be at þe ende of þe Castel.

Wes[t].
Mund[us]
skaffo[ld].

¶ Mankynde-is bed schal be vnder þe Castel, & þer schal þe sowle lye vnder þe bed tyl he schal ryse & pleye.

þis is þe watyr a-bowte þe place, if any dyche may be mad, þer it schal be pleyed, or ellys þat it be strongely barryd al a-bowt; & lete nowth ouer many styterys be with-Inne þe plase.

Northe-est.
Coveytyse
Skaffold.

Northe.
Belyal
skaffold.

(Reproduced from Furnivall and Pollard, 1904: 76)

19

of Perseverance. It is the earth where, after the fall of the angels, God placed Adam and Eve, vulnerable to evil, able to be redeemed.

The stage plan shows a circle surrounded by water 'if any dyche may be mad'. If not it must be 'strongly barryd al a-bowt'. At the centre of the circle is the castle and below it Mankind's bed. At various compass points on the circumference are the scaffolds of the World, the Flesh and the Devil, Covetousness and God.

Medieval maps of the world show a circle surrounded by the great ocean. Despite a scholarly consensus from the thirteenth century onwards that the world was a sphere, Christian iconography continued to place the holy city of Jerusalem at the centre of a disc displaying the three continents of Europe, Africa and Asia. The first printed *mappa mundi* (1472) shows a flat circle with a rim labelled *mare-oceanum* (Bricker and Tooley, 1969:45), precisely the shape of the drawing of the stage plan. This may explain why a ditch is preferable to bars. The water is not indispensable: the circle itself makes the point; but it would complete the visual image of the earth which is the scene of the play.

The inhabitants of this world include, of course, the audience within the circle, who are implicated in the progress of their representative, Mankind. The play opens with the World's address to the denizens of his realm which is also the playing area, the 'place':

Worthy wytys in al this werd wyde,
   Be wylde wode wonys and every weye-went,
Precyous prinse, prekyd in pride,
   Thorwe this propyr pleyn place in pes be ye bent!
Buske you, bolde bachelerys, under my baner to abyde
   Where bryth basnetys be bateryd and backys are schent.
Ye, syrys semly, als same syttyth on syde ...

(ll.157–63)

A sweeping gesture might indicate the wild woods and

pathways which the spectators are invited to visualize within the place. The dialogue consistently expands the space of the playing area. References to 'walking and wending' along streets and roads, through fields and groves, indicate vast landscapes. The personifications travel across hills and dales, through towns and cities, floods and fens in pursuit of their object, the possession of Mankind.

The world of the stage has its own emblematic geography. Like paradise, and like the altar, God's scaffold is in the east, the source of the Second Coming. Opposite is the scaffold of the World. The Devil, as is conventional, dwells in the north (Rudwin, 1931:63–5), and the Flesh in the warm south. Mankind is free to choose the direction of his journey. Only one way leads to God. On all other sides are the scaffolds of his enemies, including Covetousness, who offer worldly enticements to ensure his damnation. The distribution is appropriate, 'for wide is the gate, and broad is the way, that leadeth to destruction, and many there be which go in thereat: because strait is the gate, and narrow is the way, which leadeth unto life, and few there be that find it' (Matt. 7:13–14). If Southern's reconstruction of the performance is accurate, the disposition of the audience according to sight-lines would automatically provide paths to the scaffolds (Southern, 1957:74ff.). One way would lead to God, the remaining four to the forces of evil.

In the allegory virtue is possible only through withdrawal into the castle, a stronghold which represents a wall against the three adversaries who command the seven sins. The castle is within the world of the play, on earth, but presumably raised above the level of the ground, since it must be supported on posts if the bed below it is to be visible. No escape from the earth is possible until death, and temptation cannot be prevented but only resisted. But the castle represents a way of life which is nearer to perfection than any available in the world. Mankind 'hauntyth now heven halle/That schal bryngyn hym to hevene' (ll.1709–10). Withdrawal into the ascetic castle represents the victory of heavenly impulses over worldly values, of the divine soul over the flesh which is earth. The castle rises above the world of the play's main conflict, a symbol of isolation and aspiration.

At the end of the play, his salvation secured, Mankind's soul mounts the scaffold of God. Meanwhile, the World's Boy has threatened to throw his body into a lake (l.2913). Possibly this lake is the water which surrounds the earth. The body was to be thrown over the edge of the world into oblivion.

The stage plan precisely defines the relationship between human beings and life in the world which constitutes the moral analysis of the play. The circle surrounded by water represents the earth on which Mankind is born and dies, the place in which he is tempted and where he determines his eternal future. In the centre of the circle is the stronghold of virtue to which the protagonist withdraws. This is raised above the level of the ground. The bed, which is probably the place of the major physical events of the play, is firmly on the ground. Here Mankind puts on and discards the body which links him with the earth and its pleasures. Ranged round the circumference of the circle are the powerful figures of the sources of salvation or damnation.

The spectators are here offered an image of Mankind's condition and their own, and invited to identify in his perplexity a mirror of their own being. But the play also establishes a distance between the audience and the protagonist. The spectators participate in his choices; they are enlisted in the debate between good and evil; they are asked, in other words, to take sides; but at the same time, to the extent that they are able to see the visual network of meanings established by the stage plan, as Mankind is evidently not, they are offered a single, stable position from which to understand the nature of human life. This is not, it is important to stress, a position of detachment from the events of the play: the audience is not outside the world which is the arena of struggle; the spectators do not in any sense transcend the conflict which takes place in the playing area. The project of the play is both to ask the audience to 'recognize' in Mankind's discontinuity as a configuration of fragments their own condition, and simultaneously to close off the anarchic possibilities which that recognition releases. The play is at once analysis and exhortation. As analysis it shows human beings dispersed, unfixed, not in control; as exhortation it requires the spectators to make choices, precisely as if they were unified agents of their own actions. It therefore offers the audience a coherent pattern of emblematic meanings defining their disunity and at the same time provides a single and thus unified position from which that pattern is intelligible.

The playhouse opened by Sir William Davenant in 1661 inaugurated the epoch of classic realism in the commercial theatre. The first play to be performed in this converted tennis court in Lincoln's Inn Fields was *The Siege of Rhodes*, a work expressly written for 'representation by the art of prospective in scenes', as the title page of 1656 made clear. The scenic theatre with its proscenium arch and perspective backdrops was ultimately to close the gap the moralities had opened between protagonist and spectator precisely by drawing a clear demarcation line between them. Classic realist theatre isolates the world of the fiction from the world of the audience, and shows the first as an empirical replica rather than an emblematic representation of the second. The spectators recognize in the unified subjects who perform, apparently oblivious of them, within the lighted, framed space of the stage, the depiction of their own imaginary unity.

The change did not take place all at once. It was Inigo Jones who first introduced the Italian fashion of perspective scenes at the English court in 1605. Some of the spectators had difficulty in grasping what was going on in *The Masque of Blackness*. Ben Jonson, who understood the project, saw a sea which seemed to move, with waves and seahorses; Sir Dudley Carleton saw 'a great Engine ... which had motion', and a series of flats with fish painted on them. 'The indecorum was, that there was all fish and no water' (Orgel and Strong, 1973, I:12).

By the 1660s, when the theatres reopened after the war and the commonwealth had closed them, scenic staging had become familiar at least to the point where the old Elizabethan and Jacobean theatres were not worth renovating. But the action on the whole took place on the forestage in front of the proscenium arch, and there was some degree of uncertainty about the precise relationship between the actor and the scenes (Southern, 1976:93). Both stage and auditorium were lit by candles. The two (or more) doors at the back of the Elizabethan public stages, descendants of the screen doors of the Tudor halls which provided indoor morality theatres, survived in the Restoration playhouses but were transferred to the sides of the forestage, flush with the walls of the auditorium. Nonetheless, despite these signs of continuity, there was a radical difference between the old playhouses and the new. In the Restoration theatre the action took place in front of a painted scene which simulated in perspective, with whatever uncertainty, the place (and time) of a specific fictional event. The curtain rose after the prologue and was not lowered until after the epilogue. In the meantime state apartments gave way to forests and squares, harbours to palaces and prisons. The scenic spectacle offered an illusion of the world of the spectator's real or imagined experience with the object of persuading the audience 'for the time, that what they behold on the theater is really perform'd' (Dryden, 1978:14).

The project of monocular perspective, first developed by Brunelleschi in the humanist context of Renaissance Italy, was the faithful reproduction in painting of what the eye sees. While emblematic staging displays the signified, makes meaning visible, illusionism reproduces the referent, replicates what is already visible, already known. In consequence, certain coherences of social and spatial relationship are taken for granted on the scenic stage. The actors portray concrete individuals who interact with each other as unified subjects. Eventually objects defined on the painted scenes are in proportion to the size of the actors; props are in proportion to both; but proportion is defined from the point of view of an optimum position in front of the stage, from which the fictional world is visible, recognizable and separate. Even before the nineteenth century, when the auditorium finally darkened and the whole stage retreated behind the frame of the proscenium arch, the perspective theatre thus offered an internally coherent and unified spectacle to a single and unified point of view which was outside the autonomous world of the fiction.

The development of the scenic stage at court in the first decade of the seventeenth century accompanied the development of Stuart absolutism. Inigo Jones's masques focused the theatrical event and directed it to the single place in the auditorium from which the spectacle achieved its fullest effect, the throne.

> Through the use of perspective the monarch, always the ethical centre of court productions, became in a physical and emblematic way the centre as well. Jones's theatre transformed its audience into a living and visible emblem of the aristocratic hierarchy: the closer one sat to the King, the 'better' one's place was, and only the King's seat was perfect. It is no accident that perspective stages flourished at court and only at court, and that their appearance there coincided with the reappearance in England of the Divine Right of Kings as a serious political philosophy.
>
> (Orgel and Strong, 1973, 1:7)

The scenic theatre unfolds as an object of sight for a subject who is held in place by the spectacle. The pleasure of the gaze is the pleasure of an imaginary plenitude, a 'mapping of space' (Lacan, 1979:86) in which the viewing subject masters unchallenged the objects of its vision. The promise of uninterrupted receding perspective is a disclosure which offers the spectator an absolute (and illusory) transcendence. At the absolutist court of James I this transcendence was the property of the monarch and to varying degrees his courtiers. Only the royal subject was truly sovereign. After the revolution the hierarchy of transcendence identified by Orgel and Strong was offered at a price, or a range of prices, to those, including increasing numbers of the bourgeoisie (Hume, 1976:23–7), who were willing to pay between one and four shillings for seats and who, we may assume, generally possessed property sufficient to guarantee their representation in the House of Commons. The scenic stage of the Restoration period addressed a unified and unifying spectacle to a series of unified spectator-subjects who, as guardians of the liberties of the people of England, each possessed a degree of sovereignty in the new regime.

But in the period between the precarious unity offered by the moralities and the stable, transcendent unity of the Restoration stage, from 1576 when Burbage built the Theatre to 1642 when the playhouses were closed, the stage brought into conjunction and indeed into collision the emblematic mode and an emergent illusionism. The effect was a form of drama capable at any moment of disrupting the unity of the spectator. Not, of course, that it could compel this disruptive reading. No form can unilaterally determine the response of the audience. The moralities could not guarantee their emblematic intelligibility; the scenic theatre could not insist on a humanist reading; Ben Jonson and Sir Dudley Carleton were present at the same rendering of *The Masque of Blackness*; and Simon Forman shows no sign of having been disturbed by the mixture of modes in *Macbeth* in his account of a visit to the Globe in 1611 (Muir, 1962:xiii–xiv). None the less, it is possible to identify, especially in the public theatres of the late sixteenth and early seventeenth centuries, a form of staging that can be read as withholding the certainty which offers to unify in different ways both the medieval and the Restoration spectator.

Unity

It is generally agreed that when Hamlet, speaking in the Globe, defines the earth as a promontory beneath the canopy of the o'erhanging firmament, he is invoking the familiar metaphor of the world as a theatre, and identifying the apron stage itself and the roof which protected it, the 'heavens' from which divinities were lowered to the stage when the play required them:

> this goodly frame, the earth, seems to me a sterile promontory; this most excellent canopy, the air, look you, this brave o'erhanging firmament, this majestical roof fretted with golden fire – why, it appeareth no other thing to me than a foul and pestilent congregation of vapours. What a piece of work is a man! How noble in reason! how infinite in faculties! in form and moving, how express and admirable! in action, how like an angel! in apprehension, how like a god! the beauty of the world! the paragon of animals! And yet, to me, what is this quintessence of dust? Man delights not me – no, nor woman neither, though by your smiling you seem to say so.
>
> (*Hamlet*, ii. ii. 300–9)

Man is present in the speech, and his other, woman, uneasily there in the concluding joke which draws attention to the way that then, as now, the term 'man' both includes ('embraces', they say, inviting us to laugh) and simultaneously excludes women. Anatomy is made both difference and destiny, comedy and oppression. Man, meanwhile, is another paradox: like a god and at the same time a quintessence of dust. Which half of the paradox is vindicated by the fiction? Which case does the play as a whole support? And who is speaking? Is the audience invited to see Hamlet expressing his deepest feelings, displaying the subjectivity, complex and contradictory, of the sensitive prince? Or, since he is talking to Rosencrantz and Guildenstern here, is this a pose, an antic disposition designed to delude them, an assumed melancholy? Or, if the world is a stage, what is Hamlet but an actor,

27

expressing and concealing nothing, but offering a performance, a form which does not imply an anterior substance? Or, since conversely the stage must be a world, does this fiction, this conceit, lay claim to a kind of truth? But which of the possible truths?

The plurality of the speech depends on the multiple meanings of this play performed on this stage. The promontory which represents the earth is also Elsinore; Hamlet is a concrete individual with a particular history; the autonomous world of the fiction is geographically and chronologically specific, and separate from the world of the audience. At the same time, the promontory is between 'the heavens' and 'hell', the space below the stage from which infernal figures appeared through a trapdoor as necessary, and where old Hamlet's Ghost cries in the cellarage (*Hamlet*, I. v. 151). Most of the public theatres, with the exception of the Fortune, were round – or perhaps polygonal, since horizontal timbers do not easily produce a circle (Orrell, 1983:119). Orrell suggests that the Globe may have had twenty-four sides (pp.158–67), and this would certainly give the impression of a circle. Within this representation of the macrocosm, a circular earth containing the audience, microcosmic human figures on the stage, poised between heaven and hell, conducted and reconducted the struggles of which they were part and with which they were continuous.[1]

Props were indiscriminately emblematic or illusionist. The properties of the Admiral's company in 1598–9 included three trees, three rocks, three animals, two tombs, a cage, a hellmouth, a cauldron, a chariot and a rainbow (Wickham, 1963:310). The audience was on three sides of the raised stage, and sometimes four, but for a higher price spectators could sit on the stage and become part of the spectacle. And above all there were no backcloths, no perspective scenes, focusing and containing the gaze, and offering a single and unifying coherence to a single and unified point of view. In consequence, the plays are able to move between two kinds of spectacle, one emblematic, implicating the spectator in its meanings, the signified, and the other illusionist, showing the transcendent spectator sense-data, referents which constitute the raw material of experience. The conjunction of the two, or indeed the superimposition of one on the other, is capable of generating a radical uncertainty precisely by withholding from the spectator the single position from which a single and unified meaning is produced. From what place does Hamlet's speech make a unitary sense to a spectator outside the fictional world of Elsinore, inside the emblematic macrocosm of the Globe, at once observing Hamlet the Dane and implicated in Hamlet's account of man (and woman)?

Three instances will, I hope, give some indication of the kind of uncertainty in question. *Tamburlaine* (1587) is in any case a notoriously plural text. Is the rebellious Scythian shepherd who conquers the world a popular hero or an imperialist tyrant? Is he more appropriately seen as an aspiring individual or a ruthless butcher? The play, I believe, does not answer these questions, but poses them with a certain sharpness to an Elizabethan society preparing to embark on a series of colonialist adventures. It is Tamburlaine's rhetoric, his high astounding terms, which prove persuasive both for the audience and for the fictional characters. Theridamas, sent out to bring Tamburlaine under control, seems to speak for the audience when in the event he succumbs without a struggle to the hero's 'stronge enchantments': 'Won with thy words, and conquered with thy looks/I yeeld my selfe, my men and horse to thee' (*I Tamburlaine*, I. ii. 224–9). Inscribed in Tamburlaine's rhetoric is a heroic aspiration which offers to legitimate the bloodshed of his career:

> Nature that fram'd us of foure elements
> Warring within our breasts for regiment,
> Doth teach us all to have aspyring minds:
> Our soules, whose faculties can comprehend
> The wondrous architecture of the world:

And measure every wandring plannets course:
Still climing after knowledge infinite,
And alwaies mooving as the restles spheares,
Wils us to weare our selves and never rest,
Untill we reach the ripest fruit of all,
That perfect blisse and sole felicitie,
The sweet fruition of an earthly crowne.

(II. vii. 18–29)

There are, as is widely recognized, certain ambiguities here. The 'warring' of the elements which seems obliquely to justify Tamburlaine's militarism is an effect of the Fall. An earthly crown seems an anti-climactic fulfilment of such cosmic and 'infinite' aspiration. But more significant still, easily ignored by a reader but not by a spectator, this speech is delivered over the body of the dying Cosroe whose defeat and death are precisely the means to the fruition in question, the Persian crown. But 'over' is perhaps the wrong word. Tamburlaine, rhetorically measuring every planet's wandering course, takes no account whatever of the death-agony Cosroe insists that his sword has inflicted. The spectacle, however, presents the hero and his bloody victim side by side.

How is an audience to read this episode? As signifying Tamburlaine's military prowess? This is to ignore the incongruity between the rhetoric and the spectacle. As an evocation of Fortune's wheel, showing Tamburlaine's rise while Cosroe is thrown to the ground (Potter, 1980:257)? Perhaps. Or (and?) as an emblem of tyranny? The episode – and the play as a whole – seem to leave the issue unresolved, and with it the question of the heroics of military conquest.

A humanist reading of *Tamburlaine* sees the play as a challenge to the limits arbitrarily imposed on human freedom. A later and more predominantly illusionist play, *'Tis Pity She's a Whore* (c.1630?), can also be read as a plea for human freedom – here the freedom to love unhampered by a narrow and constricting Christian morality. Giovanni's final emblematic appearance, however, holding on his dagger the heart of the sister he has killed, keeping the fictional spectators at bay while he proclaims himself 'a happy monarch of her heart and her' (v. vi. 45), calls in question the romantic interpretation. This love is here defined as a bitter and destructive form of domination. The emblem does not, on the other hand, obliterate the difficulties in the way of reading the text as an unequivocal condemnation of forbidden love. From what unified place does the spectator read, 'map', master this final scene of the play, this disclosure without closure?

In these cases the collisions between emblem and illusion which offer to disrupt the spectator's unified understanding constitute isolated episodes within the plays. In *The Revenger's Tragedy* (1607), however, the collision is a structural one, and the entire action of the play is simultaneously intelligible on two distinct planes. In his opening speech Vindice addresses revenge itself: 'Vengeance, thou murder's quit-rent, and whereby/Thou show'st thyself tenant to tragedy' (I. i. 39–40). On one plane Vindice is here a wronged man, committing himself to avenge his murdered love; on another he is vengeance, as his name implies, addressing himself as personified abstraction, the rate of exchange for murder in the tragic order of cosmic justice.

Vindice achieves revenge for murder – inevitably, since vengeance is what emblematically he is. As human agent he brings about the execution of a series of human criminals – Lussurioso, Spurio, Ambitioso, etc. As personified abstraction he inflicts divine retribution on a series of vices whose names indicate their qualities – Lussurioso, Spurio, Ambitioso, etc. But it is as human being that Vindice is himself required to pay the tragic price of his actions, since he too, as a revenger, is now a murderer. At the end of the play Antonio, newly installed by Vindice's actions as the just ruler of a cleansed state, summarily dismisses Vindice to execution for killing the corrupt Duke: 'You that would murder him would murder me' (v. iii. 105). Is the play's resolution optimistic or cynical?

Does revenge purge or perpetuate killing? Does Vindice deserve death? Are we to judge his actions right or wrong?

'Vengeance is mine; I will repay, saith the Lord' (Rom. 12:19). As emblematic instrument of divine vengeance, Vindice is no more culpable than God's Plague, who strikes down Worldly Man at the end of *Enough is as Good as a Feast* (c.1560), or God's Visitation, who puts an end to the career of Lust in *The Trial of Treasure* (1567). But as human agent, Vindice arrogates the vengeance which belongs to God and himself merits divine and human retribution. *The Revenger's Tragedy* brings into conjunction two distinct versions of history. One, where God and the Devil are finally the agents of a cosmic struggle between good and evil, is familiar from the morality tradition. In the other emerging version of history human beings strive to establish justice on earth by means of individual acts of revenge which are not morally authorized. The play poses moral and political questions which cannot be given a unitary answer in the early seventeenth century. In this sense it offers no single resolution, no one point of view from which it makes a unified sense.

All texts require interpretation; all readings are produced from the raw material which constitutes the text. In this sense all texts are plural, since no arrangement of signifiers can arrest the play of meaning. None the less, there are degrees of plurality, from the limited readability of classic realism to the relative writability of the interrogative text. Morality drama is always and inevitably plural, but its project is to contain that plurality, to arrest the play of signification in the interests of the truth it offers to teach. Illusionist drama is also plural and, as recent criticism has shown, it is possible to resist illusionist strategies of limitation, to insist on producing alternative readings of classic realist texts. But the drama of the intervening period, and particularly of the half-century before the revolution, presents a special kind of plurality in so far as it displays the intersection of the two modes, illusionist and emblematic.

We can, of course, read it either way. Inevitably the dominant critical tradition of an illusionist epoch has read Shakespeare and his contemporaries in quest of illusionism, most obviously to find the representation of humanist subjects, 'characters'. Certain elements of the texts, however, have returned to haunt those readings: Coleridge's identification of Iago's 'motiveless malignity' is a familiar instance. It is also possible to construct primarily emblematic readings: Spivack's treatment of Iago as a morality Vice in *Shakespeare and the Allegory of Evil* is an impressive example. But there is a third possibility, which is to find the plays moving between the two modes, producing for the spectator a place of uncertainty or of unresolved debate.

It is important to stress that to read the plays in this way, as interrogative to the extent that their form foregrounds the plurality of their meanings, is not to escape the constraints of interpretation. Any reading limits the play of meaning, containing it within a specific framework. 'To speak is above all to choose this restricted economy within the enclosure of discourse, in order to give oneself ways towards a development that is impossible if one says nothing' (Green, 1979:20). At the same time, to alter the conventional framework is to propose an additional perspective and thus to extend the possibilities of interpretation at a particular moment. To propose an alternative to the humanist version of literary history is to offer a contribution to that rearrangement of our knowledge which signals the end of the reign of man.

2.3 Interiority

The implication of the argument from staging is that the unified subject of liberal humanism is a product of the second half of the seventeenth century, an effect of the revolution. Broadly this seems to me to be so. Liberal humanism, locating agency and meaning in the unified human subject, becomes an orthodoxy at the moment when the bourgeoisie is installed as the ruling class. Signifying practice, however, is not so well ordered as to wait for the execution of Charles I in 1649 before proclaiming the existence of an interiority, the inalienable and unalterable property of the individual, which precedes and determines speech and action. Here, for instance, is Daniel Rogers in 1642 on the grounds of marriage:

> Its true generally, but in this point specially, that speech is the discoverer of the mind: looke what the abundance of the heart is, that will vent it selfe at the mouth .... Yea, the speech of each to other should bee (without flattery) as the glasse to behold each other in.
>
> (Rogers, 1642:189)

And in 1643 Milton identifies as the main grounds for divorce,

> that indisposition, unfitness, or contrariety of mind, arising from a cause in nature unchangable, hindring and ever likely to hinder the main benefits of conjugal society, which are solace and peace.
>
> (Milton, 1959:242)

In each case the subject is understood to be both single and stable, and thus synchronically and diachronically continuous where Mankind is discontinuous. Subjectivity manifests itself in speech and behaviour, making for compatibility or incompatibility between two given dispositions. Brathwait, writing in 1630, asserts even more firmly the diachronic continuity of the subject. People may seem to change, he insists, but this is simply a matter of appearances, like clouds covering the sun. In time people's true dispositions emerge and these are unalterable, 'being so inherent in the subject, as they may be moved, but not removed'. They are not affected by circumstances. External conditions have no influence on the nature of the individual. 'Shouldst thou change aire, and soile, and all, it were not in thy power to change thy selfe' (Brathwait, 1641a:32–4).

Milton and Rogers identify this fixed self with the mind, a space hollowed out by discourse within each person and then filled with a unified and unchanging essence. 'The mind is its own place', as Satan was later to assure his troops, though he perhaps rather overestimated its powers in what followed: 'and in itself/Can make a heaven of hell, a hell of heaven' (Milton, 1968:477). This interiority, this consciousness which is also being, defines the humanist subject, the author and origin of meaning and choice. Satan's realm of the spirit where the subject itself resides is anticipated in the Christian stoicism of Dyer in the late sixteenth century:

> My mind to me a kingdom is
> Such perfect joy therein I find
> That it excels all other bliss
> That world affords or grows by kind.
>
> (Gardner, 1972:49)

In *The Second Maiden's Tragedy* (1611) the rightful ruler, Govianus, has been deposed, but it scarcely matters to him, since 'the unbounded kingdom of the mind/Is as unlimitable as heav'n' (I. ii. 13–14). Here the mind is a place of retreat, defined by its difference from the exterior world, though at least equal to it. Later Marvell would call it an 'ocean where each kind/Does straight its own resemblance find' (Marvell, 1972:101). In Dyer's poem the mind is not yet an essence, but it is already given and inviolable.

It is possible to see, then, why it has not seemed anachronistic to find evidence of humanism in the sense in which I have defined it in the self-assertion of Elizabethan and Jacobean protagonists when they proclaim the continuity of inviolable identity: 'I am/Antony yet' (*Antony and Cleopatra*, III. xiii. 92–3); 'I am Duchess of Malfi still' (*The Duchess of Malfi*, IV. ii. 142);

35

> While I remain above the ground you shall
> Hear from me still, and never of me aught
> But what is like me formerly.
>
> > (*Coriolanus*, IV. i. 51–3)

There seems to be a direct contrast between Mankind's fifteenth-century dependency and the Renaissance affirmation of isolated personal agency and responsibility when Lorenzo declares, 'I'll trust myself, myself shall be my friend' (*The Spanish Tragedy*, III. ii. 118), or when Flamineo insists, 'at myself I will begin and end' (*The White Devil*, v. vi. 258). Coriolanus dies defiantly asserting the personal achievement which is the source of his name and thus his identity:

> like an eagle in a dove-cote, I
> Fluttered your Volscians in Corioli.
> Alone I did it.
>
> > (*Coriolanus*, v. vi. 115–17)

'I am myself alone' is the exultant cry of Gloucester, the future Richard III, as he stabs Henry VI (3 *Henry VI*, v. vi. 83).

It is tempting to read the plays in these cases as exalting human integrity, endorsing truth to the self, the inner being, as intrinsically heroic. The subject thus transcends the rules of human society, politics and, indeed, death itself, in the affirmation of its own identity. But there is, as always, the problem of interpretation here. These instances of self-assertion are simultaneously intelligible in their contexts as ironic, pathetic rather than heroic, or alternatively monstrous, precisely *in*human.

To take the last first, Gloucester, as Spivack has argued, is a direct descendant of the Vice, the ironic, deceptive, destructive representative of evil in the sixteenth-century moralities. The role of the Vice, whose importance in the plays grew with his popularity among the audience, is to entice the human hero to damnation. When in the sixteenth century the morality conventions are adapted for presentation by troupes of six or seven actors, the Vice replaces the World, the Flesh and the Devil, and the sins of *The Castle of Perseverance*. Named Iniquity, Avarice or Natural Inclination, the Vices are full, unified subjects in precisely the sense that God and the Devil are the subjects of the cosmic history dramatized in the fifteenth-century plays. The Vices and their virtuous opponents are the agents of human history, but they are not themselves human.

The defining characteristics of the Vice are precisely isolation and self-assertion. Kin only to the Devil, who often carries them off on his back at the end of the play, Vices trust no one and their friendship is always feigning. They boast of their exploits, drawing attention to the power of evil in the world. In *Lusty Juventus* (*c.*1550), for example, Hypocrisy reassures the Devil:

> Do not I yet reign abroad?
> And as long as I am in the world
> You have some treasure and substance.
> I suppose I have been the flower
> In setting forth thy laws and power.
>
> (ll.381–5)

They reveal their plans to the audience, but not to the other figures on the stage, even when these figures are their collaborators in vice. Indeed, in these circumstances they tend to affirm their identity by taking control. In *Enough is as Good as a Feast* (*c.*1560) Covetous is assisted by Precipitation, Inconsideration and Temerity. He sends Precipitation to fetch his gown, cap and chain, and then stages a quarrel:

> *Covetous.* Body of me, you are knaves all three;
> Take gown, chain, cap and all for me.
> I will be even with you all, I swear by God's
> mother.
> Choose you, shift how you can one for another.
> *Be going out.*

> I warrant you I shall be able to shift for myself,
> Or else you may say I were a foolish elf.
> *Temerity.* (*hold him*) Why brother, you said you would all
> things well take.
> *Covetous.* Yea, but I would not have you your fool me to
> make,
> *Come in again.*
> For you know well enough that of you all three
> I am worthy the governor and ruler to be.
> Covetous (saith the wise man) is the root of all
> evil;
> Therefore, Covetous is the chiefest that cometh
> from the devil.
> (ll.423–34)

Covetous threatens, sulks, distances himself from his brothers in evil, all in the interests of power. When Gloucester asserts his own identity and agency he is declaring a total and unified commitment to evil rather than defining an emerging interiority, an independent realm of consciousness.

> I have no brother, I am like no brother;
> And this word 'love', which greybeards call divine,
> Be resident in men like one another,
> And not in me! I am myself alone.
> Clarence, beware; thou keep'st me from the light,
> But I will sort a pitchy day for thee;
> For I will buzz abroad such prophecies
> That Edward shall be fearful of his life;
> And then to purge his fear, I'll be thy death.
> King Henry and the Prince his son are gone.
> Clarence, thy turn is next, and then the rest;
> Counting myself but bad till I be best.
> (*3 Henry VI*, v. vi. 80–91)

The repudiation of brotherhood and the strategies devised to secure his pre-eminence align Gloucester clearly here with

the Vice. Self-assertion of this kind is the mark of evil; it is a
humanist appropriation of the texts which finds it heroic or
calls it integrity. The parallels between the traditional Vice and Lorenzo and
Flamineo are evident. Coriolanus is a more complex case, but
here too it is precisely the hero's isolation which renders him
unfit for membership of the social body as Menenius defines
it (I. i. 94–161):

> I'll never
> Be such a gosling to obey instinct, but stand
> As if a man were author of himself
> And knew no other kin.
>
> (v. iii. 34–7)

This stance drives him to betray Rome. His subsequent
(inevitable because human?) concession to 'instinct' and kin
leads him to betray the Volsces. 'Integrity' in Coriolanus
threatens destruction; the failure of integrity confines the
destruction to himself.

Antony and the Duchess of Malfi are not Vices. In each of
these instances, however, the context undermines the assertion
of continuity by stressing its irony. The Duchess, who has no
name, is claiming a political place not a personal identity.
She is in prison, facing death, wholly in the power of
Ferdinand, and in this sense the claim is in practice false. She
is at this moment politically powerless. 'Am I not thy duchess?',
she asks Bosola. 'Thou art some great woman, sure, for riot
begins to sit on thy forehead, clad in grey hairs, twenty years
sooner than on a merry milkmaid's' (*The Duchess of Malfi*, IV.
ii. 134–7). This is what it means to be Duchess of Malfi still.
Antony's assertion of his identity also marks the loss of it,
and here too it is clear that identity is not distinct from
political place in a world of meaning where public and private,
social and personal, are not yet fully differentiated:

> Authority melts from me. Of late, when I cried 'Ho!',

Like boys unto a muss, kings would start forth
And cry 'Your will?'. Have you no ears? I am
Antony yet.

(Antony and Cleopatra, III. xiii. 90–3)

The loss of political place finally entails the dissolution of the self: 'here I am Antony,/Yet cannot hold this visible shape' (IV. xiv. 13–14) (Dollimore, 1984:211). Beyond these instances it is possible to hear the poignant exchange between another politically displaced figure, a king without a kingdom, and his fool: 'Who is it that can tell me who I am?' 'Lear's shadow' (*King Lear*, I. iv. 229–30).

It is difficult, then, to read these plays simply as humanist texts, endorsing the unified human subject or affirming a continuous and inviolable interiority as the essence of each person. This does not, of course, imply that nothing had changed since the fifteenth century. Patently what it meant to be human had altered radically since *The Castle of Perseverance* displayed its fragmented protagonist. But it was to change again before a fully-fledged humanism came to assert the inalienable identity of the individual.

None the less, there are in the plays of the late sixteenth and early seventeenth centuries intimations of the construction of a place which notions of personal identity were later to come to fill. Brutus, for example, silently conscious of Portia's death, stoically refusing to speak of it, seems to give testimony to an inner being, communing with itself, independent of what is spoken. Henry V, calling in question the 'proud dream' of ceremony which distinguishes the sovereign, struggles to define a watchful interiority behind degree and form, which pays the price of sovereignty and thus legitimates it (*Henry V*, IV. i. 226–80). Ferdinand, unable to find for himself or the audience a convincing motive for his actions in his examination of their 'cause', seems – to twentieth-century criticism at least – to display in the intensity of his sexual imaginings a subjectivity unaware of its own incestuous recesses (*The Duchess of Malfi*, IV. ii. 281–7).

The classic case is, of course, Hamlet. Francis Barker has written of Hamlet's assertion of an authentic inner reality defined by its difference from an inauthentic exterior (Barker, 1984:35).

> 'Tis not alone my inky cloak, good mother,
> Nor customary suits of solemn black,
> Nor windy suspiration of forc'd breath,
> No, nor the fruitful river in the eye,
> Nor the dejected haviour of the visage,
> Together with all forms, moods, shapes of grief,
> That can denote me truly. These, indeed, seem;
> For they are actions that a man might play;
> But I have that within which passes show –
> These but the trappings and the suits of woe.
>
> (I. ii. 77–86)

'That within' is here distinguished from 'actions that a man might play', and this interiority, this essence, the heart of Hamlet's mystery, has been the quarry not only of Rosencrantz and Guildenstern, agents of the king's surveillance, but of liberal-humanist criticism of the nineteenth and twentieth centuries. Hamlet's irresolution, his melancholy, his relations with Ophelia, his career at Wittenberg and his Oedipal tendencies have all been thoroughly investigated and documented in the attempt to find the truth of Hamlet's subjectivity, the reason why he says what he says, and acts, or fails to act, as he does.

The quest is, of course, endless, because the object of it is not there. As Barker goes on to argue, 'this interiority remains, in *Hamlet*, gestural .... At the centre of Hamlet, in the interior of his mystery, there is, in short, nothing' (Barker, 1984:36–7). Hamlet is, after all, the most discontinuous of Shakespeare's heroes. Alternately mad, rational, vengeful, inert, determined, the Hamlet of the first four acts of the play is above all *not* an agent. It is as if the hero is traversed by the voices of a succession of morality fragments, wrath and reason, patience and resolution. In none of them is it possible to locate the true, the essential Hamlet. In this sense Hamlet is precisely not a unified subject.

Paradoxically, Act v presents a second Hamlet who no longer struggles towards identity and agency. This Hamlet utters no soliloquies, makes no further efforts to define the nobler course, ceases to struggle with and between reason and revenge, readily surrenders to providence (v. ii. 212–13) and the 'divinity that shapes our ends' (v. ii. 10), and in these terms is able to act. This Hamlet is an inhabitant of a much older cosmos, no more than the consenting instrument of God, received into heaven at his death by flights of angels (v. ii. 352). The play, which has begun to define an interiority as the origin of meaning and action, a human subject as agent, cannot produce closure in terms of an analysis which in 1601 does not yet fully exist. The moral and political problems are thus resolved by other means.

Or perhaps not. There is more to be said about the moral and political problems. And also, in spite of the quantities of material already devoted to the topic, just a little more to be said about the protagonist's subjectivity.

2.4 The soliloquy

How is the impression of interiority produced? Above all by means of the formal development of the soliloquy. The soliloquy, as Raymond Williams has pointed out, is the condition of the possibility of presenting on the stage a new conception of the free-standing individual (Williams, 1981:142). In conjunction with the more or less contemporaneous development of the iambic pentameter, the soliloquy makes audible the personal voice and offers access to the presence of an individual speaker. In contrast to the alliterative verse of the fifteenth century, and the 'tumbling' fourteeners characteristic of the sixteenth-century moralities, the more flexible and fluent iambic pentameter, to the degree that it does not rhyme and is not necessarily end-stopped, disavows the materiality of the process of enunciation and simulates a voice expressing the self 'behind' the speech (Easthope, 1983:51–77, 94–109). As the literal drama discards allegory, and morality personifications give way to social types, concrete individuals, the moral conflicts externalized in the moralities are internalized in the soliloquy and thus understood to be confined *within* the *mind* of the protagonist. The struggle between good and evil shifts its centre from the macrocosm to the microcosm.

In *Doctor Faustus* (1592?), for example, in spite of the play's obvious formal and thematic continuities with the morality tradition, the hero is predominantly a free-standing, literal figure in a geographically- and chronologically-specific world. Faustus first appears alone in his study, and though later Mephostophilis claims to have turned the pages of the Bible to lead him to the false syllogism (ll.1887–9), the text gives no evidence that he is visible to the audience at this point. On the contrary, Faustus is apparently alone, and it is in soliloquy that he makes his decision to seek a deity. When the Good and Bad Angels appear and address him, Faustus gives no indication that he has heard them. They appear in response to the doubts formulated by Faustus himself: unlike the corresponding figures in *The Castle of Perseverance*, they do not initiate the moral debates. In an ironic reversal of the morality tradition, Faustus summons his own destroyer, and it is Mephostophilis who pleads with him to renounce his unlawful demands (ll.309–10). The abstractions, in other words, have become relatively peripheral. The Angels are shadowy figures whose very existence might be an illusion. Mephostophilis, despite his denial, could be the product of a conjuring trick (ll.273–82). The shrunken personifications and the pliant Vice are diminished in proportion to the dominance of a human hero whose conflict is largely internalized.

But the Renaissance soliloquy shows evidence of its own genealogy, rendering precarious precisely the unified subjectivity which it is its project to represent. The repressed discontinuities of the allegorical tradition return to haunt the single voice which speaks. In the struggle between resolution and remorse which structures the soliloquies of Faustus the distinct voices of the allegorical tradition are clearly audible. In the following instance, though Faustus is alone and the speech is formally a soliloquy, it is as if the Bad Angel addresses him – by name and in the second person – while Faustus, like Mankind a century and a half before, hesitates, hearing the voice of the Good Angel urge him in the opposite direction. I give the soliloquy with the 'voice' of the Bad Angel in italics to show the effect of dialogue:

> *Now Faustus, must thou needs be damn'd,*
> *And canst not now be sav'd.*
> *What bootes it then to thinke on God or Heaven?*
> *Away with such vaine fancies, and despaire,*
> *Despair in GOD, and trust in Belzebub:*
> *Now go not backward: no, Faustus, be resolute:*
> *Why waverst thou?* O something soundeth in mine eares,
> Abjure this Magicke, turne to God againe.
> I and Faustus will turne to God againe.
> *To God? he loves thee not ...*

(ll. 389–98)

The 'voice' of the Bad Angel combines reasoning, coaxing and imperatives, like the traditional Vice. Meanwhile the 'voice' of the Good Angel sounds in his ears and Faustus responds. The three figures of the traditional morality debate have clearly differentiated roles within this soliloquy.

The final speech of the play is an internalized psychomachia between despair and repentance, the certainty of death and a longing to escape. Its closest analogue in the moralities is

44

the dialogue between Death and Everyman (*Everyman, c.*1500, ll.85–183). Everyman's terror mounts gradually. He begs at first for twelve years to repent, and later pleads, 'Spare me till tomorrow'. Eventually he learns the meaning of death: it is eternal, irrevocable, solitary. Everyman turns to flee, but in vain. Death's repeated 'nay' is stern and implacable, preventing all escape. Finally Everyman comes close to despair, wishing he had never been born. In Faustus's last soliloquy two voices are also distinguishable, one cold, rational, certain, the other pleading and bargaining like Everyman. I give a section of the speech with the voice of Death in italics. Here the unease of the formal disjunction between unity and discontinuity is evident in the fact that Death identifies Faustus now in the second person, now in the third, and once in the first person:

Ah Faustus,
Now hast thou but one bare houre to live,
And then thou must be damn'd perpetually.
Stand still you ever moving Spheares of heaven,
That time may cease, and midnight never come;
Faire natures eye, rise, rise againe and make
Perpetuall day: or let this houre be but
A yeare, a month, a weeke, a naturall day,
That Faustus may repent, and save his soule.
O lente lente currite noctis equi:
The stars move still, time runs, the clocke will strike,
The devill will come, and Faustus must be damn'd.
O, Ile leape up to my God: who pulls me downe?
See see where Christs bloud streames in the firmament,
One drop would save my soule, halfe a drop, ah my Christ.
Rend not my heart, for naming of my Christ,
Yet I will call on him: O, spare me Lucifer.
Where is it now? *'tis gone. And see where God*
Stretcheth out his arme and bends his irefull browes:
Mountaines and hils, come, come and fall on me,
And hide me from the heavy wrath of God.

No, no?
Then will I headlong run into the earth:
Gape earth; *O no it will not harbour me.*

(ll.1926–48)

Who, then, is speaking, when Faustus speaks of – or to, or about – himself? The speaker, the subject of the enunciation, is there before us on the stage, palpably a unity. But the subject of the utterance, the subject inscribed in the speech, is fragmented, discontinuous. In a similar way Hieronimo in soliloquy in *The Spanish Tragedy* (*c.*1590) is at once unified and discontinuous (iii. xiii. 1–44). Hieronimo cites to himself the scriptural prohibition on human revenge, 'Vindicta mihi', and replies to himself, 'Ay, heaven will be reveng'd of every ill.' And then in the imperative, 'Then stay, Hieronimo.' But in another and contradictory imperative, 'Strike, and strike home, where wrong is offered thee'. Six lines in the second person lead to resolution in the first: 'And to conclude, I will revenge his death'. There follow eighteen lines defining in the first person a strategy for avoiding detection and then, the choice of action settled, an imperative addressed to himself to assemble in a single cause the fragments which constitute the human being:

Hieronimo, thou must enjoin
Thine eyes to observation, and thy tongue
To milder speeches than thy spirit affords,
Thy heart to patience, and thy hands to rest,
Thy cap to courtesy, and thy knee to bow,
Till to revenge thou know, when, where and how.

In the tradition of the psychomachia the fragments of being are predominantly abstract moral or psychological qualities, but the distinction between physical and psychological properties is a modern one – the effect of the humanist isolation of the mind as the essence of the subject. In the 'little world made cunningly/Of elements', where the blend of humours

46

defines disposition, the physical and the psychological are continuous. The repentant Everyman greets his own Beauty, Strength and Five Senses, as well as Discretion and Knowledge, only to be parted from them all as he crawls into the grave. Lady Macbeth's invocation to cruelty displays the contradictory nature of the subject in the early seventeenth century:

> Come, you spirits
> That tend on mortal thoughts, unsex me here;
> And fill me, from the crown to the toe, top-full
> Of direst cruelty. Make thick my blood,
> Stop up th' access and passage to remorse,
> That no compunctious visitings of nature
> Shake my fell purpose nor keep peace between
> Th' effect and it. Come to my woman's breasts
> And take my milk for gall, you murd'ring ministers,
> Wherever in your sightless substances
> You wait on nature's mischief. Come, thick night,
> And pall thee in the dunnest smoke of hell,
> That my keen knife see not the wound it makes,
> Nor heaven peep through the blanket of the dark
> To cry 'Hold, hold'.
>
> (*Macbeth*, I. v. 37–51)

The speaker, Lady Macbeth, the subject of the enunciation, is visible on the stage, there before us as a unity, performing the invocation. But the subject of the utterance is barely present in the speech. It is not the grammatical subject of the actions – the spirits are – and the moment it appears (as 'me') in the third line of the text, it is divided into crown, toe, cruelty, blood, remorse, nature, breasts, milk. The speech concludes with the opposition between heaven and hell, reproducing the morality pattern of the human being as a

deground between cosmic forces, autonomous only to the
int of choosing between them.

The contradictions between unity and discontinuity produce, from a humanist point of view, some odd effects. When
Sir Charles Mountford in *A Woman Killed with Kindness* (1603)
kills two men in a fight, he exclaims:

> My God! what have I done? what have I done?
> My rage hath plung'd into a sea of blood,
> In which my soul lies drown'd.

Remorse is instantaneous and induces what sounds to a
modern interpretation suspiciously like equivocation: 'It was
not I, but rage, did this vile murder'. But the line that follows
makes it clear that the isolation of rage is not an evasion of
the consequences: 'Yet I, and not my rage, must answer it'
(*A Woman Killed with Kindness*, III. 42–52). The episode is
parallel in some ways to the end of *Othello*, where Othello the
Venetian executes Othello the pagan in the name of Venetian
justice (v. ii. 341–59).

Leavis, from a humanist perspective, reads Othello's final
speech as 'un-self-comprehending' 'self-dramatisation' (Leavis,
1962:152). This assumes, of course, not only a self to be
comprehended and dramatized, but also an anterior self to do
the dramatizing and comprehending (or not). What makes
such a reading not only possible but persuasive? The answer,
again, is that it is above all an effect of the formal development
of the soliloquy. The precariously unified protagonist of
Renaissance drama is in practice marked by another division
which points forwards to a fully-fledged humanism rather
than backwards to the Middle Ages, and this is the source of
the subject's imaginary interiority. Even, or indeed perhaps
especially, when the soliloquy is all in the first person,
when the subject defined there is continuous and non-
fragmentary, the occurrence of 'I' in speech is predicated on
a gap between the subject of the enunciation and the subject
of the utterance, the subject who is defined in the speech.

Since the subject of the enunciation always exceeds the subject of the utterance, the 'I' cannot be fully present in what it says of itself. It is this gap which opens the possibility of glimpsing an identity behind what is said, a silent self anterior to the utterance, 'that within which passes show'. The project of humanist criticism is to fill this gap.

The gap is inevitable; whether we set out to fill it is a matter of choice. In his opening speech in *The Castle of Perseverance* the newborn Mankind defines his own helplessness: 'I not wedyr to gon ne to lende/To helpe myself mydday nyn morn' (ll.281–2). He goes on to define his predicament. Like everyone else he has two angels, one who comes from Christ and the other who is his inveterate enemy and will lead him to hell (ll.301–9). If we attend primarily to the state of mind of the speaker, the subject of the enunciation, the speech is absurd. No baby knows these things. And if Mankind knows them he is not as helpless as he pretends. The precocious infant is evidently seeking attention and is probably prone to paranoia. In this he bears some resemblance to Leavis's Othello. But of course in this instance we do not read the text in this way. To make sense of *The Castle of Perseverance* is to identify Mankind with the figure defined *in* the speech, ignorant of the world, torn between conflicting imperatives, possessing some knowledge and a great deal of uncertainty. It is to read the speech primarily as information for the audience about what a human being is, rather than as access to a personal consciousness at a particular moment. In other words, it is to focus on the subject of the utterance and not on the subject of the enunciation.

But when the fragments are internalized the gap between the two subjects is prised open in a way which seems to invite a different kind of reading. Where is the focus of the audience's attention when Wendoll in *A Woman Killed with Kindness* struggles to resist his desire for Anne Frankford, wife of his friend and benefactor?

I am a villain if I apprehend
But such a thought; then to attempt the deed –
Slave, thou art damn'd without redemption.
I'll drive away this passion with a song.
A song! Ha, ha! A song, as if, fond man,
Thy eyes could swim in laughter, when thy soul
Lies drench'd and drowned in red tears of blood.
I'll pray, and see if God within my heart,
Plant better thoughts. Why, prayers are meditations,
And when I meditate – O God, forgive me –
It is on her divine perfections.

(vi. I–I I)

Who is speaking here? A villain? No, because the speaker
repudiates this villain as damned, as foolish. The villain
becomes 'thou' – precisely not the speaker. A virtuous man,
then? No, because the figure defined in the speech cannot
pray but only submit to his own desire. I have already
suggested a way in which we might read the speech in terms
of two distinct voices, two conflicting imperatives addressed
to a scarcely defined third figure, but it is easy to see how a
humanist criticism foregrounds this third figure, the 'real'
Wendoll, neither good nor evil but knowing in his uncertainty
and so imaginative, tormented.

Who is speaking when Hamlet castigates himself for his
inaction? A rogue and peasant slave? The 'I' of the utterance
is here identified as other, the 'I' of misrecognition, in contrast
to the 'I' which recognizes the failure to act as inadequate,
something to castigate. That 'I', the distinct, differed subject
of the enunciation, is the humanist subject, the sensitive
prince. And yet Hamlet's subjectivity is itself un-speakable
since the subject of the enunciation always exceeds the subject
of the utterance. Hamlet cannot be fully present to himself or
to the audience in his own speeches and *this* is the heart of
his mystery, his interiority, his essence.

One final instance: Macbeth contemplating the deep dam-

nation which is the inevitable consequence of Duncan's
murder.

> And pity, like a naked new-born babe,
> Striding the blast, or heaven's cherubin hors'd
> Upon the sightless couriers of the air,
> Shall blow the horrid deed in every eye,
> That tears shall drown the wind. I have no spur
> To prick the sides of my intent, but only
> Vaulting ambition, which o'er-leaps itself,
> And falls on th' other.
>
> (I. vii. 21–8)

An early seventeenth-century audience, well-versed in the
emblematic tradition, might have attended primarily to two
major figures: on the one hand, pity, 'like a naked new-born
babe', and on the other a common medieval representation
of pride, a knight who spurs his horse forward beyond its
powers until he is thrown to the ground. For such an audience
the imagery linking the elemental and the human ('tears shall
drown the wind'), and the human and the supernatural (the
babe and heaven's cherubin), might indicate that the hero's
choice between pity and pride/ambition is a moment in the
cosmic struggle with which he is continuous and which
is duplicated in his own being. This is conjecture. Less
conjecturally, a humanist criticism attends to two quite
different figures, the subject of the utterance confronting a
moral choice, and the subject who speaks, who identifies in
cosmic imagery the perils of his own ambition. In the gap
between them it constructs the feeling, self-conscious, 'poetic'
Macbeth, a full subject, a character. The text, of course,
internalizing the emblems, reproducing them as verbal imagery, faces both ways. There is no single, correct 'historical'
reading. But the reading we choose is produced by and
produces in its turn a specific history which is always a
history of the present. Liberal humanism finds its own
reflection, its own imaginary fulness everywhere.

Whichever reading we choose there is a price to pay. To read these Renaissance soliloquies in their historical difference is to surrender liberal humanism's claims to universality and nature. Conversely, the subject of liberal humanism can never in practice control meaning, never mean exactly what is said, say exactly what is meant. Because the speaker necessarily exceeds the 'I' of the utterance, the unity promised by humanism inevitably eludes it. The humanist subject is always other than itself, can never be what it speaks. However much Hamlet tries to define the nature of true heroism, to analyse whether it is nobler to act or to suffer, a humanist knowledge finds that he is really thinking about suicide in the famous soliloquy. However he struggles to define revenge, to differentiate it from hire and salary, to identify it as an act which sends its victim to hell, humanist criticism finds him really rationalizing his own continued delay. The sensitive prince does not mean what Hamlet says because the self is always ultimately un-speakable, unuttered.

And so the unified and unique subject of liberal humanism is forever tragically locked within its own silence, uncommunicating, granted the gift of language only in order inevitably to betray itself. In twentieth-century literature, where at last there is nothing that cannot be said, where the final barriers of censorship and self-censorship have fallen, there is in the end nothing worth saying because words finally fail to render the subject transparent to itself: for Prufrock, 'It is impossible to say just what I mean'; Beckett's doomed figures speak without signifying; Pinter's alienated characters bombard each other with empty cliches in a discourse which is always and evidently the discourse of the Other.

Humanist criticism is predicated on the subject's inability to express the meaning of which the subject is nonetheless the origin. Treating all texts as utterances, it undertakes to redouble them with another meaning, what the author really meant, what we as readers are meant to understand. The project is to remedy the author's inevitable failure. The quarry is the enunciating subject itself, source of the meaning only shadowed in the text. Literary criticism is thus a choric elegy for lost presence.

It is also, however, a way of controlling knowledge, of ruling out the plurality of readings the text as text is able to release, in favour of a single meaning which must always be uncovered by a certain expertise, a fineness of judgement not given to all readers, because the meaning in question is neither in the text nor produced by the text but is always elsewhere. Lost presence is reconstructed by a knowledge which comes from outside both the text and the consciousness of the enunciating subject.

True meaning is thus unconscious. And if humanist literary criticism offers to control our reading of texts, a humanist psychoanalysis is also there to control from outside the meaning of what we say, to identify what is really being said on that other scene beyond the censoring mechanisms of condensation and displacement. In psychoanalysis 'a thing must always mean something other than itself'; the truth of the utterance is to be found only 'by juggling with clues and significances' (Guattari, 1984:55). But there is *a* truth, a meaning, which arrests the play of signification. And this truth is always familial, always located in the patient's childhood, always in the past and not the present, with the effect of negating a present whose real meaning is somewhere else. What is more, the practice of psychoanalysis is directed inwards towards the absent self. In the process of transference the patient's emotions are relived and redirected to the silent analyst.

The psychoanalytical transference, like a kind of churn for creaming off the reality of desire, leaves the patient dangling in a vertigo of nothingness, a narcissistic passion which, though less dangerous than Russian roulette, leads if successful to the same sort of irreversible fixation on unimportant details which ends by withdrawing him from all other social investments.

(ibid.)

It all helps, of course, and this is Guattari's point, to keep us off the streets. The quest for the truth of the self, our own and others', endlessly fascinating, is precisely endless, since the subject of liberal humanism is a chimera, an effect of language, not its origin. Meanwhile, the social and political are placed as secondary concerns – naturally, since our democratic institutions are so clearly expressive of what we essentially are. In the subject's hopeless pursuit of self-presence politics can safely be left to take care of itself. And we can be sure that the institutions in question will in consequence stay much as they are.

3
KNOWLEDGE

3.1 Discursive knowledge

The subject of liberal humanism is required to know. Its knowledge is won, possessed, an entitlement, a definition. Knowledge is the ground of the democratic right of electoral choice, and its analogue in the marketplace, consumer choice. It is not innate, but is planted in the subject by 'experience' as well as by education, the press, advertising and all the other sources of information indispensable to the free west. But the growth of knowledge in the individual depends on the condition of the subject itself – its sanity and maturity (lunatics and children are not entitled to vote), and its intelligence (there is no point in educating a person beyond his or her capacity). Some subjects are thus more knowing than others and this entitles them to audibility, authority and a relatively high price for their labour-power. Knowledge is knowledge of things and people – science, technology, psychology, worldly wisdom. It thus differentiates the subject from the objects of its knowledge, defines the subject as that which knows in contradistinction to that which is known. But knowledge is also the abstraction and introjection of the essence of the object. The subject thus contains the world it knows, the world of its knowledge. When it achieves self-knowledge, knowledge in its highest form, the subject becomes its own object and thus expands to touch the horizon of its understanding. And then, still climbing after knowledge infinite, it pushes back that horizon too, exceeding all known limits. The subject of liberal humanism literally knows no bounds.

It was not always so. In the Middle Ages knowledge was ultimately knowledge not of the world and the self but of God, by means of theology, the queen of the sciences, culminating discipline of the trivium and the quadrivium. To know God was not to master an object of knowledge, but to apprehend a meaning which was also truth. God, the *Logos*, at once divinity, concept and word, was pure meaning and pure being, the transcendental signified and referent, and fully to know God was not to differentiate oneself from the objects of knowledge but, on the contrary, to become absorbed in total presence, to be transformed and ultimately dissolved. Knowledge was also practice, uniting meaning and being in submission to the discourse and the discipline of salvation. It was thus absorption into the institution of the church and the body of the faithful. Knowledge was release into dispossession.

At the beginning of *Everyman* (*c.*1500) God, 'the High Father of Heaven' speaks from his throne:

> I perceive, here in my majesty
> How that all creatures be to me unkind,
> Living without dread in wordly prosperity.
> Of ghostly sight the people be so blind,
> Drowned in sin, they know me not for their God.
>
> (ll.22–6)

Ignorance imposes a distance between the creator and his 'unkind' (alienated) creatures. Not to know God is to be 'drowned in sin'. Conversely, knowledge is 'dread', since absolute truth is also absolute authority, and death is the instrument by which this majestic God maintains his power. God sends Death to apprehend Everyman.

The confrontation throws into relief Everyman's failure to

grasp the meaning of death. 'I know thee not', he protests (l.114), and offers to come to an arrangement satisfactory to them both.

Death.	What! weenest thou thy life is given thee,
	And thy worldly goods also?
Everyman.	I had weened so, verily.
Death.	Nay, nay; it was but lent thee.

(ll.161–4)

Death's 'thou shalt know' (l.96) and 'wete thou well' (ll.112, 143) underline the process by which Everyman gradually learns the meaning which is also the referent: death is inevitable, universal, final; it is also a personal destiny. But the meaning of death in isolation from the discourse of redemption is not enough. Overwhelmed by the sense of God's infinite power, Everyman comes close to despair: 'though I mourn it availeth nought . . . . I wot not well what for to do' (ll.193–5).

It is the entry of Knowledge which constitutes the turning-point of the play. Knowledge conducts Everyman to Confession in the House of Salvation and tells him to kneel down and ask mercy; she instructs him to fulfil his penance; and subsequently she hands him the garment of contrition:

Knowledge.	Put on this garment to thy behoof,
	Which is wet with your tears,
	Or else before God you may it miss,
	When you to your journey's end come shall.
Everyman.	Gentle Knowledge, what do ye it call?
Knowledge.	It is the garment of sorrow;
	From pain it will you borrow;
	Contrition it is
	That getteth forgiveness;
	It pleaseth God passing well.

(ll.638–47)

Everyman puts it on. Fully to learn the name of contrition is to encounter contrition as presence and in consequence to become contrite. Knowledge, not merely God's messenger but his surrogate, knows no distinction between theory and practice. There is therefore no subject outside what Everyman knows, no independent self which betrays his understanding. What he is at any specific moment (worldly, despairing or contrite) is an effect of the degree of his ignorance or knowledge at that moment. In other moralities it is evident that meanings can be lost as well as gained. Knowledge is not instrumental but constitutive; it is a condition of being. Truth is guaranteed by God. To learn is to recognize the *Logos*, meaning-which-is-truth (or Wisdom who is Christ); understanding is neither reflective nor creative; it is not, in other words, an activity of the subject.

Everyman is a drama of subjectivity in which the subject itself is perpetually deferred. The protagonist begins from a position of plenitude, of oneness with his world, which is explicitly illusory, an effect of misrecognition. His encounter with Death is a moment of precipitate entry into the symbolic order, into a new world of meaning which is also a world of difference. In the symbolic order being implies the possibility of non-being, presence the possibility of absence. Not to know difference is not to know God: but to know God is to know separation from the world. Everyman's companions, Fellowship, Kindred, Cousin and Goods, abandon him, leaving him to face death alone. The entry of Knowledge at this point to teach him the meaning of penitence specifies Everyman as a figure whose being is determined outside him by a discursive and institutional system of differences beyond his control.

The repentant Everyman, securely placed within the knowledge and the discipline of the church, greets for the first time his own faculties, and rejoices in a new-found plenitude:

I have hither brought
Strength, Discretion, Beauty and Five Wits. Lack I naught;
And my Good Deeds, with Knowledge clear,

All be in company at my will here.
I desire no more to my business.

(ll.679–83)

Once again, however, he encounters absence as his faculties desert him on the brink of the grave. But this time his response is prompt and correct: 'O all thing faileth, save God alone' (l.841). This recognition of the transcendental presence which holds the symbolic order in place is the guarantee of his own continued existence in a world beyond absence and death and without difference, a world of total presence. The self which is an effect of Christian knowledge finally melts away in the salvation which is the goal of that knowledge. Countless Christian mystics, glimpsing such a state of being, have shared the desire of St Paul in the Vulgate 'to be dissolved and be with Christ' (Phil. 1:23). Absolute presence, eliminating difference, is precisely the dissolution of the subject. The nearest approach to such a condition in this life is in the cloud of unknowing, where the soul moves beyond preliminary earthly understanding, beyond the instruction of the church, and in knowing only that it knows nothing, knows all that can be known of God (Hodgson, 1982:70).

The cloud of unknowing is a special prerogative, a way of perfection, of ecstasy which is neither available nor necessary outside the life of contemplation. But the knowledge which is a necessary prelude to unknowing is a condition of salvation. This knowledge is inscribed in a discourse which does not pretend to transparency since it is itself the location of truth. The effectivity of the (Latin) liturgy lies not beyond it in a process which it *expresses*, but in the participation of the faithful in its performance, in the process which it enacts and re-enacts. When in *Mankind* Mercy invites the audience to live in accordance with the implications of the Atonement, he does so in an aureate manner which invests his words with weight and authority:

O soverence, I beseche yow yowr condycyons to rectyfye

Ande wyth humylite and reverence to have a remocyon
To this blyssyde prynce that owr nature doth gloryfye,
That ye may be partycypable of his retribucyon.

(ll.13–16)

Clarity, more or less synonymous with transparency, is highly
prized only later, when language becomes a *medium* through
which, as through glass, thought is made visible.

If virtue foregrounds the signifying process in this way, it
is also at the level of signification that the Vices work to efface
the knowledge which leads to salvation. Newguise taxes
Mercy with using English Latin, offering him obscenities to
translate and nonsense to deliver 'in clerycall manere'
(*Mankind*, l.124ff.). The effect is to draw attention to the
signifier at the expense of the meaning. Mercy in return
reproaches the Vices with their idle language and they agree
to leave, commenting that Mercy is evidently irritated by their
'eloquence' (ll.147–50). The characteristic eloquence of vice
in the morality plays is a strongly accentual, incantatory
nonsense, which celebrates the process of enunciation itself.
Nowadays in the 1470s is cheerfully irrelevant as well as
irreverent:

> Cum wynde, cum reyn,
> Thow I cumme never ageyn!
> The Devll put out both yowr eyn!
> Felouse, go we hens tyght.
>
> (*Mankind*, ll.154–7)

This engaging nonsense which scrambles the discourse of
salvation reverberates through the moralities. The effect of
the Reformation was to transform the discourse of redemption
from a liturgical to a scriptural one, but not immediately to
challenge the notion of knowledge as inscription. The guarantee of virtue was the Word of God. Correspondingly, the Vices
continue the practice of obscuring the signified. Nearly a
hundred years after *Mankind* when Haphazard, the Vice of

Apius and Virginia, has driven Conscience out of Judge Apius,
he confirms his victory by dissipating in nonsense the meaning
of the event:

> For Conscience was carelesse, and sayling by seas
> Was drowned in a basket and had a disease.
> Sore mooved for pitye when he would graunt none
> For beyng hard harted was turned to a stone,
> And sayling by Sandwitche he sunke for his sin.
> Then care not for Conscience the worth of a pin.
>
> (ll.438–43)

As Robert Weimann points out, Vice-nonsense sometimes
indicates an alternative set of meanings, points to another
knowledge which is in conflict with Christian teaching. In
this sense it is not only impertinent, subverting the authority
of virtue, and not merely im-pertinent in its irrelevance, but
a grotesque inversion of the otherworldly knowledge which
leads to salvation. Thus in *Mankind* Mercy concludes his
address to the audience with an invocation of John the
Baptist's prophecy that the corn will be saved but the chaff
will be burnt (Matt. 3:12; Luke 3:17). Mischief counters this
by announcing that he has been taken on as a cornthresher
and invoking an alternative authority who reveals that 'Corn
servit bredibus, chaffe horsibus, straw fyrybusque'. Which is
to say, he explains, that corn is used to make bread, chaff to
feed horses, and straw to provide fire in winter (ll.54–9).
Mischief here not only celebrates the play of signification but
in doing so confronts the symbolism of Christian knowledge
with the literal, secular, physical knowledge which has to do
with survival in an agricultural community (Weimann,
1978:119–20). Vice in this instance is not simply nonsense,
though it is that; it is also a parody of sense which offers at
the same time a competing and contradictory sense.

Vices characteristically disguise their own significance – for
their victims but not of course for the audience – by changing

their names. The Vice of *Respublica* (1553) takes the spectators into his confidence:

> But now what my name is and what is my purpose,
> Taking you all for friends I fear not to disclose:
> My very true unchristian name is Avarice,
> Which I may not have openly known in no wise.

His name offends those who secretly practise what he preaches. To legitimate the practice of avarice the Vice will call himself Policy:

> The name of Policy is of none suspected,
> Policy is ne'er of any crime detected,
> So that under the name and cloak of Policy
> Avarice may work facts and 'scape all jealousy.
>
> (ll. 11–28)

Avarice here invites the audience to identify – and his victim to submit to – an alternative to Christian knowledge in which 'unchristian' avarice-as-policy is an acceptable way of life.

The project of the Vices from the beginning is to replace the discourse of salvation with the wisdom of this world which is foolishness with God (I Cor. 3:19). In *The Castle of Perseverance* Covetousness wins Mankind not in the outright battle against the virtues but by persuading him that in his old age he will need the comforts money can bring. In *Wisdom* Lucifer works by appropriating patristic discussions of scripture. The adoption of pseudonyms, an almost invariable practice of the Vices in the sixteenth-century moralities, is an elaboration of this identification of the process of temptation as the construction of a rival discourse which legitimates sin and leads to hell. *Enough is as Good as a Feast* includes a characteristically complex use of pseudonyms. Covetous, who calls himself Policy, is supported by Inconsideration, known as Reason, Precipitation, called Ready Wit, and Temerity, called Agility. Worldly Man succumbs to their joint persuasion and with wit and agility succeeds in heaping up great wealth.

When his exploited servants and tenants appeal to him for relief, he refuses in the name of reason. Struck down at last by God's Plague, he is carried off to hell, concerned to the end with his policy for disposing of his worldly goods.

The contest between these rival discourses is nowhere more evident than in the parapraxes which are a recurrent feature of Vice-comedy. The Vice proffers his victim a glimpse of what is at stake, then hastily withdraws it, insisting that he really said something quite different. In *The Nature of the Four Elements* Sensual Appetite promises Humanity,

> And yf that I ever forsake you,
> I pray God the devyl take you!
> *Humanity.* Mary, I thanke you for that othe.
> *Sensual Appetite.* A myschyfe on it! my tongue, loo,
> Wyll tryp somtyme, what so ever I do –
> But ye wot what I mene well.
>
> (ll. 532–7)

Courage in *The Tide Tarrieth No Man* (1576), whose ambiguous name demonstrates the moral sliding of the signified, inadvertently reveals that the Devil's kindness to his adherents is motivated by the hope 'after death to have body and soul'. But the Vice rapidly recovers his proper ground:

> Tush, what mean I thus of soul for to speak?
> In vain with such talk my brains I do break.
> For soul there is none when the body is dead –
> In such kind of doctrine my scholars I lead.
> Therefore, say I, take time while time is,
> For after this life there is nothing but bliss.
> There is no soul any pain to abide,
> The teachers contrary from truth are far wide.
>
> (ll. 514–21)

Two antithetical knowledges are set side by side before the audience, with the effect of drawing attention to the implications of the opposition between divine and worldly wisdom.

The most famous exponent of the parapraxis of evil is almost certainly Shakespeare's Duke of Gloucester, who quickly withdraws the sentence of death he delivers on the young Prince of Wales:

> *Gloucester.* So wise so young, they say, do never live long.
> *Prince.* What say you, uncle?
> *Gloucester.* I say, without characters, fame lives long.
> Thus, like the formal vice, Iniquity,
> I moralize two meanings in one word.
>
> (*King Richard III*, iii. i. 79–83)

Two meanings, two knowledges. The play of meaning in the world after Babel permits evil to challenge the knowledge which is guaranteed by God and ensures salvation. The gap opened by the Fall, the space between signifier and signified, signifier and referent, the place of difference, is also the place of death. Emptied of God, the discourses of evil circulate endlessly about an eternal absence. Discursive knowledge is constitutive of being. The wisdom of this world, *self*-centred, is finally centred on an eternal absence, the dissipation of the self imaged in the torments of hell. The knowledge of salvation, centred on God, implies the ultimate dissolution of the self in undifferentiated presence. Discursive knowledge does not recognize the knowing subject of liberal humanism, differentiated from the objects of its knowledge, the unified self which is the origin and proprietor of what it knows.

3.2 Empirical knowledge

But there was meanwhile an alternative tradition which can be traced back to Plato by way of St Paul. The creator, author of the book of nature, is intelligible in and through his creation. The natural world is thus a signifying system, offering access to the transcendental signified, the divine authorial intention: 'For the invisible things of him from the creation of the world are clearly seen, being understood by the things that are made, even his eternal power and Godhead' (Rom. 1:20). In this form the tradition of empirical knowledge is not in conflict with discursive knowledge since in each case the project is the same: to read God in his inscriptions, the world or the church. In the Middle Ages empirical knowledge was subordinate to discursive knowledge and was constantly policed by the church wherever it threatened to lay claim to an alternative institution or institutional powers. But the ideological and institutional uncertainties which immediately followed the breakdown of control by the Catholic church offered a space in which empirical knowledge, not apparently in conflict with either Catholic or Protestant orthodoxy, was developed and modified to the point where experience was finally to supplant discourse as the source of truth.

In the course of this development and modification certain areas of conflict with the earlier orthodoxy gradually emerged and proved to be decisive for the history of the subject. First, the book of nature requires a reader as well as a writer. Empirical knowledge thus inaugurates a difference between the knowing subject and the objects of its knowledge, and this difference becomes definitive for the subject. The subject is now defined as that which knows, in contradistinction to that which is known. Secondly, language ceases to be the location of knowledge and becomes its instrument. Discourse is thus no longer constitutive but expressive. Since things themselves, now differentiated as objects, cannot in consequence implant knowledge of themselves in the subject, it is experience, lodged in the subject itself, which is now the source of knowledge and thus constitutive of being. The subject consequently takes the place of God and becomes the author and guarantee of its own (subjective) truth. And thirdly, the question, 'what can it *do?*', always implicitly addressed to discursive knowledge and confidently answered by the promise of salvation, is also addressed to empirical knowledge but, then as now, more evasively met. (Or perhaps more plurally met, since now the promise held out to the social body by empirical knowledge is alternatively the mastery of nature, imperial power, boundless economic growth or mutually assured destruction.) The resolution in the late seventeenth century of these three areas of conflict was the triumph of liberal humanism – and the subsequent interrogation of the resolution then adopted has consistently been identified as a threat to its hegemony.

In John Rastell's humanist play, *The Nature of the Four Elements* (*c.*1520), Nature, Studious Desire and Experience, equipped with a globe, a model of the cosmos and a map, provide for the instruction of Humanity and the audience an exposition of the received scientific wisdom of the moment. Their main areas of concern in the incomplete text which survives are the elements, geography, cosmology, and a series of compelling arguments, logical and empirical, that the earth is a sphere. This is essentially a popularization of the knowledge familiar to scholars, in the manner of Caxton's *Mirror of the World* (1480). Knowledge as defined in *The Nature of the Four Elements* is natural philosophy, and nature is seen as a means to knowledge of the creator:

> But man to knowe God is a dyffyculte,
> Except by a meane he himselfe inure,
> Which is to knowe Goddys creaturys that be:
> As furst them that be of grosyst nature,
> And than to know them that be more pure,
> And so by lytyll and lytyll ascendynge
> To know Goddys creaturys and mervelous werkinge.
>
> And thys wyse man at the last shall come to
> The knowlege of God and his hye mageste.
>
> (ll.92–100)

The project of empirical knowledge is thus the same as the

project of discursive knowledge. But their methods are different. Experience, who has travelled the world and can in consequence confirm the accuracy of maps, adduces evidence rather than God as the guarantee that the world is a sphere. He argues on the basis of the apparent movement of the stars in relation to ships and the longer visibility of tall objects on the horizon (ll.1060–1118). He is about to provide a demonstration of the point, using the globe and a candle, when the text unfortunately breaks off. But not before Experience has insisted that Humanity already knows all this (l.1059): he has only, therefore, to draw the appropriate conclusion from the familiar facts. In other words, the subject as defined in this text of about 1520 produces knowledge out of its own resources, simply by recognizing the implications of its experience.

Language in *The Four Elements* is an instrument of communication, and the only problem that might arise is its adequacy to the material. Happily, the text patriotically announces, the vernacular is now sufficiently developed for the task of explaining matter of such gravity (ll.25–8). The style of exposition in the play is exactly the style of a good lecture – vigorous, colloquial and transparent.

In response to the implicit question, 'what can it do?', a humanist text naturally claims that there is a connection between knowledge and virtue. But the nature of the connection is slightly elusive:

> And this wyse man at the last shall come to
> The knowledge of God and his hye mageste,
> And so to lerne to do his dewte, and also
> To deserve of his goodnes partener to be.

> (ll.99–102)

The complex structure which holds together meaning, practice and redemption in *Everyman* has no place outside the discursive model of knowledge. Science does not self-evidently lead to duty and salvation. The play hurries over this difficulty, while offering to motivate Humanity by urging that ignorance is contemptible (ll.1441–2), that the desire for knowledge is 'natural' (ll. 213, 289–95), and that understanding differentiates Humanity from the beasts and legitimates his dominion over them (ll. 211–12). The text betrays its unease about the link between knowledge and virtue precisely by drawing attention to the fact that the connection is not inevitable. It insists at some length that God will not reward those who become wise only in order to heap up wealth. This is easily done, it is true, but far too much value is currently attached to riches. The virtuous use their knowledge for the benefit of the commonwealth, and this is best achieved by bringing knowledge to the ignorant (ll.52–91). Thus by a triumphant circularity – knowledge is beneficial and therefore virtuous when it is put to work to dispel ignorance – the text evades the obligation to theorize the moral and eschatological value of the knowledge it offers, while at the same time allowing it to become apparent to the audience that wisdom is a means not only to dominion over nature but also to worldly wealth.

A similar uncertainty about whether the value of knowledge is primarily moral or material can be traced through a group of allegorical plays which seem to have been designed for school performance at intervals during nearly fifty years of the sixteenth century. These concern the adventures of Wit, who is in love with Science or Wisdom. In John Redford's *Wit and Science* (early 1530s) the hero, who is the son of Nature, wants to marry Science, the daughter of Reason and Experience. At his second attempt Wit overcomes the giant, Tediousness, climbs Mount Parnassus and wins the lady. The beginning of the play is lost, but the text as it stands gives no indication that knowledge leads to God. There is, however, a connection between Science and virtue, in the sense that it 'goth/In her of kynd to do good to all' (ll.1060–1). Wit is evidently to grow up to resemble Gaius Flaminius, virtuous scholar, the humanist hero of Medwall's *Fulgens and Lucres* (*c.*1500). And like Humanity in *The Four Elements* he is to care more for the common good than for personal advancement. Science rejects the services of Fame, Favour, Riches and Worship, emissaries of the World (ll.620–72).

And yet this is the only episode in this elegant, economical and coherent allegory which is difficult to interpret. It takes place at a moment when Wit has abandoned his quest for Science and submitted instead to the whore, Idleness. Science rejects worldly values on the grounds that she has no need of them, 'beyng as I am a lone wooman' (l.661). In any case, she continues, she has little reason at this moment to care for worldly favours, 'Seeyng the wyytys of the worlde be so waveryng' (l.674). Later, when Wit realizes his folly, it is one of his chief regrets that in place of Fame, Favour, Riches and Worship he is likely, by losing Science, to have won 'Hatred, Beggry, and Open Shame' (ll.841–2). At the beginning of the play Reason had explained that he was content to bestow his daughter on the devoted but impecunious Wit: Science had enough for them both to live on (ll.11–26). The difficulty of making a single sense of the play's position here seems to be an effect of its own hesitation between commitment to the ascetic values of a life of learning and recognition of the worldly rewards becoming available to the educated as the construction of a nation state and the transition to an economy based on the circulation of commodities created a need for clerical skills at all levels.

Knowledge leads to virtue but also to wealth and power. This is more clearly evident in *The Marriage of Wit and Science* (*c.*1569), a largely prudential remake of Redford's play. Here Wit is resentful that Nature has not made learning easier to attain. Nature explains, however, that the element of difficulty sustains the scarcity-value of knowledge. Without this great and rich employers would no longer need the services of the educated, so that those born poor would have no means of improving their social position (ll.136–43). Wit's love of Science is profoundly ambiguous:

O pearle of passing pryse, sent downe from god on hye,
The swetest beauty to entise that hath bene sene with eye.
The wel of wealth to all, that no man doth annoye:
The kaye of kingedomes and the steale of everlasting joye.
The treasure and the store, whom all things good began,
The nurse of Lady Wysedoms lore, the lincke of man and
                                                    man.
                                          (ll.799–804)

The last line is conventional, but the rest of the speech, and
indeed the play as a whole, make it impossible to decide for
certain whether the wealth, the kingdoms and the treasure
are figurative or real. The play concludes with a great deal
of rejoicing that Wit is to marry Science and much emphasis
on the worldly recognition he has secured in consequence.
Science tells him, 'The world shall know doubt not, and shal
blow out your fame' (l.1536).

In *The Marriage Between Wit and Wisdom* (1579) a substantial part of the action concerns the comic activities of Idleness,
who in this play has become male. Idleness picks Wit's pocket,
steals a porridge pot, appears disguised as a quack doctor, a
ratcatcher and then a priest, is outwitted by Snatch and Catch
who are cleverer criminals, and is finally repudiated when
Wit marries Wisdom. These exploits display the shifts that
must be made in order to survive without education. Though
Idleness insists on his 'mother wit' (l.148), he is a ready
victim for Snatch and Catch with their superior cunning, and
at the end of the play he becomes an outcast. Like *Nice Wanton*
(c.1550), *The Disobedient Child* (1560s) and Gascoigne's *The
Glass of Government* (1575), the text sets out to demonstrate
that idleness in youth leads to enforced idleness and so to
crime in adult life. Conversely, the market value of knowledge
guarantees those who possess it a good, steady job.

3.3 Knowledge in conflict

The education Idleness neglects remains primarily discursive. Latin grammar, rhetoric and logic constituted the school curriculum, and in the universities divinity retained its pre-eminence as the culminating discipline of the quadrivium. Knowledge is thus the place in this period of a major contest for meaning. Either empirical or discursive, dissolving the self on the one hand or installing the subject on the other, its motivation may be eschatological, moral or material. These meanings converge and conflict in a number of plays of the period in specific but distinct ways, with implications in each case for the identity of the subject.

Knowledges in conflict produce the tragedy of Doctor Faustus who, from inside the framework of a predominantly discursive knowledge, repudiates its promise of salvation and seeks the worldly fruits of empirical knowledge. Within a framework which allots sovereignty to heaven or hell, Faustus, in quest of wealth and dominion, sets out to become more than man – and ends longing to be less.

The implied question which runs through Faustus's opening soliloquy is, 'what can knowledge do?' One by one he rejects the traditional disciplines on the grounds that the power inscribed in them is not absolute, not transcendental:

> Is to dispute well logickes chiefest end?
> Affoords this art no greater miracle?
> Then read no more ....
>
> Couldst thou make men to live eternally,
> Or being dead, raise them to life againe,
> Then this profession were to be esteem'd.
>
> (Doctor Faustus, ll.36–8, 52–4)

Only God can legitimately transcend nature, and the miracle promised by the discourse of salvation is precisely eternal life. But when Faustus finally reaches divinity, he dismisses it in a false syllogism which rejects exactly that promise:

> The reward of sin is death ....
> If we say that we have no sinne we deceive our selves, and
> there is no truth in us. Why then belike
>   We must sinne, and so consequently die,
>   I, we must die an everlasting death.
>   What doctrine call you this?
>
> (ll.67–74).

In invoking each of these premises, Faustus omits the second half of the quotation, which in each case tempers the divine justice with Christian mercy and promises redemption (Rom. 6:23; 1 John 1:8–9). He concludes that orthodox knowledges can do nothing worth doing, and turns to magic as a source of riches and power:

> Oh, what a world of profite and delight,
> Of power, of honour, and omnipotence,
> Is promised to the studious artizan?
> All things that move betweene the quiet poles
> Shall be at my command: emperors and kings
> Are but obey'd in their severall provinces:
> Nor can they raise the winde, or rend the cloudes:
> But his dominion that exceeds in this,
> Stretcheth as farre as doth the mind of man.
>
> (ll.80–8)

The syllogism, which for Faustus is decisive, is the primary instrument of deduction in scholastic logic, and within the framework of discursive knowledge logic itself is an authoritative source of truth, 'an arte to try the corne from the chaffe, the truthe from every falshed' (Wilson, 1551, sig. B 2v). Both Bacon and Locke would later resist the attribution of such importance to the syllogism, on the grounds that it demonstrates no truth which is not already implied in the premises. The empiricist separation of meaning from truth renders the syllogism merely instrumental, since it 'commands assent ... to the proposition, but does not take hold of the thing' (Bacon, 1960:41). While modern logic is seen as a formal system for testing the validity of an argument on the basis of the relations between the propositions, where the criteria for judging the truth of the propositions lie outside the sphere of logic itself, scholastic logic holds dialectics to be a ground of knowledge. In a problematic which defines language as opaque and identifies (true) meaning with truth, the syllogism is not transparent but is the location of truth. Where God is the transcendental meaning-as-truth, falsehood is synonymous with evil, and consequently finds its signified, which is also its referent, in hell. Here is the entire chapter on logic from Caxton's *Mirror of the World*:

> The seconde science is logyke whyche is called dyalectique. This science proveth the 'pro' and the 'contra': that is to saye the verite or trouthe, and otherwyse. And it preveth wherby shal be knowen the trewe fro the fals and the good fro the evyll, so veryly that for the good was created heven and maad, and on the contrarye wyse, for the evyll was helle maad and establisshyd, whiche is horryble, stynkyng and redoubtable.
>
> (Caxton, 1913:34)

Faustus rejects the discourse of salvation anchored in heaven and replaces it with the hellish signifying nonsense of magic:

> These metaphisicks of magitians,
> And negromantick bookes are heavenly.
> Lines, circles, signes, letters, and characters,
> I these are those that Faustus most desires.
>
> (*Doctor Faustus*, ll.76–9)

Later we see him performing the ceremonies and Latin invocations which constitute a travesty of the signifying practices of Christian knowledge. But the discourse of salvation constantly returns to haunt him, not only in the words of the Good Angel and the Old Man, but in the very moment when, in a parody of the Atonement, Faustus seals his difference from God in writing and in blood. His blood congeals and the words 'Homo fuge' are momentarily inscribed on his body. The devils distract him with 'crownes and rich apparell', the emblems of wealth and power (l.471 S.D.).

In the problematic of discursive knowledge understanding is a preparation for the dissolution of the self. It is empirical knowledge which promises dominion. In empiricism as Locke would define it a century later, the subject of humanism takes, in effect, the place of God. Faustus seeks to be a knowing subject. He has mastered the objects of knowledge to a certain point, yet he is still 'but Faustus, and a man' (l.51). His project is a greater one: 'Here tire my braines to get a deity' (l.90). When he seeks empirical knowledge, however, Faustus is rapidly brought up against its limits. The discourse of evil cannot tell him anything he does not already know: 'These slender questions Wagner can decide:/Hath Mephostophilis no greater skill?' (ll.600–1). The signifying practices of hell forbid him to know who made the world (ll.618–23). In the sphere of satanic knowledge the book of nature does not point to eternal power and Godhead. And human dominion is in practice no more than a series of conjuring tricks.

The anguish Faustus constantly rehearses, and dissipates in vain delights, is a recognition of the limits which confine the subject who usurps the place of God. The play is poised between two problematics, a discursive knowledge which does not lead to power, and an empirical knowledge which is not yet certain of its own project or its authority. Faustus, aspiring to more than discursive knowledge permits, cannot become an autonomous, knowing subject, because as yet the only fully articulated, coherent alternative to Christian knowledge is the discourse of hell which is service to Lucifer. At the critical moment when his blood congeals it is this autonomy that is in question:

What might the staying of my bloud portend?

74

Is it unwilling I should write this byll?
Why streames it not, that I may write a fresh?
Faustus gives to thee his soule: ah there it staid.
Why shouldst thou not? is not thy soule thine owne?

(ll.453–7)

From the moment of his signature, as the rest of the play makes clear, his soul, previously heaven's, belongs to hell. Lucifer is now his sovereign lord, and though a return to the service of God remains a perpetual possibility until the point of death, there is as yet no place of full ownership, no place of true and legitimate dominion for the knowing subject. At last, in terror, Faustus, who sought a deity, longs to be a beast without a soul (l.1964), or to be dissolved, though not with Christ (ll.1970, 1977–8). He is finally torn to pieces by the devils, dispersed in hell.

In *The Spanish Tragedy* (*c.*1590), which is probably more or less contemporary with *Doctor Faustus*, though the dates of both texts are uncertain, Hieronimo constitutes himself a knowing subject in relation to the objects of his knowledge. But haunted by the sovereignty which resides outside the self, uncertain whether he speaks in the name – the discourse – of heaven or hell, or neither, Hieronimo finally bites out his own tongue, repudiating the right which defines the subject, the right of speech itself.

Hieronimo sets out to identify the murderers of his son and bring them to justice. He appeals for help to heaven and in apparent consequence a letter falls to the stage (III. ii. 23 S.D.). In it Belimperia reveals the names of the murderers. Afraid that the letter may be a trap, Hieronimo determines to assemble further information which will confirm its contents (III. ii. 48–9). While he is lamenting heaven's seeming indifference, the Hangman brings him Pedringano's letter to Lorenzo which provides conclusive evidence that Lorenzo and Balthazar are the murderers. Barred from access to the king, Hieronimo is unable to secure justice. The knowledge he possesses is thus ineffectual: it can *do* nothing. His despair leads to madness and in this condition he resolves to reunite truth with action in revenge, which belongs to hell:

> Though on this earth justice will not be found,
> I'll down to hell, and in this passion
> Knock at the dismal gates of Pluto's court....
> Till we do gain that Proserpine may grant
> Revenge on them that murdered my son:
> Then will I rent and tear them thus and thus,
> Shivering their limbs in pieces with my teeth.
>
> (III. xiii. 108–23)

Hieronimo has written a tragedy which he, Belimperia and the two murderers are to play before the king. But each is to perform in a different language. Balthazar reasonably protests that this will create considerable confusion, 'And hardly shall we all be understood' (IV. i. 181). But the occlusion of the signified is a device to withhold meaning and truth from the participants and the (fictional) spectators until, the action completed, Hieronimo himself, as author, will 'make the matter known'(IV. i. 187). The epilogue abandons the sundry languages. Hieronimo shows the body of his son and tells in the vernacular the story of the murder. The actors, he now makes clear, are really dead, uniting signifier and signified (Hieronimo's play and its meaning), signified and referent (the meaning and the event). He runs to hang himself but the king and his companions intervene to make him 'inform', 'speak', explain the truth. He tells the story again, but still they press him to speak. This time he refuses: 'never shalt thou force me to reveal/The thing which I have vowed inviolate' (IV. iv. 187–8). He bites out his tongue, and when urged to write the truth instead, he calls for a knife to mend his pen and kills himself.

What is the secret that Hieronimo bites out his tongue to conceal, the thing which he has vowed inviolate? There is apparently nothing left to tell. He has twice told the story of the murder and his revenge. But what is impenetrable, unknown, unknowable is the explanation which lies beyond the narrative, the justifying answer to the insistent and repeated 'why?'. He dies in defence of this secret, which is as yet no secret at all, but is none the less the unspeakable secret of an emergent humanism.

The question that inaugurates Hieronimo's silence is Castile's, 'But who were thy confederates in this?' (IV. iv. 176). The literal answer is that he had none. Belimperia was an accomplice but she knew nothing of the nature of Hieronimo's planned revenge. What is left uncertain in this play is what is so clearly defined in *Faustus*, the role of heaven and hell. It is his confederacy with the forces of good or evil, and thus the legitimacy of his knowledge-action, that Hieronimo will not – cannot – reveal.

The first piece of knowledge Hieronimo acquires is contained in the letter from Belimperia. The provision of the letter, which begins the constitution and isolation of Hieronimo as a knowing subject, this 'miracle', as he calls it (III. ii. 32), may or may not be the work of heaven. The cryptic stage direction gives no clue: 'A letter falleth' (III. ii. 23 S.D.). Does the letter fall from 'the heavens' above the stage without human agency? An illusionist director might make Belimperia drop it from her window in the gallery above the stage and in this way move the fiction into a fully humanist world. As it stands, the text leaves the question open.

Hieronimo solicits help from the heavens but they are 'counter-mur'd with walls of diamond' (III. vii. 16). Or are they? Is the Hangman who brings Pedringano's letter an agent of good or evil? Or neither?

In his madness Hieronimo turns to hell, but is the author of the tragedy of Soliman and Perseda mad or sane? Hieronimo himself invokes heaven as the agent of tragic justice: 'Now shall I see the fall of Babylon,/Wrought by the heavens in this confusion' (IV. i. 195–6). But the audience might wonder quite what part the heavens play in the tragedy of Soliman and Perseda. Hieronimo, author and director of the play, obscuring the signified in the device of the sundry languages, holding the signifier on to both signified and referent, has made himself absolute by taking control of meaning, truth and action.

Hieronimo, in possession of the documentary evidence, the objects of his empirical knowledge, stands on the threshold of modern subjectivity. He appropriates the right to act on what he knows, becomes the agent of events, takes control without seeking justification in a knowledge guaranteed outside him by either heaven or hell. He has no confederates. And yet the play cannot break with the terms of the discursive model of knowledge. Heaven and hell remain presences in the text, constantly reopening the question of the legitimacy of Hieronimo's actions.

In the world of empirical knowledge, in relation to the knowledge he possesses, Hieronimo is a speaking subject. In the world of discursive knowledge, where truth and action are authorized outside the self, Hieronimo has finally no certain and identifiable place from which to speak. But the knowing, speaking subject is also finally reduced to silence. Seeking authority for its actions ultimately from within, in what it *is*, the subject of humanism can never find a guarantee of legitimacy. The self which knows exists only in the process of knowing, and in contradistinction to the objects of its knowledge. Produced from moment to moment, but never fully present to itself in any of those moments, the subject cannot authorize what it knows or know what it is. It cannot therefore justify itself. Hieronimo cannot tell 'why' in this sense. He cannot tell what he does not know. But to be a subject is precisely to know and to speak. He bites out his tongue to conceal what the subject of humanism is compelled to banish from its knowledge and therefore from its utterance, the absent legitimation of its own actions.

Hamlet evidently owes a good deal to *The Spanish Tragedy*. As Lacan points out (twice), the difference between *Oedipus* and *Hamlet* is that Hamlet knows (Lacan, 1982:19–20, 43). Like Hieronimo, Hamlet distrusts the auspices of this knowledge and devises ways of putting it to the test. But confirmation of the facts does not in the world of empirical knowledge legitimate action, does not determine whether it is nobler to suffer or to take arms. Here again knowledge is ineffectual: it can do nothing. The soliloquies puzzle over and fail to resolve the divorce between knowledge and action. When he returns from England it is in the light of an older knowledge, a submission to the divinity that shapes our ends, that Hamlet is able to kill Claudius.

Prospero is an altogether more confident subject, in possession of and dispensing a humanist knowledge which both brings about and legitimates his dominion on the island. And yet here too, in *The Tempest*'s single dramatic crisis, it seems that what is at stake is the limits of knowledge-as-power. Prospero can cause tempests and mitigate their effects; he can charm the conspirators into immobility; he can enslave the inhabitants of the island; and he can control, with their consent, the courtship of Ferdinand and Miranda. But where consent is lacking, as it is in Caliban's case, Prospero's dominion depends on an elaborate system of rewards and punishments, and on perpetual vigilance.

When Prospero calls a sudden halt to the marriage masque of Ferdinand and Miranda, he is 'in some passion/That works him strongly' (*The Tempest*, IV. i. 143–4), 'touch'd with anger', 'distemper'd' (l.145), 'vex'd' (l.158) and 'troubled' (l.159). The intensity of these terms is hard to account for in the light of Prospero's own explanation:

> I had forgot that foul conspiracy
> Of the beast Caliban and his confederates
> Against my life; the minute of their plot
> Is almost come.
>
> (IV. i. 139–42)

The episode leads into Prospero's meditation on mutability

and mortality, a reflection on the instability of a world doomed to 'dissolve' (l.154) and the insubstantiality of the self which must die: 'We are such stuff/As dreams are made on' (ll.156–7).

The (emblematic?) dissolution of the masque, and the insistence on the inevitable dissolution of the self and the world, seems in excess of the sudden recollection of a plot by Caliban and his two drunken companions, unless we take into account the conflict between knowledges and the rewards they promise, between the knowledge of salvation which offers immortality and the knowledge of the world which offers dominion.[2] Prospero's humanist magic is not forbidden knowledge and its power is great. The text spares no rhetorical force in defining it:

> I have bedimm'd
> The noontide sun, call'd forth the mutinous winds,
> And 'twixt the green sea and the azur'd vault
> Set roaring war. To the dread rattling thunder
> Have I given fire, and rifted Jove's stout oak
> With his own bolt; the strong-bas'd promontory
> Have I made shake.
>
> (v. i. 41–7)

There is no lack of confidence here as the humanist subject takes the position of God and asserts a dominion over nature. But it is at the end of this speech that Prospero resolves to break his staff and bury it certain fathoms in the earth. 'And deeper than did ever plummet sound/ I'll drown my book' (ll.56–7). Again the excess – the fathoms and the plummet – if Prospero is simply announcing that he no longer needs his arcane knowledge now that he has achieved the project of recovering his dukedom.

At the end of the play, in a reference strangely at odds with the comic resolution of the narrative, Prospero speaks of a retirement to Milan, 'where/Every third thought shall be my grave'(v. i. 310–11). 'Retire' is as unexpected as the renewed reference to mortality. And his Epilogue goes on to allude to two distinct realms, invoking two different vocabularies, with the effect of juxtaposing worldly dominion and submission to an otherworldly order:

> Now I want
> Spirits to enforce, art to enchant;
> And my ending is despair
> Unless I be reliev'd by prayer,
> Which pierces so that it assaults
> Mercy itself.
>
> (ll.13–18)

This double evocation of death, apparently unmotivated either by the conclusion of the narrative or by the conventions of the epilogue, points perhaps to one of the strands of meaning in this extremely plural play. This is the crisis brought about by an encounter with the limits of apparently unlimited empirical knowledge, precipitated by Caliban's threat to Prospero's life.

3.4 The triumph of empiricism

The adaptation of *The Tempest* by Davenant and Dryden was remarkably popular in the Restoration period. Pepys saw it eight times between 1667 and 1669 (Spencer, 1965:17). An operatic version appeared in 1673, probably revised by Shadwell. In the Restoration *Tempest* there is no crisis of knowledge. Indeed, Caliban's revolt, along with Prospero's mutability speech, the burial of his staff and the drowning of his book have all disappeared. Knowledge is now knowledge of sexual difference, and it is not only empirical but fully empiricist in the sense that it stems from the experience of the individual. It is a property of the subject and a legitimate source of dominion.

Miranda has a younger sister, Dorinda. Neither has ever seen a man (in this pre-Freudian world their father evidently doesn't count as a *man*). They therefore have difficulty in grasping what the word means. Meanwhile, in another part of the island, Prospero has concealed Hippolito, whose dukedom has been usurped by Alonzo, and who has never seen a woman. Lacking experience of the referent, he too is unable to master the signified. The collision between the knowing Ferdinand and the innocent exiles creates much comic confusion, especially when Hippolito rapturously discovers first what a woman is and secondly that the world contains more than one of them. He consequently resolves that he must have them all. This leads to a duel with Ferdinand until, weak from loss of blood, Hippolito agrees to confine himself to Dorinda. Restored to their rightful property, the exiles return home rejoicing, after an uninterrupted entertainment produced by Prospero's magic.

The rewriting of *The Tempest* erases the problem of knowledge. The central comic structure is the movement from innocence through experience to the knowingness that Prospero and the audience have possessed all along. Similarly, when *Doctor Faustus* is rewritten as a farce in 1697 the crisis of knowledge has virtually disappeared. Faustus's transgression is that he has sold his soul for pleasure, and since forbidden pleasure is far less scandalous in 1697 than forbidden knowledge in 1592, the play ends with a celebration in hell, where the dismembered hero is reassembled as a unified subject: 'Faustus Limbs come together. A Dance, and Song'.

The transformation of the meaning of knowledge, and the concomitant installation of the subject of liberal humanism, is most fully documented by Bacon and Locke. It was Locke who was to prove the authoritative theorist of liberal humanism, and his work on knowledge was a development and streamlining of certain aspects of Bacon's, taking particular account of Descartes's on the way. As I have tried to suggest, philosophical texts do not exist in isolation from the meanings concurrently in circulation. I cite them here as markers rather than determinants of the movement of meaning.

The empiricist subject as Bacon defines it is radically distinct from the objects of knowledge, and experience is the means by which it comes to know them. Locke begins *An Essay Concerning Human Understanding* (1690) with the project of analysing how *we* come to attain the notions *we* have of *things* (I. i. 2, my italics), and although in the course of the work it becomes evident that there is a serious problem about whether the notions can be said to match the things, the separation – indeed, isolation – of the subject from objects is not in question. Language for both Bacon and Locke is entirely instrumental, the means by which the subject finds labels for its experience and communicates (with whatever difficulty) with other subjects. For Locke words are signs of ideas, which are ideas of things (III. ii. 1), and the ideas they label are those of the speaker (III. ii. 2). Communication depends on exciting in the listener the same idea as the speaker has (III. iii. 3; III. ix. 4). The subject is thus the origin and guarantee of meaning. The project of knowledge is control. Bacon in 1620 stresses that the power in question is not personal and individual but social – 'for the benefit and use of life' (Bacon, 1960:15). But for Locke seventy years later what knowledge can do is so obvious and so unproblematic that the *Essay* can begin by taking it for granted: 'Since it is understanding that sets man above the rest of the sensible beings, and gives him all the advantage and dominion which he has over them ...' (I. i. 1).

Following Descartes, Locke identifies the existence of the thinking (and feeling) subject as self-evident, and as the ground of all other knowledge (IV. ix. 3). Since nothing can come of nothing, the existence of the subject proves that there must be an eternal being which is the source of the subject and its powers (IV. x). The existence of God thus depends on the logically prior existence of the subject. The new metaphysics of the human essence produces an identification of good with that which causes pleasure in us and evil with what causes pain (II. xx. 2), though something like conventional religion reappears when the *Essay* proposes the possibility of an afterlife as a motive to virtue (II. xxi. 70). The mind of man, 'which takes its flight farther than the stars, and cannot be confined by the limits of the world' (II. vii. 10), capable of thoughts 'which towre above the clouds, and reach as high as Heaven it self' (II. i. 24), effectively supplants God in the humanist cosmos.

And yet Locke's majestic and triumphant subject is at the same time a poor, desolate creature, sure of nothing but its own existence, and uncertain of the real nature even of that. The following elegiac sentence stands in marked contrast to the Cartesian confidence from which it is derived: ''Tis past controversy, that we have in us something that thinks, our very doubts about what it is, confirm the certainty of its being, though we must content our selves in the ignorance of what kind of being it is' (IV. iii. 6). As for the knowledge of objects, this is not available at all. All we have is the *idea* of the *sensation* produced by the object. There is no guarantee that the idea matches the object itself. If we had more acute senses, objects would almost certainly produce quite different ideas in us. The microscope has made this clear. What if we could magnify things a thousand times more (II. xxiii. 11)? Anyone who had much sharper senses might well inhabit a quite different world, with a wholly different set of ideas (II. xxiii. 12). What is more, accurate communication cannot be guaranteed. There is no certainty either that the names we use match the same ideas in different minds, or that the same object produces the same idea in the minds of different people. The only standard is the ideas 'of those, who are thought to use those names in their most proper significations' (II. xxxii. 12). The knowing subject is unable to be sure of communicating, at the mercy of its own sensations, imprisoned by its ideas, which may or may not correspond to other people's. In order to have any certainty that its ideas are 'right' (II. xxxii. 26) it must have recourse to those who 'are thought' to have got theirs right. In order to speak intelligibly it should make strenuous efforts to conform to 'common use' (III. ix. 8; III. xi. 11). Definition of terms helps (III. xi. 17), though since definition consists of other words it is not entirely clear how.

The repeated emphasis on the authority of established figures and common use shows the extent to which the knowing subject of liberal humanism is held in place by the norms of the social body. But this subject is at the same time strangely anti-social, egocentric. Discussing the relationship between sleeping and waking, Locke explains that when the dreamer wakes he has no more knowledge of or concern for the emotions he has felt in dreams 'than he has for the happiness, or misery of a man in the Indies, whom he knows not' (II. i. 11). The man in the Indies, who is not even an object of knowledge, can hardly be expected to elicit concern or sympathy. The only delights the text alludes to are sad, unsocial pleasures – eating, drinking, or heaping up knowledge itself.

Puzzlingly, Locke's analysis leads ultimately to an infinite regress. The subject derives the materials for understanding from reflection on things, or rather, from reflection on its own ideas of things (II. i. 1). 'Since the mind, in all its thoughts and reasonings, hath no other immediate object but its own ideas, which it alone does or can contemplate, it is evident, that our knowledge is only conversant about them' (IV. i. 1). But since the mind is like a blank sheet of paper until ideas are imprinted on it (II. i. 2), the problem presents itself of what precisely it is that does the reflecting and contemplating. There are, Book I of the *Essay* insists, no innate ideas. The cabinet of the mind, to cite another of Locke's metaphors, is progressively stocked, and the stock labelled (I. ii. 15), but the mind which so busily does the sorting and labelling has no resources other than the stock itself. It has nothing to reflect *with*. The subject which is an effect of its experience has, according to the theory, no independent means to the reflection on that experience which produces understanding. At the heart of the protagonist of Locke's *Essay* there is an absence which humanist philosophers, most notably Kant, have subsequently struggled to fill.

The tragic hero of humanism, subject of empiricist knowledge, who has taken the place of God, is an isolated figure, uncertain of the knowledge of the self, the world and others which legitimates its lonely dominion. Bacon's project for knowledge was the formation of an institution for the development and exchange of scientific information, and the Royal Society was established in 1660. Since then it has become customary for knowledges to be based in institutions which define and delimit by a process of exclusion what is admissible as constituting the knowledge in question. They also have the effect of alleviating the loneliness humanism imposes, as the subject finds confirmation of its own knowledge, and thus its own identity, by participating with other subjects in the same discourse, colluding with them in the recognition of the same objects of knowledge. Other subjects (themselves an effect of discourse) fill the vacancy left by the disappearance of the absolute, legitimating presence of heaven when the subject takes the place of God. But the price of humanist legitimation is precisely the recognition of existing objects of knowledge and participation in existing discourses. It is, in other words, a high degree of conformity to what is already known, already authorized.

3.5 The production of knowledge

Liberal humanism thus establishes a confederacy of knowledge which, by affirming that experience is shared, reaffirms both the knowledge which is the effect and the subject which is the origin of the knowledge. This shared recognition is the project of classic realist drama, the dominant mode of the Restoration stage. It may seem perverse to characterize the rhymed heroics of Restoration tragedy in this way, but what the term classic realism implies is not fidelity to the real, since the recognition of reality in fiction is primarily a matter of familiarity with the conventions used to depict a recognizable world. Rather, classic realism identifies an illusionist mode which struggles to efface its own textuality, and which depends on a structure of enigma leading to closure which is also a disclosure. The project is a final moment of recognition for the characters and for the audience from which the events of the story are in retrospect fully intelligible. The spectator thus participates in a moment of collusion with the dramatist in which the experience of the events of the story is seen to lead to a shared intelligibility.

It is important that the knowledge produced in this way should be an effect of the spectator's personal experience. The humanist subject, as Locke pointed out, learns most effectively in this way: 'For, I think we may as rationally hope to see with other mens eyes, as to know by other mens understandings'. The opinions of others, though they may ratify knowledge empirically acquired, cannot take its place. 'Such borrowed wealth, like fairy-money, though it were gold in the hand from which he received it, will be but leaves and dust when it comes to use' (Locke, 1975: I. iv. 23). It is for this reason that illusionism progressively eliminates the evidence of its own textuality in order to present (an illusion of) the events themselves, offered up to be directly experienced by the audience. But of course the spectator's interpretation is to a large extent an effect of the specific events selected and the terms in which they are presented. And this too is necessary in the interests of the production of a sense of intersubjective confirmation between the author and the spectator.

Classic realism, which reaches its apotheosis in film, seems in the twentieth century so natural, so inevitable, that it is important to remind ourselves that it is in practice a quite specific form. In the medieval morality tradition emblematic staging and direct address to the audience draw attention to the fact that the play is a performance before spectators. Suspense is minimal. There is narrative – characteristically the story of mankind's temptation, fall and repentance – but no vital clues are withheld until the end, and there is in consequence no climactic moment of sudden recognition which is shared by the characters and the audience. On the contrary, nothing which would facilitate interpretation is concealed at any point. The prologue which so often recounts the story in advance, the homiletic mode of address and the allegorical names of the characters act as markers of the meaning of the play. If the audience learns from the moralities, it does so in terms of the detailed analysis they offer of a familiar moral framework. The knowledge of the audience may be put to the test, of course, by the charm or the persuasiveness of the Vices. In *Enough is as Good as a Feast*, for instance, Covetous induces Worldly Man to abandon his new-found asceticism on the grounds that wealth will enable him to be more charitable (ll.817ff.), an argument which has proved compelling even in the twentieth century. The sixteenth-century audience is, of course, invited to resist it. In this sense the audience is enlisted in the moral choices of the protagonist, asked to cast its vote for good and against evil. But the moments of choice are distributed through the play. Unless we are to imagine that the damnation of a figure called Worldly Man, who has succumbed to the temptation of a figure called Covetous, comes as a surprise to the audience, a supposition which would imply that a great deal of the play was largely unintelligible to them, there is in *Enough* no moment of closure which is simultaneously a disclosure. There is a shared knowledge between the dramatist and the audience but it is primarily discursive – a matter of meanings – rather than empiricist – a consequence of participation in the experience of the events staged.

In the Elizabethan plays I have discussed suspense is not a major element. The Chorus of *Faustus* tells us what will happen. As far as narrative is concerned, the play is no more than an amplification of the prologue. *The Spanish Tragedy* is framed by a discussion between Andrea and Revenge. Revenge's opening words are, 'Then know, Andrea' (I. i. 86). He goes on to promise that Belimperia will kill Balthazar. His choric function at the end of each act is to predict the main events of the next. In addition, the audience witnesses the murder of Horatio. No enigma withholds the identity of the murderers. What is characteristically concealed in Renaissance drama is the 'future' as it is defined in relation to the 'present' of any specific moment in the play, and in cases like *Doctor Faustus* it is only the details of that future which remain unknown. But the present and the past as they account for the future, make it intelligible, are not normally withheld. Imagine, for example, a version of *King Lear* in which the audience does not know until the final scene that Edgar's plot was Edmund's invention, that Poor Tom is Edgar and that Gloucester has not really jumped off Dover cliff.[3] And consider by contrast *The Conquest of Granada* (1670–1), where neither the audience nor the hero discovers for the first nine acts of this two-part play that the hero is not in reality a Moor, but the long-lost son of a member of the Spanish royal family.

True identity is an obvious instance of explanatory information which classic realism commonly withholds. The late sixteenth and early seventeenth centuries produced a good many plays and romances which depend on the device of a woman disguised as a boy. Five heroines of Shakespearean comedy and the corresponding figures in their sources and analogues come readily to mind. When this motif occurs in the drama or in the narrative fiction of this earlier period, the audience or reader usually knows the identity of the 'boy' from the moment of the disguise. But there is at least one exception. In *Philaster* (1609?) by Beaumont and Fletcher the hero is in love with Arethusa. She returns his love but is accused of a liaison with Bellario, formerly Philaster's page, now Arethusa's. The lovers are reunited in Act v only when Bellario proves Arethusa's innocence by revealing that 'he' is in fact Euphrasia, the daughter of Dion, who is believed to have gone on a pilgrimage, but has actually disguised herself as a page for love of Philaster. Fletcher was probably the most highly regarded of the earlier dramatists on the Restoration stage (Hume, 1976:234–5).

Philaster is not pure classic realism. We know from the beginning, for example, that Philaster is the rightful heir to the Sicilian throne. But the way in which the play handles the enigma it does construct is highly sophisticated. Euphrasia's 'pilgrimage' is prepared for early on, in what appears to be no more than a polite exchange between Philaster and her father, Dion (I. i. 318–22). Dion shows a marked partiality for Bellario (IV. vi. 113). Dion is the most loyal supporter of Philaster's right to the throne, and it was his praise that made his daughter fall in love with Philaster in the first place (v. v. 158ff). All this is intelligible retrospectively from the moment of closure. It constitutes a kind of vista back through the play, bringing together apparently trivial details and investing them with their 'true' significance. The effect is the creation of a gap between what the spectator has seen on the stage and what was 'really' happening. The truth of the fiction is thus a narrative which is not exactly given in the text, but which is produced by the mind reflecting retrospectively on its experience of the events, and which is shared with the dramatist who evidently knew all along that Bellario was Euphrasia.

Enigma, suspense and disclosure become the characteristic structural determinants of the drama after the Restoration. The consequent confederacy of knowledge inevitably operates at the level of morality as well as plot, since questions of justice, propriety and decorum are imbricated with the resolution of the narrative. Renaissance tragedy, with its looser plot structure, does not necessarily close off quite so surely the questions it raises, as I have suggested in Chapter

2. In addition, a good many post-Restoration 'tragedies' have happy endings, a strategy which also foregrounds questions of poetic justice and thus of ethics: courage (moral and physical), fidelity and integrity are highly valued and duly rewarded. If we take the subtitles as evidence, the moral knowledge constructed to be shared between dramatist and audience is not particularly esoteric: *All for Love, or The World Well Lost*; *Troilus and Cressida, or Truth Found Too Late*; *Love Triumphant, or Nature Will Prevail*. It must have been fairly easy to produce – or reproduce – a confederacy of common sense on the basis of such insights.

But in practice the ethics may be both more elaborate and more subtle. *The Conquest of Granada*, for instance, can be seen as staging a sequence of moral debates, where in each case the audience is nudged in the direction of the choice which is subsequently confirmed by the plot as correct. Should a man seize his brother's crown for the sake of the woman he loves (I Act II)? Clearly not. And it emerges that Abdalla's is not true (romantic) love: Lyndaraxa, a wicked and ambitious woman, can only inspire a qualitatively different emotion. Should a man betray a king who rewards his service with ingratitude (I Act III)? Evidently not. Almanzor has nothing to gain from an alliance with the treacherous Abdalla. Here is a more difficult case: should a father give permission for his son to marry the daughter of his oldest enemy when she has saved the son's life (I Act V)? Yes, because, as the play makes clear, the marriage will eventually reconcile the parties to the quarrel. Should a son in these circumstances resist his duty to his father for the sake of the woman he loves (ibid.)? Yes! (True love is almost always to be trusted as a moral guide in heroic drama.) The play sustains this mode for ten acts. Mrs Evelyn, who saw it in 1671, found it 'full of ideas', Utopian in its refinement and profoundly instructive (Dryden, 1978:411).

If the morality stage is a place of exhortation, the late seventeenth-century theatre has become a place of confirmation and legitimation of common knowledge, and thus of its source, personal experience, as an affirmation of individual subjectivity. The unresolved questions of the Renaissance plays and the Vice-nonsense of the moralities are not here admissible. Coherence – of utterance and of knowledge – marks and displays the unity of the knowing self, and lucidity offers the best hope of the intersubjective collusion which dispels the solitude and uncertainty that haunt the humanist subject. Clarity of expression, elegance of plot and the resolution of moral issues are the virtues of classic realist drama. There should be no unanswerable questions. And nonsense is now banished to the madhouse, censored as symptomatic of the psychosis which constantly threatens to demonstrate the precariousness on which humanist knowledge is founded.

4

AUTONOMY

4.1 Tyranny

The project of the Tudor and Stuart monarchies was absolutist. From the centre of the nation-state, as Head of the Church, the most powerful of the ideological apparatuses, the sovereign would dispense law and order in return for absolute control. The project was never realized. There was no standing army to enforce the royal will; and the monarchy depended on parliamentary approval for revenue from taxes. Under pressure from an emergent mode of production which, while it welcomed the markets and communications guaranteed by a unified state, nevertheless resisted control from the centre in the interests of the free development of the forces of production, the monarchy finally gave way in the 1640s before an alliance of otherwise conflicting groups. Economic depression united the people and their employers; many of the country gentry, outside the patronage of the court, found common cause with the petty bourgeoisie who opposed the controls on free enterprise; the national church, adhering to a relatively individualist creed in order to differentiate itself from Rome, tended to legitimate the concept of individual dissent, but at the same time succeeded by its authoritarianism in uniting the dissenters against the monarch as its Head. Magnificence, the primary signifier of absolute monarchy, was expensive. To reduce their reliance on taxation, and therefore on parliament, the Tudors sold former church estates, and then royal lands, thus losing the income from them. The Stuarts

93

sold offices and monopolies, thus reducing their own control. Ultimately absolutism was revealed as dependent for money, as it was for legitimation, on parliament, one of the institutions it most needed to control. Its other major rival was the common law. When the monarchy was reinstated in 1660 it was on different terms and in a different climate. The new terms were cemented by the revolution of 1688. Absolutism, the power of the sovereign to make law and to impose it on the people with or without their consent, was in practice based, in its British manifestation, precisely on consent. A constant possibility or threat, absolute rule never succeeded in becoming a reality.

The Tudor and Stuart theory of absolutism was as unstable as the practice. The arguments, which vary in detail, have in common a tendency to fix difference as antithesis, to restrict the imaginable possibilities to two: on the one hand, this government, or on the other, no government, the present order or its opposite, which is always chaos. This is an elementary ideological strategy. The twentieth-century equivalent can be seen in its crudest form in the identification of the Soviet Union (or Eastern Europe) as the only imaginable alternative to the present political and economic arrangements of the west. The project is, of course, in both cases, to close off any consideration of a third possibility, perhaps as yet unrealized, which might offer to remedy the defects of the one without reproducing the evils of the other. In the Renaissance this third possibility was democracy.

The weakness of the strategy is that the terms of the antithesis fail to stay in place, constantly slide away from polarity and back towards difference, recreating a margin where the trace of the other, the repudiated antithesis, insists within the definition of what is endorsed. Absolute monarchy depends for its propaganda on absolute meaning, and both are constantly threatened by the return of the repressed.

The strategy and the problem it involves are evident in the Homily on Obedience, one of *Certain Sermons or Homilies*

94

Appointed by the King's Majesty, to be Declared and Read by All Parsons, Vicars or Curates Every Sunday in Their Churches. The argument of the Homily on Obedience is that kings, rulers and judges are set in authority over the people by God, that resistance to them is therefore resistance to God as well as to the sovereign, and that God (as well as the sovereign) will punish it. The alternative to the order God has imposed is anarchy:

> Take away kings, princes, rulers, magistrates, judges, and such estates of God's order; no man shall ride or go by the highway unrobbed; no man shall sleep in his own house or bed unkilled; no man shall keep his wife, children, and possessions in quietness: all things shall be common: and there must needs follow all mischief and utter destruction both of souls, bodies, goods and commonwealths.
>
> (Corrie, 1850: 104–5)

Disorder leads to the perpetual possibility of disquiet, injury and death. Fortunately, 'we in this realm of England' have succeeded in avoiding all distress, thanks to the excellence of the reigning monarch, King Edward VI. (The names were changed as the *Homilies* were reissued at regular intervals in the reigns of Elizabeth, James I and Charles I.) But even if 'we' (the inclusive and unifying pronoun holds together the nation-state even while it separates the grateful subjects from the sovereign) were not so privileged, but were governed by ministers who abused their power, we should still be forbidden to withstand them. And for confirmation of this principle the Homily cites the highest examples:

> Our Saviour Christ himself and his apostles received many and divers injuries of the unfaithful and wicked men in authority: yet we never read that they, or any of them, caused any sedition or rebellion against authority.

On the contrary, they suffered in patience, without resistance, 'troubles, vexations, slanders, pangs, and pains, and death itself' (Corrie, 1850: 108).

The theory of absolutism requires obedience even to tyrants, since the alternative would permit the people to judge which sovereigns deserve obedience, and thus call in question the absolute power of the monarch and the corresponding subjection of the people. But as the Homily on Obedience ingenuously reveals, the effects of tyranny include the perpetual possibility of 'troubles, vexations ... pains, and death', precisely the evils which lie in wait outside the existing regime, which are excluded by obedience to the present order. Tyranny, it appears, closely resembles anarchy, at least from the point of view of the people. The remedy for anarchy is absolutism. Absolutism offers no remedy for tyranny.

When Hobbes produced an apology for absolutism over a century later in 1651, the terms of the discourse had changed in certain crucial respects. Most obviously, in *Leviathan* the divine authority for sovereignty has given way to the concept of popular consent. Power is given to the sovereign by the people for their own protection. In this respect Hobbes is closer to Locke than to the Homily. But the power once given, is absolute, and here *Leviathan* confronts some of the structural problems encountered by the Homily. It does so, of course, at much greater length, and with a good deal more rhetorical sophistication.

Hobbes devotes very little explicit attention to tyranny. He concedes that the sovereign may err (Hobbes, 1968:323), may strip one subject of property and possessions to enrich another who is a favourite or flatterer (p.243), or may be an infidel (p.625). He admits that it may be a miserable condition to be at the mercy of 'the lusts, and other irregular passions' of one who has unlimited power (p.238). But these are minor evils compared with the real misery of the only thinkable alternative, the state of nature. The direct historical context of *Leviathan* is, of course, the civil war, and it is this cataclysm which takes mythic form in Hobbes's account of the natural condition of human beings, the war of all against all. Motivated by appetites and aversions, people in a state of nature constantly threaten each other's liberty, goods and security. Their inevitable and necessary condition is 'a perpetuall and restlesse desire of power after power' (p.161), since the only way to increase their safety is to reduce the threat from others by augmenting their own power. The state of nature is a regime of constant fear. At last, 'weary of irregular justling, and hewing one another' (p.363), people agree to submit entirely to a ruler (or an assembly, but assemblies have serious drawbacks) who will impose order on this chaos. Any government is preferable to the 'miseries and horrible calamities' of lawlessness (p.238). In the state of nature there is no agriculture, no trade, no architecture, 'no arts, no letters, no society', but only 'continuall feare, and danger of violent death' (p.186). The promise of Hobbes's commonwealth is, by contrast, peace and civilization.

But if the civil war is mythically present in *Leviathan*, all the instabilities of Stuart absolutism are also there in mythic form in the logic of the text. Monarchs enforce order by fear of punishment (p.223), by 'terror' of their power and strength (p.227). But monarchs, like their subjects, participate in human nature. Indeed, they offer evidence precisely of the insatiable desire for power:

> And from hence it is, that kings, whose power is greatest, turn their endeavours to the assuring it at home by lawes, or abroad by wars: and when that is done, there succeedeth a new desire; in some, of fame from new conquest; in others, of ease and sensuall pleasure; in others of admiration, or being flattered for excellence in some art, or other ability of the mind. (p.161)

Who or what, then, restrains the natural propensities, the appetites and aversions, of kings? Theoretically, the interests of the monarch, which are synonymous with the interests of the commonwealth, since the sovereign's success arises only from the success of the subjects. But in practice, the text concedes, rulers 'may ordain the doing of many things in pursuit of their passions, contrary to their own consciences' and subjects have no right even to protest, because in surrendering their power they have authorized whatever actions the sovereign may take (p.297).

Government eliminates the perpetual fear which is the consequence of the desire for power by restraining the people. But the price of this restraint is the installation of a monarch who has total power – and whose subjects have no redress against a regime of perpetual fear. Traces of war thus reappear within the commonwealth, calling in question the contrast between civilization and the state of nature on which the argument depends.

The rhetoric of *Leviathan* depends on a series of oppositions. It is by art that men transform nature to make civil society, an artificial man, the common wealth, leviathan itself. Thus the multitude of wills become one will, the voices one voice and the people one person (pp.227–8). Each member of the commonwealth is the author of the words and deeds of this single person (p.232) and thus conflict is eliminated. At the same time, however, 'he that carryeth this person, is called SOVERAIGNE, and said to have soveraigne power; and every one besides, his SUBJECT' (p.228). In other words, the unity necessarily dissolves in the analysis into its constituent parts, sovereign and subjects, a duality, and the text reinforces the point by going on to consider independently the rights of sovereigns and the rights of subjects, and their respective obligations and liberties. Power, it thus implicitly acknowledges, is always a relation, always power over another. It is inevitably divisive, unequal, a disequilibrium. It is thus inherently unstable. *Leviathan* concedes that the unified commonwealth it defines can be destroyed by its own duality, since 'through the ignorance, and passions of men, it hath in it, from the very institution, many seeds of a naturall mortality, by intestine discord' (p.272). Power is relational, and *this* relation, made by art (the artificial man who represents all men) is subject to destruction by the very nature – the passions of men – that necessitated it. In consequence, the monarch must exercise power still more firmly in order to eliminate the possibility of disobedience, intensifying division by forcing sovereign and subjects still further apart. The promised unity turns out to be opposition, and tyranny becomes not merely the shadow of absolutism but its norm.

Filmer's *Patriarcha*, which was written between 1635 and 1642, but not published until the monarchy was again in jeopardy in 1680, is compelled by its own logic to argue that tyranny is not really such a bad thing after all. Patriarchalism, which elicited some support in the sixteenth century, but gathered strength in the seventeenth, proposed an analogy between the obedience naturally due to fathers of families and submission to the monarch in the interests of the people: 'As the father over one family, so the king, as father over many families, extends his care to preserve, feed, clothe, instruct and defend the whole commonwealth' (Filmer, 1949:63). Like *Leviathan*, *Patriarcha* thus uses the rhetoric of unity (the family), but it is similarly forced by its own absolutism to recognize that, as Charles I was to put it, 'a subject and a sovereign are clean different things' (Lockyer, 1959:135). Within a short space, therefore, Filmer finds himself weighing up the relative evils of tyranny and sedition. Tyranny, he concludes, is preferable. After all, the cruelty of tyrants is usually confined to a few specific people who offend them (Filmer, 1949:92). And he calculates, in support of this proto-Utilitarian case, that all the murders carried out by Tiberius, Caligula, Nero, Domitian and Commodus put together could not match the number of lives lost in the Roman civil wars (p.91). In any case, 'there is no tyranny to be compared to the tyranny of a multitude' (p.93). To judge from the history of *Patriarcha*, which was reissued three times between 1680 and 1696, and which Locke thought worthy of detailed refutation in *Two Treatises of Government* (1690), these arguments must have had some appeal for Tories of the post-Restoration period.

James I in *Basilikon Doron* (1599) takes a different position on tyranny, but one which leaves certain apparently unconscious ironies in the text. A good king and a tyrant, it urges, are quite contrary to each other. Good kings are *subjected* to the well-being of their subjects; tyrants seek only their own interests. Good kings therefore reign happily and generally die in peace, while tyrants incur rebellion (James I, 1965:18–19). Much of the rest of the text, which defines the duties of a king for the benefit of the young prince Henry, the heir to the throne, gives advice on how to handle the rebellion that is apparently constantly imminent in Scotland from unruly members of the clergy and from nobles who suppose themselves above the law (pp.22–6). Meanwhile, the common people do nothing but complain (p.27). Again antithesis seems to slide back towards difference and the inscription of the excluded other in what is endorsed.

These imperative texts, propaganda on behalf of monarchy, cannot afford to recognize the possibility of democracy, or any case for revolution. The drama of the period, however, is not so inhibited. This is not because the dramatists were more radical (though they probably were: it's hard to see how anyone could be less radical than Filmer). It is primarily because narrative depends on the existence of obstacles, while propaganda depends on their elimination. The smooth and successful operation of absolute power does not generate a story. It is notable that in *Measure of Measure*, which Franco Moretti, in a fascinating essay on tragedy and sovereignty, cites as an instance of absolutist drama (Moretti, 1983:57–61), the astute benevolent despot has precisely to abdicate, to hand over his power, or at least the official aspects of it, to Angelo, in order to produce a plot. More strikingly still, in Shirley's *The Cardinal* (1641), a royalist revenge play, it is only the (totally unexplained) absence of the sovereign which ensures the continuity of the narrative.

In *The Cardinal* the contradiction between the ideological project and the requirements of the story creates a play which verges on incoherence. On the wedding day of the Duchess Rosaura to D'Alvarez, the bridegroom is murdered in a masque by his rival, Columbo. The King, who is present and in control, promises justice and imprisons Columbo. As Act III ends, guards escort Columbo from the stage, and the Duchess declares, 'This shows like justice' (III. ii. 248). Immediately afterwards, at the beginning of Act IV, Columbo is at large again and vowing to kill at the altar any future bridegroom of the Duchess. The King is conspicuously absent at this point, and he remains so until the final scene, when he reappears at the climactic moment, authoritatively interrogates all those present, encourages the innocent Duchess to take poison by mistake, expresses amazement at the extraordinary wickedness of the intriguing Cardinal, and concludes that kings should be more careful. If the King's promise had stood uncontradicted and Columbo been executed, the play would have ended with Act III. It is only the otherwise unaccountable absence of the sovereign which makes revenge imperative and sustains the narrative for another two acts. The effect, of course, is that the royalist project is severely undermined.

More commonly the plays foreground tyranny, which is an endless source of narrative. In many instances the tyrant's innocent victims have no redress, and the story is one of helpless suffering. But occasionally, as in *Julius Caesar*, tyranny and sedition are brought into confrontation, with the effect of raising the issue the absolutist texts are compelled to exclude, the question of freedom. Roman history, by contrasting the liberty of the Republic with Imperial tyranny, introduced into the range of what it was possible to consider the third model of political organization which absolutist propaganda, based on antithesis, effaced. The Roman Republic in its Renaissance representation was to all intents and purposes a democracy.

To have the concept is not, of course, to have a commitment to the concept. *Julius Caesar* brings into conjunction, and indeed into collision, two distinct orders of sovereignty. It does not (cannot in 1599?) choose decisively between them, but it offers its audience the opportunity to reflect on the differences. The speeches of Brutus and Mark Antony in the marketplace focus and point the contrast. Antony's account of Caesar identifies him with Rome, much as Hobbes identifies the sovereign with the commonwealth. Caesar is presented as the city's champion and its benefactor: 'He hath brought many captives home to Rome,/Whose ransoms did the general coffers fill' (III. ii. 88–9). The people are his heirs: he has left the citizens 75 drachmas each and his private arbours and orchards for their common recreation. The conspirators can have had no motives other than 'private griefs' (l.213). They have isolated themselves from Rome, become its enemies, 'traitors' (ll.153, 185). This is precisely the strategy of the apologists for absolutism: opposition to the regime is treason against the realm itself, since the realm *is* the sovereign, and treason is therefore the work of 'unnaturall subjects' (James I, 1965:19). And so, Antony triumphantly declares, using the inclusive and unifying pronoun to its fullest effect:

> what a fall was there, my countrymen!
> Then I, and you, and all of us fell down,
> Whilst bloody treason flourish'd over us.
>
> (III. ii. 190–2)

Brutus too speaks in the name of Rome: 'Not that I lov'd Caesar less but that I lov'd Rome more' (l.19); 'I slew my best lover for the good of Rome' (l.43). But he employs much less familiar terms, identifying Rome with the Republic and the Republic with freedom:

> Had you rather Caesar were living, and die all slaves, than that Caesar were dead, to live all free men? ... Who is here so base that would be a bondman? If any, speak; for him have I offended. Who is here so rude that would not be a Roman? (ll.24–30)

The speech in the marketplace echoes the terms in which the conspirators define the assassination itself: 'Liberty! Freedom! Tyranny is dead!' (III. i.78); 'Liberty, freedom and enfranchisement!' (l.81); 'Peace, freedom and liberty!' (l.111); 'The men that gave their country liberty' (l.119).

The content of these phrases is not very specific in the play. No golden world of lost liberty is depicted; no political project for the future of Rome is discussed. The Senate is barely delineated. The people are more sharply defined, but the relationship between Senate and people is not specified. Of course, the assassination does not bring peace or freedom. Equally it is not clear whether Caesar is the tyrant the conspirators believe him to be. Antony is (IV. i), but there is in any case no evidence that Antony has any legitimate claim to the power he appropriates. Perhaps the play condemns usurpation rather than tyranny? Or tyranny but not absolutism?

These issues are not clear-cut. This is not surprising: the play is not a political tract. But it is the location of certain meanings, evidence of what can be said and understood in 1599. And here the implication is that it is possible to present on the stage with some degree of sympathy the commitment to an alternative to absolutism, indeed to monarchy itself, in which to be a member of the commonwealth is also to be 'free'.

Ben Jonson's *Sejanus* (1603) reads in some respects like a sequel to *Julius Caesar*, and there is evidence that Jonson was summoned to appear before the Privy Council, possibly on a charge of treason. *Sejanus* is not much more specific about liberty but it is far less equivocal than *Julius Caesar* about its value, and unambiguous in its condemnation of tyranny. Sejanus, favourite of the Emperor Tiberius, systematically eliminates or removes his political opponents and those in the line of succession to the throne. Tiberius becomes suspicious of his designs when Sejanus contemplates marrying Livia, widow of the heir apparent. The Emperor therefore elevates

Macro, in effect a second Sejanus, who engineers the fall of his rival. Sejanus is torn to pieces, reduced to dust and scattered abroad by the mob.

For the opponents of Sejanus, most of whom become his victims, the Republic is a precious period of their history:

> We, that (within these fourescore yeeres) were borne
> Free, equall lords of the triumphed world,
> And knew no masters but affections,
> To which betraying first our liberties,
> We since became the slaves to one mans lusts.
>
> (I. 59–63)

The Republic was good. And yet a virtuous emperor would be better still (I. 400–9). But this Emperor, subject to flatterers, is thereby subject to vice (I. 410–24). Something ought to be done: 'It must be active valour must redeeme/Our losse' (IV. 157–8). And yet nothing should make a subject rise against a sovereign (IV. 163–4). On the other hand, the Emperor's subjects are worse than slaves (IV. 171).... This debate runs all the way through the play. Sejanus's opponents praise Brutus and Cassius for their heroism (I. 93–104; III. 411–60); his flatterers condemn Brutus as 'an enemie of his countrie' (III. 397).

But in the event no one emulates Brutus and Cassius. The fall of Sejanus is an effect of the political structure itself. The increasingly decadent, increasingly absent Emperor needs a surrogate, but to delegate his power is to risk being supplanted. He therefore appoints Macro to check Sejanus. Macro recognizes that in these circumstances he must strike first if Sejanus is not to destroy him (IV. 89–92). This is the war of all against all, in which power is secured only by more power, but here the cause is absolutism, not the state of nature. At the end of the play Sejanus is annihilated, but Macro has replaced him. There is no evident difference between them: powerful flatterers are interchangeable in the political economy of the absolutist state. The tyranny, the corruption and the time-serving continue.

By 1619 the sympathetic invocation of the Roman Republic on the stage had become unacceptable to the censor. In *Sir John Van Olden Barnevelt*, a play based on contemporary events, the hero is executed for resistance to the Prince of Orange. At the end of his trial Barnevelt draws a parallel between the Prince and the first of the emperors:

> Octavius, when he did affect the Empire
> And strove to tread upon the neck of Rome
> And all hir ancient freedoms, tooke that course
> That now is practisd on you; for the Catos
> And all free sperrits slaine or else proscribd
> That durst have stir'd against him, he then sceasd
> The absolute rule of all. You can apply this:
> And here I prophécie I, that have lyvd
> And dye a free man, shall when I am ashes
> Be sensible of your groanes and wishes for me;
> And when too late you see this goverment
> Changd to a monarchie youll howle in vaine
> And wish you had a Barnevelt againe.
>
> (p.292)

Probably on the grounds that the audience could indeed 'apply this' all too well, the Master of the Revels first altered the most offensive phrases and then, evidently recognizing that modifications would not solve the problem, drew a line through the whole passage down to 'howle in vaine' (Gildersleeve, 1961:117–18).

By this time reference to the assassination of Caesar had become a commonplace of plays concerning tyrannicide. Clermont d'Ambois resembles Brutus (*The Revenge of Bussy d'Ambois*, II. i. 103–12). The event is also present in the margins of *Hamlet*, when Polonius with unwitting irony foreshadows his own death: 'I did enact Julius Caesar; I was kill'd i'th' Capitol; Brutus kill'd me' (III. ii. 100–1). No wonder

Hobbes believed that one of the causes of rebellion, to be countered by the strongest measures, was the practice of reading books about (Greek and) Roman history. These books, he argued, make a false distinction between regicide and tyrannicide, and say that the latter is not only lawful but laudable. Furthermore, 'from the same books, they that live under a monarch conceive an opinion, that the subjects in a popular commonwealth enjoy liberty; but that in a monarchy they are all slaves.' And so, he concludes, 'I cannot imagine, how anything can be more prejudiciall to a monarchy, than the allowing of such books to be publikely read' (Hobbes, 1968:369).

But it must be Fulke Greville's closet-drama, *Mustapha*, which offers the most radical dramatic critique of absolutism in the period. *Mustapha* was written in the mid-1590s, but considerably revised – and politicized – sometime before its first publication in 1609. Here, as in *Sejanus*, the analysis is structural. In this instance the ruler, Soliman, is not wicked, decadent or absent. But, the play implies, unless the sovereign is omniscient, to rule is to depend to some degree on advice. On the other hand, to be an adviser is to possess power, and to possess power is to threaten the absolute power of the sovereign. In consequence, absolute monarchs inevitably go in perpetual fear: 'they, that all men feare, are fearefull too' (*Mustapha*, II. iii. 64). At the same time, to be the subject of such a monarch is also to be in perpetual danger: 'dreadfull is that power that all may doe' (II. iii. 63). And the only way for either the sovereign or the subject to overcome fear and danger is to possess total control:

> Where one man ruleth all,
> There feare, and care are secret wayes of wit;
> Where all may rise, and only one must fall,
> There pride aspires, and power must master it.
>
> (II. ii. 83–6)

The 'must' of the final line is important: the political economy of absolutism renders inevitable the endless cycle of fear, aspiration, mastery and fear. 'Greatnesse must keepe those arts by which it grew' (II. ii. 4); 'Princes must be ours, or we their tombe' (Chorus Primus, l.182). Monarchy in *Mustapha* is again the precise equivalent of the state of nature in *Leviathan*.

The plot is relatively simple. Rossa, Soliman's wife, persuades him that his son, Mustapha, threatens his life. Camena, Soliman's daughter, and Achmat, his adviser, maintain Mustapha's virtue. Rossa kills Camena and declares Achmat a traitor. She induces Soliman to have the innocent Mustapha killed. Her son, Zanger, the intended beneficiary of Rossa's plot, kills himself. Rebellion threatens. In the version of 1609 long choruses between each act analyse the political implications of these events. The first chorus in particular offers a remarkable denunciation of the way tyranny harnesses the virtue of obedience, engrossing it to itself with the effect of corrupting law, religion and even language, to the destruction of the people.

As in *Julius Caesar* and *Sejanus*, it is not entirely clear whether anything can properly be done. Here too the answer is, *probably* not. But there is a certain – and increasing – hesitation. At the end of the play fury at Soliman's action and pity for Mustapha's Christ-like death have brought the people to a state of rebellion. Achmat debates his obligations to his sovereign. According to the first version of the text, the obedience of the subject is conditional on the monarch's obedience to God (ms. C, v. ii. 203–4). The virtue of obedience becomes a weakness when it reinforces tyranny (ll.204–5). Since it appears that the king must be ruled by someone, better the people than his wife: 'Yf kinges will needes be ruled who are more fitte/then people who have intereste in it?' (ll.210–11). Should Achmat then encourage rebellion? But this glimpse of a legitimate popular sovereignty almost immediately gives way before the orthodox argument that it is for God alone to take action against tyrants. In consequence, the debate ends with Achmat resolved:

> Kinges are the roddes or blessinges of the skye
> God onlye judge. Hee knowes what they deserve.
> Solyman shall still be safe, or I will dye.

$$(\text{ll.}319\text{--}21)$$

But in the later version this conclusion is not quite so firmly specified. Achmat rehearses in solitude an encouragement to the people: 'Question these thrones of tyrants;/Revive your old equalities of nature/... Lend not your strengths to keepe your owne strengths under' (*Mustapha*, v. iii. 92–5). And yet rebellion brings only ruin and disorder, not freedom (ll.105–8). He ought, therefore, to support the regime. But how? How are the people to be brought under control (ll.115–20)? The play ends with Achmat uncertain, Rossa lamenting and the realm apparently in chaos. There is no closure.

Each of these plays interrogates absolutism and finds it wanting. Absolutism slides towards tyranny, but paradoxically the central problem of tyranny is that it is finally *in*effectual. Julius Caesar is perhaps only a tyrant in embryo ('in the shell', as Brutus puts it (II. i. 34)), but his susceptibility to flattery is ominous. Tiberius and Soliman are disastrous for the commonwealth not because they have too much power, but because in the end they have too little. According to absolutist theory, the sovereign has total power, the subject none. There is no room in the absolutist texts for the subject to possess any degree of autonomy. But the plays offer a very different (though no less political) analysis. Here God's representative on earth conspicuously lacks divine virtue, or omniscience, or omnipotence. The sovereign is human, deaf, decadent or uxorious – or simply incapable of knowing everything, and therefore dependent on advice. (The Duke of Vienna sees and controls what is going on in his dominion only on condition that he surrenders his office and becomes Friar Lodowick.) This gap between the human monarch and the God who authorizes monarchy creates a space in which the subject becomes the sovereign's rival: 'For worlds repine at those, whom birth, or chance,/Above all men, *and yet but men*, advance' (*Mustapha*, II. ii. 87–8, my italics). Brutus, Sejanus and Macro, Mark Antony and Rossa (and Friar Lodowick) are in practice the powerful figures in these plays. They are for a moment autonomous. In most cases it is a usurped, unauthorized autonomy that they possess. Freedom is only an idea, popular sovereignty no more than a momentary possibility. The civil war is still forty years off.

And yet is it not clear in *Julius Caesar* or in *Sejanus* that Brutus is simply mistaken or wicked. Friar Lodowick is certainly more knowing, more effective and of more use to the commonwealth than the Duke of Vienna. And Achmat not only knows the truth which Soliman cannot see; at the end of *Mustapha* it is Achmat, the subject, not Soliman, who confronts the question whether and how to control the people, and who is thus to determine the future of the state. Absolutism, the plays imply, produces precisely the resistance it sets out to exclude. And the dramatization of absolutism gives birth, however tentatively, to the concept of the autonomous subject.

4.2 The limits of sovereignty

There were, of course, challenges to the theory of absolutism outside the theatre, and here too there began to exist, beyond the limits of sovereignty, an area of self-determination for the subject. On the one hand, it was widely assumed that the subject was not obliged to obey a command from an earthly ruler which was contrary to the will of God. And on the other, it was held that the sovereign was broadly subject to the law. The power of the monarch, according to these arguments, was confined within the limits of justice, divine and human.

Tyndale's *Obedience of a Christen Man* (1528) urges sub-

mission to the higher powers (Rom. 13:1), and this requirement is absolute. None the less, there may be circumstances
in which the command of the sovereign is in direct conflict
with the will of God. In this situation the appropriate Christian
response is a passive refusal to obey and the patient endurance
of whatever punishment the sovereign imposes. Ironically,
The Obedience thus becomes a guide to disobedience (Greenblatt,
1980:92). The Homily on Obedience includes a similar
reservation, and similarly stresses that the right to disobey is
not a right of active resistance or insurrection (Corrie,
1850:112). This position, which had the authority of Luther
(Skinner, 1978, II:3–19), was to be expected in the early days
of European Protestantism. In England where, after the
Reformation, the sovereign was Head of the Church, it was
taken up by the Puritans, in terms which gave marginally
more prominence to the autonomy of the individual conscience
as the faculty which identifies the will of God. Thus in
Cartwright's version, 'If there be anything wherein we do not
according to that which is commanded (by magistrates), it is
because we cannot be persuaded in our consciences that we
may do so (whereof we are ready to render a reason out of
the word of God)' (Little, 1970:87). And more decisively still,
for Perkins,

> Now the courts of men and their authorities are under
> conscience. For God in the heart of every man hath erected
> a tribunal seat, and in his stead hee hath placed neither
> saint nor angel, nor any other creature whatsoever, but
> conscience itselfe, who therefore is the highest judge that
> is or can be under God.
>
> (Little, 1970:123)

The religious debates thus carve out a space in which to
know the will of God and from which to disobey the will of
the sovereign. In Puritan theory this space is the province of
the individual subject, authorized by Puritanism itself. Not
surprisingly, *Basilikon Doron* constantly reverts to the problem

of 'rash-headie' Puritans and 'fierie spirited men in the ministerie' as the natural enemies of the sovereign (James I, 1965:6, 23, 38).

The Anglican position did not allow for disobedience, but it did tend to locate the sovereign within rather than above the law. This medieval principle (Holdsworth, 1924:209; Ullman, 1967:78–80) subsisted into the sixteenth and seventeenth centuries as at once a limitation on the development of absolutism and a guarantee of the continuity of kingship: 'Lex facit regem', in Hooker's phrase (Hooker, 1888, III:353). The king, as York explains to Richard II, is not entitled to ignore the law of the land, since it is this law which guarantees the king's own succession and rule (*King Richard II*, II. i. 195–9). In abrogating the law, Richard overthrows the main barrier to his own deposition. Charles I was to be executed on the grounds that he had been found by a court of law to have broken the law of his own kingdom.

But though the bounds of sovereignty are fairly clearly specified, doubt and uncertainty surround the limits of the subject's autonomy, as is evident in the moral and political insecurity of the fictional Henry IV, and the recorded hesitation and fears of some of the non-fictional regicides. Political theory more commonly defines the legal obligations of the sovereign than the subject's right to implement the law when the sovereign fails to do so. But here too the drama is less inhibited because, while the project of theory is to eliminate problems, narrative depends on them. On the stage revenge was the specific problem which brought together these issues. The problem of revenge involved precisely the question of the obligations and responsibilities of the subject in the implementation of divine and human justice.

In the revenge plays in the half-century before the civil war it is the sovereign's failure to administer justice which inaugurates the subject's quest for vengeance. Hieronimo rips the bowels of the earth with his dagger, calling for 'Justice, O justice, justice, gentle king' (*The Spanish Tragedy*, III. xii.

63). Titus Andronicus urges his kinsmen to dig a passage to Pluto's region, with a petition 'for justice and for aid' (*Titus Andronicus*, IV. iii. 15). The Duchess Rosaura appeals direct to the monarch:

> Let me have swift and such exemplar justice
> As shall become this great assassinate.
> You will take off our faith else, and if here
> Such innocence must bleed and you look on,
> Poor men that call you gods on earth will doubt
> To obey your laws.
>
> (*The Cardinal*, III. ii. 104–9)

In each case, however, the sovereign fails to enforce the law. Indeed, in *Antonio's Revenge* (c.1600), *The Revenger's Tragedy* and *Hamlet* the ruler is the criminal. In the absence of justice the doubt Rosaura defines propels the revenger to take in the interests of justice action which is itself unjust.

Revenge is not justice. Titus is a man 'so just that he will not revenge' (*Titus Andronicus*, IV. i. 129). Acting outside the legal institution and in defiance of legitimate authority, individuals have no right to arrogate to themselves the role of the state in the administration of justice: 'never private cause/Should take on it the part of public laws' (*The Revenge of Bussy d'Ambois*, III. ii. 115–16). Conscience, which permits passive disobedience, forbids murder, and thus makes cowards of some revengers (*Hamlet*, III. i. 83–5).[4] Others, more resolute, like Laertes are deaf to its promptings:

> To hell, allegiance! Vows to the blackest devil!
> Conscience and grace to the profoundest pit!
> I dare damnation. To this point I stand,
> That both the worlds I give to negligence,
> Let come what comes; only I'll be reveng'd
> Most throughly for my father.
>
> (*Hamlet*, IV. v. 128–33)

When Hamlet differentiates revenge from hire and salary

(III. iii. 79), he specifies the gap between vengeance and justice. Revenge is always in excess of justice. Its execution calls for a 'stratagem of ... horror' (*Antonio's Revenge*, III. i. 48–50). Titus serves the heads of Chiron and Demetrius to their mother and the Emperor in· a pastry coffin. Antonio massacres the innocent Julio and offers him in a dish to his father, after cutting out the tyrant's tongue. Vindice prepares for the Duke a liaison with the skull of the murdered Gloriana, and the 'bony lady' poisons him with a kiss (*The Revenger's Tragedy*, III. v. 121). Hippolito holds down his tongue and compels him to witness his wife's adultery while he dies.

The discourse of revenge reproduces the violence and the excess of its practice: 'Look how I smoke in blood, reeking the steam/Of foaming vengeance' (*Antonio's Revenge*, III. v. 17–18); 'Then will I rent and tear them thus and thus,/Shivering their limbs in pieces with, my teeth' (*The Spanish Tragedy*, III. xiii. 122–3); 'Now could I drink hot blood,/And do such bitter business as the day/Would quake to look on' (*Hamlet*, III. ii. 380–2); 'I should 'a fatted all the region kites/With this slave's offal' (*Hamlet*, II. ii. 574–5). As Claudius assures Laertes, it is in the nature of revenge to 'have no bounds' (*Hamlet*, IV. vii. 128). The rugged Pyrrhus – avenging *his* father's death, 'roasted in wrath and fire,/And thus o'er-sized with coagulate gore' (*Hamlet*, II. ii. 455–6) – is not, after all, entirely a caricature of the stage revenger.

And yet the act of vengeance, in excess of justice, a repudiation of conscience, hellish in its mode of operation, seems to the revenger (and to the audience?) an overriding imperative. Not to act is to leave crime unpunished, murder triumphant or tyranny in unfettered control. The orthodox Christian remedy is patience: 'Vengeance is mine; I will repay, saith the Lord' (Rom. 12:19). *The Spanish Tragedy* offers two contrasting models, dramatizes, in effect, two antithetical worlds, one authoritarian, divinely ordered and controlled, and the other disordered, unjust, incipiently secular and humanist. In Portugal Alexandro is accused of the murder of

Balthazar. Alexandro is not permitted to speak (I. iii. 88), but patience and heaven are invoked in his defence (III. i. 31–5). As he is bound to the stake, insisting that his death will be avenged on his accuser, Villuppo, an ambassador arrives with letters for the King which show that Balthazar is alive. Heaven is evidently ordinant in Alexandro's providential last-minute release, and in the consequent execution of Villuppo. In Spain the murder of Horatio initially elicits a parallel response: 'The heavens are just, murder cannot be hid' (II. v. 57); 'Ay, heaven will be reveng'd of every ill' (III. xiii. 2). But when Hieronimo appeals to heaven for justice a letter 'falleth' (III. ii. 23 S.D.). Its auspices are uncertain; it is addressed to the subject and not to the sovereign; it reveals the identity of the murderers, and thus inaugurates Hieronimo's quest for justice, which becomes an act of revenge. The place of heaven – or hell – in this process is, I have suggested in Chapter 3, unclear.

Whatever the requirements of Christian patience, the imperatives of fiction demand that heaven delays the execution of justice, and in the interim crime continues. Belimperia is imprisoned, Pedringano is suborned, Serberine murdered. In *Hamlet* Claudius is still in possession of the crown and Gertrude, and is planning the death of the hero in addition. Vindice has waited nine years and meanwhile crime at court is met with a travesty of justice. In these circumstances revenge is a political as well as a moral issue. Thus Hamlet asks,

> Does it not, think thee, stand me now upon –
> He that hath kill'd my king and whor'd my mother;
> Popp'd in between th' election and my hopes;
> Thrown out his angle for my proper life,
> And with such coz'nage – is't not perfect conscience
> To quit him with this arm? And is't not to be damn'd
> To let this canker of our nature come
> In further evil?

(v. ii. 63–70)

The question, like most of the questions raised in *Hamlet*, is not answered. But even Clermont d'Ambois, model of Stoic virtue, is persuaded by Bussy's Ghost that he has a moral obligation to punish the murder the king leaves unpunished, and so to do in this world 'deeds that fit eternity':

> And those deeds are the perfecting that justice
> That makes the world last, which proportion is
> Of punishment and wreak for every wrong,
> As well as for right a reward as strong.
> Away, then! Use the means thou hast to right
> The wrong I suffer'd. What corrupted law
> Leaves unperform'd in kings do thou supply.
>
> (*The Revenge of Bussy d'Ambois*, v. i. 91–8)

And in consequence, the Ghost concludes, 'be above them all in dignity' (l.99). The bloody masques and Thyestean banquets are hellish, but they have the effect, none the less, of purging a corrupt social body, and in the process installing the subject as autonomous agent of retribution.

Revenge exists in the margin between justice and crime. An act of injustice on behalf of justice, it deconstructs the antithesis which fixes the meanings of good and evil, right and wrong. Hamlet invokes the conventional polarities in addressing the Ghost, only to abandon them as inadequate or irrelevant:

> Be thou a spirit of health or goblin damn'd,
> Bring with thee airs from heaven or blasts from hell,
> Be thy intents wicked or charitable,
> Thou com'st in such a questionable shape
> That I will speak to thee.
>
> (I. iv. 40–4)

The Ghosts in revenge plays consistently resist unequivocal identifications, are always 'questionable' in one of the senses of that word. Dead and yet living, visitants at midnight (the marginal hour) from a prison-house which is neither heaven nor hell, visible to some figures on the stage but not to others, and so neither real nor unreal, they inaugurate a course of action which is both mad and sane, correct and criminal. To uphold the law revengers are compelled to break it. The moral uncertainty persists to the end. Vindice's execution by Antonio either punishes or perpetuates injustice: 'You that would murder him would murder me' (*The Revenger's Tragedy*, v. iii. 105). Hamlet dies a revenger, a poisoner, but also a soldier and a prince (*Hamlet*, v. ii. 387–95). Clermont d'Ambois survives the duel with Montsurry but kills himself thereafter. Antonio, to his (and the audience's?) 'amazement' (*Antonio's Revenge*, v. vi. 28), is greeted by the Senate as a hero, but the play ends with his retirement to a monastery.

The question whether it is nobler to suffer in Christian patience or to take arms against secular injustice is not resolved in the plays. It is ultimately a question about authority – God's, the sovereign's or the subject's. To the extent that the plays condemn revenge, they stay within an orthodoxy which permits only passive disobedience and prescribes no remedy for the subject when the sovereign breaks the law. But in order to be revenge plays at all, they are compelled to throw into relief the social and political weaknesses of this ethical and political position. To the extent that they consequently endorse revenge, they participate in the installation of the sovereign subject, entitled to take action in accordance with conscience and on behalf of law.

4.3 The sovereign subject

At the end of Act III of *Julius Caesar*, after Antony has delivered his address to the people, inciting them to loot and burn the city in whose name he unites them against the 'treason' of the conspirators, there is a short scene in which Cinna the poet, initially mistaken for Cinna the conspirator, is lynched by the people for his bad verses, for his name, for no reason at all (III. iii). The contest between Brutus and Antony is a conflict for the allegiance of the people. Both speak in their name or on their behalf, but neither consults them. None the less, it is the power of the people, destructive and uncontrollable once it is released, which is decisive for the future of Rome. The violence here depicted leads directly to war, to the suicides of Brutus and Cassius and, as many of the audience at the Globe would have known, to the ever more violent history of the Roman Empire. The allegiance of the people is decisive but the people are not in any sense autonomous. From the beginning of the play they are shown to be motivated from outside – by Caesar's staged triumph and then by the Tribunes, by Brutus and then by Antony. In each case the context of the competition for their allegiance is violence: Caesar's victory over Pompey, the assassination of Caesar.

The 'people' (that is, property-owning men) had long had a role, however indirect, in the English constitution, through their representatives in parliament. Though parliament did not on the whole initiate legislation, it had to approve it, and it was entitled to discuss freely all matters submitted to it (Holdsworth, 1924:90–1). On this basis it was understood that the people played a part in the affairs of the realm since, as Sir Thomas Smith put it in 1583, in parliament

> everie Englishman is entended to be there present, either in person or by procuration and attornies, of what preheminence, state dignitie, or qualitie soever he be, from the prince ... to the lowest person of Englande. And the consent of Parliament is taken to be everie mans consent.
> (ibid., p.182)

The constitutional struggles of the early seventeenth century concerned the respective powers of the crown and parliament. Ironically, it was Charles I who declared in 1642 that the three estates of the realm, crown, Lords and Commons, had equal powers in the making of laws, had, in other words, equal sovereignty, and that this excellent arrangement was attributable to the wisdom of his ancestors' subjects, the

117

people (Weston and Greenberg, 1981:36). Subsequent royalist attempts to retreat from this position were ineffectual and the king's analysis more or less immediately became orthodox.

Meanwhile, there had developed in Europe a theory of popular sovereignty which held that power was only delegated to the monarch by the people, and a counter-reformation analysis which authorized the deposition of the sovereign by a representative assembly of the whole commonwealth (Skinner, 1978, II:113–73). At the same time, radical Protestantism produced in response to the Emperor Charles V and to Queen Mary Tudor a theory of popular resistance which constituted a move beyond passive disobedience. Sovereigns who defied the law of God could be brought to account, and the people were entitled to act as God's instruments in their arraignment. There was a direct line of descent from the Calvinism of the 1550s to Locke's argument in *Two Treatises of Government* (1690), by way of the revolution of the 1640s (ibid., pp.189–241).

In 1642 Henry Parker, a lawyer of Lincoln's Inn, called for the supremacy of the people through their representatives in parliament (Prall, 1966:17). In January 1649 the House of Commons declared 'that the people under God are the original of all just power'. God is included here, but the grammatical subject, the presence which is the source and guarantee of just power, has become the people. The House went on to declare 'that the Commons of England assembled in Parliament, being chosen by and representing the people, have the supreme authority of this nation' (Lockyer, 1959:76). A fortnight later the Lord President addressed the King:

> The Commons of England ... according to the debt they did owe to God, to justice, the Kingdom and themselves, and according to that fundamental power that is vested, and trust reposed in them by the people ... have ... constituted this Court of Justice before which you are now

brought, where you are to hear your charge, upon which the Court will proceed according to justice.

(ibid., pp.81–2)

Charles I was tried and executed in the name of the people of England, represented by the House of Commons.

The House of Commons had been severely purged. The electorate consisted of male forty-shilling freeholders. Women and 'servants' (employees) were understood to be represented by the heads of their households. None the less a radical change had been effected: the monarch was now accountable to the social body. In consequence, Charles I's assertion that 'a subject and a sovereign are clean different things' took on a new meaning unknown to him. The people, however narrowly understood, were now sovereign, and the way was open for their subjection to that sovereignty.

Their sovereignty is the natural heritage of the people, 'being originally and naturally in every one of them, and unitedly in them all'. As a result,

the power of kings and magistrates is nothing else, but what is only derivative, transferr'd and committed to them in trust from the people, to the common good of them all, in whom the power yet remains fundamentally and cannot be tak'n from them, without a violation of thir natural birthright.

(Milton, 1962:199–202)

Law and order is now firmly grounded in human nature and guaranteed by civil society. Liberal humanism is installed, and with it the autonomous subject, the 'free' individual, subject to and subjected by new but equally ruthless mechanisms of power.

In Locke's classical analysis the project of liberalism is to overcome the instability of absolutism by redistributing the power. What is missing from *Two Treatises* is any recognition that the sanctity of property produces a new inequality between those who have only their labour-power to sell and those who are in a position to buy it – or not to buy it. Free enterprise, the economic system which promotes the autonomy of the subject, thus depends on a conflict of economic interests which leads to a new form of instability. In spite of this, or perhaps because of it, liberal humanism allows no place for dissent. In any dispute the community acts as umpire, by 'settled standing rules', and through its representatives punishes what it defines as offences (Locke, 1967, II:87). To be a member of a society is to give tacit consent to its rules (ibid., 119), and the only alternative to accepting the rules is to sell up and leave (ibid., 121). Dissent is automatically anti-social. Resistance from within the social body is deviant or delinquent, legitimately ignored or penalized as the work of the enemy within. The autonomy of the individual subject is thus conditional on conformity to certain norms by which the individual can be measured, sifted, classified, ranked or disciplined.

Venice Preserved (1682), probably still among the most widely known of Restoration tragedies, retained its popularity long after its immediate context – the Popish Plot and the Tory celebration of the fall of Shaftesbury – had been forgotten. Though it satirizes the Whigs, its values are not particularly Tory, and its popularity in the eighteenth and nineteenth centuries may be an effect of the fidelity with which the play reproduces the central meanings of the new liberal humanism. *Venice Preserved* does not, of course, concern itself with the class struggle, but it is a play about the inadmissibility of dissent and the conditional nature of liberal 'freedom'. Jaffeir, financially ruined by his father-in-law, who is a member of the Senate, is persuaded by his friend Pierre to seek vengeance by joining a conspiracy to overthrow the Senate. Subsequently induced by his wife to confess all to the Senate, he is repudiated by the conspirators, and is able to reassert his integrity only by killing himself, after stabbing Pierre to death to save him from being broken on the wheel as a traitor. *Venice Preserved* thus brings together the main concerns of both the revenge tradition and the tyrannicide plays, but the radical differences between this text and the earlier ones mark the ideological distance which is an effect of the transfer of sovereignty from the monarch to the social body.

Revenge and freedom are closely interwoven in the motives of the conspirators:

> *Jaffeir.* from this hour I chase
> All little thoughts, all tender human follies
> Out of my bosom. Vengeance shall have room.
> Revenge!
> *Pierre.* And Liberty!
> *Jaffeir.* Revenge! Revenge!
> (*Venice Preserved*, II. ii. 127–30)

The politics of the conspiracy are not very clearly defined. Pierre maintains that the people are deluded with 'a show/Of liberty' while the Senate is arbitrary and tyrannical (I. i. 153–60). The cause is 'our liberties, our natural inheritance' (II. ii. 90); the purpose is 'to restore justice and dethrone oppression' (II. iii. 126). But the evident corruption of the Senate does not mean that the audience is invited to sympathize with insurrection. The anti-social means to be employed betray Pierre's high, if vague, ideals. The rebels plan 'the destruction/Of a whole people' (III. ii. 226–7). Venice will become a smoking ruin, a spectacle of horror (III. ii. 373–82). (In *Julius Caesar* it was absolutism not freedom which was shown initiating the destruction of the city.) And it emerges that the real project of the conspirators is not only to destroy the tyrants but to take their places, to 'possess/That seat of empire which our souls were framed for' (II. iii. 82–3).

The terms are Renault's. As the most corrupt of the conspirators, and their leader, he is clearly motivated by the desire for personal power and glory. Pierre, perhaps naively, seems to be committed to liberty. But he too, like Jaffeir, is 'really' motivated by personal bitterness: Antonio, a Senator, has stolen the woman he loves. In other words, the commitment to political change, we are to understand, is 'really' personal, an effect of the hunger for power, or resentment, or psychological instability.... The play reproduces the liberal-humanist construction of an antithesis between public and private, political and personal, in which the latter is always privileged, and always ultimately determining. Both the Senators and the conspirators are corrupt and self-seeking. There is nothing to choose between contestants for power in the public world. Wise people keep aloof from politics. Jaffeir and Pierre become involved in the affairs of the state only under the stress of private grief.

Indeed, it could be argued that the play's primary interest is not in politics at all but in personal relationships, and specifically in Jaffeir's inner conflict between love and friendship. The politics is merely a context for this. Jaffeir's marriage to Belvidera for love is the source of his father-in-law's antagonism, and he interprets his financial ruin as tragic because it is a betrayal of Belvidera's right to comfort and protection. It is as Pierre's friend that he joins the conspiracy, but in response to Belvidera's persuasions that he betrays him. Friendship finally triumphs when Jaffeir kills Pierre at his own request, thus saving him from dismemberment and ignominy.

Thanks to Jaffeir's intervention, Pierre dies a unified (literally) and autonomous subject. Jaffeir too is an autonomous subject in the sense that he is not represented as the battleground of conflicting cosmic forces, like Mankind, or of contradictory political imperatives, like the earlier revengers. Unlike his predecessors, prompted to their revenge by heaven and hell, Jaffeir is motivated by individual psychological impulses. Bitterness and hatred well up uncontrollably from within him. He is thus the origin of his own actions. At the same time, however, he loses all autonomy once he excludes himself from the social body, dissents from its rules and thus

identifies himself as a deviant, a traitor, a 'foe .
iii. 141). From then on he is at the mercy of ot.
outside the commonwealth and thus unprotected
community:

> How cursed is my condition, tossed and jostled
> From every corner; fortune's common fool,
> The jest of rogues, an instrumental ass
> For villains to lay loads of shame upon,
> And drive about just for their ease and scorn.
>
> (III. ii. 213–17)

Jaffeir regains his lost autonomy when, by executing himself
on the scaffold meant for Pierre, punishing himself for his
own delinquency, he acts on behalf of the commonwealth
and thus reintegrates himself into the social body. And here
there is some continuity with the earlier drama: Othello the
Venetian, for example, executes Othello the pagan in the
name of Venice (*Othello*, v. ii. 355–9); Cassius, by killing
himself, avenges Caesar (*Julius Caesar*, v. iii. 45–6). The deaths
which form the climax of *Venice Preserved* could stand as the
paradoxical emblem of liberal-humanist freedom. Pierre and
Jaffeir are punished, but not by the illegitimate and corrupt
Senate which has taken control of Venice. The play by
implication alludes to another – legitimate – community
which is not synonymous with the corrupt state. In punishing
themselves Pierre and Jaffeir, by that action itself, rejoin the
legitimate community to the extent of becoming its agents,
'work by themselves' to ensure its continuity. It is thus the
social body which executes them. Their deaths affirm the
sovereignty of the social body, revealing in the process the
severely conditional nature of individual freedom.

On these terms their deaths are also heroic, an act of
defiance against arbitrary power. When Jaffeir carries out
Pierre's request to kill him, Pierre's personal rebellion is
existentially triumphant: 'This was done nobly – we have
deceived the Senate' (*Venice Preserved*, v. iii. 99). In *Sejanus*,

too, Silius, spokesman for Republican liberty, kills himself 'to mock Tiberius tyrannie' (III. 338). And Hieronimo, choosing to die rather than reveal what the King 'requires', triumphantly preserves his unspeakable secret. Clermont d'Ambois kills himself rather than kill the king on the one hand or become 'the slave of power' on the other (*The Revenge of Bussy d'Ambois*, v. v. 192). Jaffeir kills Pierre at his own request to save him from being executed by the Senate. Pierre thus dies autonomous. Jaffeir dies as an act of free choice, by his own hand. Suicide is a means of escaping humiliation and control. In this sense it is, paradoxically, the supreme assertion of both the autonomy of the subject and the sovereignty of the social body, since it is only in so far as it is subject to the social body that the liberal-humanist subject works by itself to become heroic.

Suicide as heroism was in conflict in the Renaissance with an older view of suicide as the final sin, an act of despair, the obverse of pride in its defiance of God's power to forgive. It was also a refusal to acknowledge God's right to determine the moment of death: 'Men must endure/Their going hence, even as their coming higher' (*King Lear*, v. ii. 9–10). Death in *Everyman* is under divine control. Death comes from elsewhere. Within liberal humanism death is for this reason the ultimate threat to the autonomy of the subject: it signifies that the subject is finite, that its plenitude is illusory. 'I feel secretly close to all the other people who don't want death to be something that comes from outside themselves' (Guattari, 1984:8). But death which is self-inflicted, chosen, puts an end to finitude itself, an end to the endless desire of the liberal-humanist subject to be precisely autonomous, to be not just free, but also the origin and guarantee of its own identity, the source of being, meaning and action. Suicide re-establishes the sovereign subject: 'death in the hollow of your own hand ... willing impotence' (ibid., p.7). As the crowning affirmation of the supremacy of the self, and simultaneously the extinction of finitude, it is 'the diamond of unnamable desire' (ibid., p.8).

In the absolute act of suicide the subject itself is momentarily absolute. As an individual action, therefore, suicide is a threat to the control of the state. The democratic liberal-humanist state, claiming to represent the legitimate community, cannot afford to recognize an act of autonomy which it does not itself authorize. Suicide was illegal in Britain until 1961, and it remains illegal to help another person commit suicide or to publish information which would provide such help. But the free west has now found a new way to put an end to finitude while simultaneously holding the subject in place within the community as the state defines it. Unlike all previous forms of war, nuclear war is both an act of aggression, authorized by the social body, against the unauthorized power of the enemy, and at the same time communal suicide, an absolute act of universal sovereignty, putting an end to all desire by the extinction of the whole world. Nuclear weapons place death in the hollow of our hand, our own death, by our own hand. The nuclear apocalypse, closing off in the moment of its fulfilment the desire to be absolute, is liberal humanism's diamond of unnamable desire.

Liberal humanism, conceived as autonomy for the subject and as control by the social body, but also as violence, in the imagined revenge, insurrection and regicide produced by the drive of absolutism towards tyranny, and born in 1649 when 'bloody hands' applauded the spectacle of tyrannicide on another 'tragic scaffold' (Marvell, 1972:56), still bears in its maturity the marks of its entry into the world. The liberal-humanist state appears to be moving in the name of the people towards an act of violence which is also the supreme declaration of its own autonomy, towards a moment which holds together the aggression and the control which are the conditions of our 'freedom'. Here, as in the murder of Cinna the poet, the people have been enlisted in a course which in a different sense they have not themselves initiated.

Their allegiance, however, is now, as then, a site of struggle. It may still prove decisive.

Part II: WOMAN

5

ALICE ARDEN'S CRIME

5.1 Defining the crime

On Sunday 15 February 1551 Alice Arden of Faversham in Kent procured and witnessed the murder of her husband. She and most of her accomplices were arrested, tried and executed. The goods of the murderers, worth a total of £184.10.4½d., and certain jewels, were forfeit to the Faversham treasury. The city of Canterbury was paid 44 shillings for executing George Bradshaw, who was also present at the murder, and for burning Alice Arden alive (Ebsworth, 1895:48). At a time when all the evidence suggests that crimes of violence were by no means uncommon, Alice Arden's crime was cited, presented and re-presented, problematized and reproblematized, during a period of at least eighty years after it was committed. Holinshed, pausing in his account of the events which constitute the main material of the *Chronicles of England, Scotland and Ireland* to give a detailed analysis of the murder, explains that the case transgresses the normal boundaries between public and private, and so,

> for the horribleness thereof, although otherwise it may seeme to be but a private matter, and therefore as it were impertinent to this historie, I have thought good to set it foorth somewhat at large.
>
> (*Arden of Faversham*, p.148)

This 'horribleness', which identifies Alice Arden's domestic crime as belonging to the public arena of history is not, it could be argued, a matter of the physical details of the murder, nor even of the degree of premeditation involved. On the contrary, the scandal lies in Alice Arden's challenge to the institution of marriage, itself publicly in crisis in the period. Marriage becomes in the sixteenth and seventeenth centuries the site of a paradoxical struggle to create a private realm and to take control of it in the interests of the public good. The crime coincides with the beginning of this contest. *Arden of Faversham*, which can probably be dated about 1590, is contemporary with a major intensification of the debate about marriage, and permits its audience glimpses of what is at stake in the struggle.

There are a great many extant allusions to Alice Arden's crime. It was recorded in the *Breviat Chronicle* for 1551, in the diary of Henry Machyn, a London merchant-tailor, and in Stow's *Annals of England* (1592, 1631) as well as in Holinshed's *Chronicles* (1577, 1587). Thomas Heywood gives it two lines in his seventeen-canto poem on the history of the world, *Troia Britannica* (1609), and John Taylor in *The Unnaturall Father* (1621, 1630) invokes it as an instance of God's vengeance on murderers. In addition to the play, which ran to four editions between 1592 and 1633, '[The] complaint and lamentation of Mistresse Arden' was printed in ballad form, probably in 1633.

The official record of the murder was given in the Wardmote Book of Faversham, reprinted in Wine's Revels edition of the play, together with Holinshed's account and the ballad. According to the Wardmote Book, Arden was 'heynously' and 'shamefully' murdered, and the motive was Alice's intention to marry Mosby, a tailor whom she carnally kept in her own house and fed with delicate meats, with the full knowledge of her husband. The value-judgment established here is constant in all the accounts, and the word 'shameful' defines the crime in the *Breviat Chronicle* (*Arden of Faversham*, p.xxxvii), in Holinshed, on the title page of the first edition of the play and again in the ballad. What is contested in these re-presentations is not, on the whole, the morality of the murder, but its explanation, its meaning. Specific areas of the story are foregrounded or reduced, with the effect of modifying the crime's significance. The low social status of Mosby, and Arden's complaisance, for instance, both intensify the disruption of matrimonial conventions, and these elements are variously either accounted for or played down. Arden's role in the story differs considerably from one narrative to another.

What are the implications of the constant efforts at redefinition? In Holinshed's analysis Arden was a gentleman, a tall and comely person, and Mosby 'a blacke swart man'. According to the marginal gloss in the second edition of the *Chronicles*, Alice's irrational preference is an instance of the radical difference between love and lust, and her flagrant defiance of the marriage bond accountable in terms of human villainy: 'Thus this wicked woman, with hir complices, most shamefullie murdered hir owne husband, who most entirelie loved hir all his life time' (*Arden of Faversham*, pp.148, 155). But running through Holinshed's narrative is another account of the murder, not wholly consistent with this view of Arden as innocent victim, which emphasizes God's vengeance on his greed for property. In this account Arden's avarice, repeatedly referred to in the story, is finally his undoing. His complaisance is a consequence of his covetousness: 'bicause he would not offend hir, and so loose the benefit which he hoped to gaine at some of hir freends hands in bearing with hir lewdnesse, which he might have lost if he should have fallen out with hir: he was contented to winke at hir filthie disorder' (ibid., p.149). After Arden's death, the field where the conspirators had placed his corpse miraculously showed the imprint of his body for two years afterwards. This field was Arden's property, and in 1551 he had insisted that the St Valentine's fair be held there, 'so reaping all the gaines to himselfe, and bereaving the towne of that portion which was woont to come to the inhabitants'. For this he was bitterly cursed by the people of Faversham (ibid., p.157). The field itself had been 'cruellie' and illegally wrested from the wife of Richard Read, a sailor, and she too had cursed him, 'wishing manie a vengeance to light upon him, and that all the world might woonder on him. Which was thought then to come to passe, when he was thus murdered, and laie in that field from midnight till the morning' on the day of the fair. Again the marginal gloss spells out the moral implications: 'God heareth the teares of the oppressed and taketh vengeance: note an example in Arden' (ibid., p.159). The murder is thus part of the providential scheme.

These two versions of Arden – as loving husband and as rapacious landlord – coexist equally uneasily in the play. Here the element of complaisance is much reduced: Arden has grounds for suspicion but not certainty. Mosby's baseness is a constant theme, and underlines Alice's irrationality. But what is new in the play is the parallel between Arden's dubious business deals and Alice's. A good part of the plot is taken up with Alice's negotiations with possible murderers. Michael is to carry out the crime in exchange for Susan Mosby. Clarke is to provide a poison, and subsequently a poisoned picture, in exchange for Susan Mosby. Greene gets £10 and a promise of £20 more, with land to follow, for his 'plain dealing' in carrying out the murder (I. 517). Greene subcontracts the work to Black Will and Shakebag for £10. Finally, in desperation, Alice increases her offer to this team to £20, and £40 more when Arden is dead. They leave triumphantly with their gold when the work is completed. Mosby, too, is part of this world of economic individualism, and there are indications that his motive is not love of Alice so much as desire to come by Arden's money (e.g. VIII. 11–44). He quarrels with Alice in terms of 'credit', 'advantages', 'fortune' and 'wealth' (VIII. 80–92). If the play has any explanation to offer of Alice Arden's crime it is social and economic rather than providential. The event is primarily an instance of the breakdown of order – the rape of women and property – which follows when the exchange of contracts in a market economy supplants old loyalties, old obligations, old hierarchies.

But there are elements of the play which this reading leaves out of account. Some of the dialogue between Alice and Mosby invites a response which contradicts the play's explicit project, defined on the title page, of showing 'the great malice and dissimulation of a wicked woman, [and] the unsatiable desire of filthie lust'. In these speeches it is marriage which is identified as an impediment to true love, and images familiar from the poetry of the period seem to offer the audience a position of some sympathy with Alice's repudiation of the marriage bond:

> *Alice.* Why should he thrust his sickle in our corn,
> Or what hath he to do with thee, my love,
> Or govern me that am to rule myself?
> Forsooth, for credit sake, I must leave thee!
> Nay, he must leave to live that we may love,
> May live, may love; for what is life but love?
> And love shall last as long as life remains,
> And life shall end before my love depart.
>
> *Mosby.* Why, what's love, without true constancy?
> Like to a pillar built of many stones,
> Yet neither with good mortar well compact
> Nor cement to fasten it in the joints
> But that it shakes with every blast of wind
> And, being touched, straight falls unto the earth
> And buries all his haughty pride in dust.
> No, let our love be rocks of adamant,
> Which time nor place nor tempest can asunder.
>
> (x. 83–99)

The natural and elemental images and the Biblical echoes momentarily ennoble Alice's defiance of patriarchy. Early in the play Clarke makes explicit this other face of the crime:

133

> Let it suffice I know you love him well
> And fain would have your husband made away,
> Wherein, trust me, you show a noble mind,
> That rather than you'll live with him you hate
> You'll venture life and die with him you love.
>
> (I. 267–71)

In these instances the play presents Alice Arden's challenge to the institution of marriage as an act of heroism. Alice rejects the metaphysics of presence which guarantees the social enforcement of permanent monogamy, in favour of a free sexuality, unauthorized within the play as a whole, but glimpsed at isolated moments:

> Sweet Mosby is the man that hath my heart;
> And he [Arden] usurps it, having nought but this,
> That I am tied to him by marriage.
> Love is a god, and marriage is but words;
> And therefore Mosby's title is the best.
> Tush! Whether it be or no, he shall be mine
> In spite of him, of Hymen, and of rites.
>
> (I. 98–104)

The ballad, almost certainly derived from the play, redefines the problem yet again. For the first time the woman is the unequivocal subject of the narrative, in contrast to the play, where the title indicates that it is Arden's tragedy rather than Alice's. The ballad reduces the story to two main elements – Alice's love and the series of contracts for the murder. These negotiations are recounted in all their detail within a text of only 192 lines. Arden's rapacity is ignored, and Holinshed's 'blacke swart' Mosby becomes a man of 'sugred tongue, good shape, and lovely looke' (l.11). The ballad is a record of contracts made and broken for love. There is no explicit doubt of Alice's wickedness: her 'secret dealings' come to light and are duly punished by her death (l.167). At the same time a curious formulation, perhaps a slip of the pen, picks up something of the element of ambivalence in the play: 'And then by justice we were straight condemn'd,/Each of us came unto a shamelesse end' (ll.165-6). 'Shamelesse' here is unexpected – appropriate to their (impudent) behaviour, perhaps, but not to their (disgraceful) execution. On a reading of the word obsolete since the fifteenth century, 'shameless' could mean 'free from disgrace' (*OED*, 3). Perhaps a parapraxis betrays the unconscious of the text, a world well lost for love, and Alice Arden heroic on the scaffold, exposing herself to death through death.

However that may be, these repeated reinterpretations of the events, reproblematizations of the murder, may be read as so many attempts to elicit a definitive meaning for Alice Arden's crime. In each case this definitive meaning remains elusive, in the sense that each text contains elements not accounted for in its overall project. What is at stake in these contests for the meaning of the murder is marriage itself.

5.2 Murderous women

The existing historical evidence gives no reason to believe that there was a major outbreak of women murdering their husbands in the sixteenth century.[5] What it does suggest, however, is a widespread belief that they were likely to do so. The Essex county records for the Elizabethan period, for instance, reveal no convictions for this crime, but they list several cases of frightened husbands seeking the protection of the courts. In 1574 a Barnston man complained that his wife, 'forgetting her duty and obedience as a wife, had sundry times maliciously attempted to bereave her husband of his life, so that he stand in great fear' both of her and of two men from Dunmow, her 'adherents', who haunted his house at night (Emmison, 1970:162). In 1590 a man called Philpott complained that John Chandler, then living with Philpott's wife, had given his consent to Philpott's death, and Rowland Gryffyth deposed that he had been hired to carry out the murder (ibid., p.199). The records of the ecclesiastical courts in the same county include two cases, both in 1597, of men who refused to live with their wives for fear that they would be murdered by them (Emmison, 1973:162).[6]

When the crime was actually committed, it seems that notoriety instantly followed. In 1573 Anne Sanders (or Saunders) consented to the murder of her husband, a London merchant, by her lover, George Browne. The case rapidly became as widely known as the Arden murder. It was recorded by Arthur Golding in a pamphlet published in the same year and again in 1577; it was probably the subject of an anonymous pamphlet called 'A Cruell Murder Donne in Kent' published in 1577 (Marshburn, 1949); the story was told by Holinshed and Stow again; and it was recounted by Antony Munday in *A View of Sundry Examples* (1580). Like the Arden case, the Sanders murder elicited a play, *A Warning for Fair Women* (*c.*1590), and a ballad, 'The wofull lamentacon of Mrs. Anne Saunders, which she wrote with her own hand, being prisoner in Newgate, justly condemned to death' (Rollins, 1920). In the ballad Anne Sanders begs all women to be warned by her example; the play, unable to account in any other terms for so scandalous a crime, shows Anne, in an allegorical dumb show instigated by the furies, suddenly torn between chastity and lust, then pledging herself to Browne in a ceremony which evokes the 'sacrament prophane in mistery of wine' between Paridell and the adulterous Hellenore in *The Faerie Queene* (III. ix. 30).

In 1591 Mistress Page of Plymouth was executed with her lover and two other men for the murder of her husband. A ballad by Thomas Deloney appeared at once, recording 'The lamentation of Mr Pages wife of Plimouth, who, being forc'd to wed him, consented to his murder, for the love of G. Strangwidge'. Here the ambivalences implicit in the Arden narratives are foregrounded to produce a radical contradiction between sympathy and condemnation. The ballad gives a graphic account of the miseries of enforced marriage:

My closen eies could not his sight abide;
My tender youth did lothe his aged side:
Scant could I taste the meate whereon he fed;
My legges did lothe to lodge within his bed.

At the same time,

Methinkes the heavens crie vengeance for my fact,
Methinkes the world condemns my monstrous act,
Methinkes within my conscience tells me true,
That for that deede hell fier is my due.

(Deloney, 1912:483)

In the circumstances it is particularly regrettable that *Page of Plymouth* by Jonson and Dekker, performed by the Admiral's Men in 1599, is now lost, as is *The History of Friar Francis*, produced, according to Henslowe's diary, in 1593/4, though not necessarily for the first time (Adams, 1943:193–4). According to Heywood in 1612, when *The History of Friar Francis* was performed at King's Lynn it had the gratifying effect of inducing an apparently respectable woman in the audience to confess that seven years earlier she had poisoned her husband for love of a gentleman in precisely the same way as the protagonist of the play. Heywood is here writing in defence of the moral efficacy of stage plays, and it is worth noting that of the three instances he cites of the providential operation of the drama, two concern women murdering their husbands. In the second case it was the method of murder shown on the stage which caused 'a woman of great gravity' to shriek loudly, and after several days of torment to confess that she had driven a nail into the temples of her husband twelve years before. She was duly tried, condemned and burned (Heywood, 1612, sig. G 1v–2v).

5.3 The control of marriage

According to John Taylor, writing in 1621, 'Arden of Feversham, and Page of Plimmouth, both their murders are fresh in memory, and the fearfull ends of their wives and their ayders in those bloudy actions will never be forgotten' (Taylor, 1630:140). This was seventy years after Alice Arden's crime. The prominence allotted to these cases, the suspicion which seems to have been prevalent in Essex in the period, and Heywood's instances of the salutory effects of stage plays in bringing such crimes to light, all point to a preoccupation with the possibility of women murdering their husbands which is not accounted for in any of the individual texts. In *Arden of Faversham* Alice Arden defines her problem specifically in terms of the institutional regulation of sexuality by marriage:

> nothing could enforce me to the deed
> But Mosby's love. Might I without control
> Enjoy thee still, then Arden should not die;
> But, seeing I cannot, therefore let him die.

(I. 273–6)

It is a contest for the control of sexuality in the period which throws marriage into crisis and precipitates the instability of the institution that is evident in crimes like Alice Arden's.

The history of marriage in the Middle Ages is a history of an effort to regulate sexuality by confining it within a framework of permanent monogamy. From the twelfth century onwards the Church gradually extended its control over marriage, making efforts to contain instances of divorce and bigamy by urging with increasing insistence the public solemnization of matrimony after due reading of the banns on consecutive Sundays (Sheehan, 1971; Howard, 1904, 1:361). Since at the same time private marriage in the presence of witnesses was held to be valid and binding, it was easy enough to produce just cause or impediment after the event. The banns were no guarantee against bigamy, since they were easily evaded by those who had anything to fear. In consequence, the process of taking control was slow and laborious, so that in 1540 it was still the case that bigamy was widespread, and that 'no mariage coulde be so surely knytt and bounden but it shulde lye in either of the parties power and arbitre ... to prove a precontracte a kynnerede an alliance or a carnall knowledge to defeate the same' (Powell, 1917:62). Many of the cases which came before the ecclesiastical courts depended on such ingenuities, but Michael M. Sheehan finds, after investigating the late fourteenth-century register of the consistory court of the Bishop of Ely, that there at least 'the court was primarily a body for the proof and defence of marriage rather than an instrument of easy annulment' (Sheehan, 1971:263). The commitment of the court to the stability of marriage above all other considerations may be illustrated by one of the cases Sheehan cites. The marriage between John Poynant and Joan Swan was annulled on the grounds of the husband's impotence. Joan married again, and John took up with Isabel Pybbel. When Isabel became pregnant John prepared to marry her, but the court investigated the matter and found that, since John was apparently not impotent after all, his marriage to Joan Swan should be restored. John protested, claiming affinity within the forbidden degrees between Joan and Isabel, but the court was not impressed, and the original marriage was eventually reinstated.

The Anglican church took over on behalf of the sovereign this effort to control the institution of marriage through the ecclesiastical courts, but not without a struggle which generated a high degree of uncertainty about the nature and permanence of marriage. The introduction of registers of births, marriages and deaths in 1539 was a move towards central control of the population, but at the same time the Reformation introduced a liberalization of marriage which found a focus in a debate about divorce that remained legally unresolved, apart from a brief interlude during the commonwealth, until the nineteenth century.[7]

The Catholic church had permitted separation *a mensa et thoro* (from bed and board) for adultery, cruelty, apostasy or heresy, and divorce *a vinculo matrimonii* on the basis of impotence or of a prior impediment to valid marriage on grounds of consanguinity, affinity or precontract. The act of 1540 attempted to abolish precontract as grounds for divorce, but had no practical effect. Meanwhile, most of the newly Protestant states had introduced divorce with remarriage for the innocent party in cases of adultery and desertion. Similar legislation was urged in England, and was incorporated in the *Reformatio Legum Ecclesiasticarum* of 1552. This was defeated in the House of Commons, but the divorce provision had been sanctioned independently, when a commission under Cranmer had approved the remarriage of the divorced Northampton in 1548, and this was confirmed by parliament in 1552. In practice, however, the ecclesiastical courts largely refused to put the law into operation, and in consequence the position of marriage remained extremely confused and controversial for the rest of the century. The divorce debate reached a high point in the 1590s, with the result that in the Canons of 1597 Convocation declared all remarriage after divorce illegal. These were not sanctioned by Elizabeth, but the principle was reiterated in the Canons of 1604 which were approved by James I, though without silencing the controversy.

The divorce debate polarized already conflicting definitions of marriage. Broadly, the Anglican and absolutist position was that marriage was indissoluble, that couples were joined by God for the avoidance of fornication and the procreation of children, and there was no remedy but patience for marital disharmony and discontent. The liberal position of the Puritans is familiar from Milton's divorce tracts, which carry the radical Protestant arguments to their logical climax. Equally broadly, the Puritans defined marriage as a civil covenant, a thing indifferent to salvation. It depended on consent, and where this was lacking the couple could not be said to be joined by God, and could therefore justly be put asunder. The Reformers varied in the causes of divorce they were prepared to admit.

Only Milton gave real prominence to discord as a cause, while Henry Smith, at the other extreme though still within the pro-divorce lobby, recognized divorce for adultery but vigorously repudiated incompatibility as grounds:

> If they might bee separated for discorde, some would make a commoditie of strife; but now they are not best to be contentious, for this lawe will hold their noses together, till wearines make them leave struggling, like two spaniels which are coupled in a chaine, at last they learne to goe together, because they may not goe asunder.
>
> (Smith, 1591:108)

Not all the Reformers were so optimistic about the couple learning to go together. According to Martin Bucer, whose *De Regno Christi* was addressed to Edward VI when the author was Professor of Divinity at Cambridge, the Church's refusal to permit divorce compelled it to tolerate 'whordoms and adulteries, and worse things then these', 'throwing men headlong into these evils'. 'Neither', he argued, 'can God approve that to the violation of this holy league (which is violated as soon as true affection ceases and is lost,) should be added murder' (Milton, 1959:447, 470). John Rainolds, writing in 1597, insists that if divorce is forbidden, crimes like Alice Arden's are bound to follow: a husband may be forced to live in permanent suspicion, or worse –

> And how can he choose but live still in feare and anguish of minde, least shee add drunckennesse to thirst, and murder to adultery: I meane least she serve him as Clytemnestra did Agamemnon, as Livia did Drusus, as Mrs Arden did her husband?
>
> (Rainolds, 1609:88)

There is some evidence for the bitterness of the struggle. John Dove, who preached a sermon against divorce in 1601, records that many people found his view offensive, 'as unseasonable for the time, and unpleasing to the auditory'

(Dove, 1601: Preface). Rainolds wrote his plea for divorce in 1597, but explains in a letter to Pye published in 1606 that the Archbishop of Canterbury at that time 'thought it not meete to be printed: as containing dangerous doctrine'. He urges Pye to cut out any references to him (Rainolds) in his own argument if he wants to get into print, especially since the Canons of 1604 have hardened the orthodox line (Howson, 1606: n.p.). Rainolds's own *Defence of the Judgment of the Reformed Churches* was published in 1609. The Archbishop's censorship seems to have been even-handed, since at about the same time he also discouraged Edmund Bunny from publishing his case against divorce – in order to avoid controversy, on the grounds that he had already 'staied' one of the contrary persuasion (Bunny, 1610: Advertisement). Bunny's book appeared in 1610. Later William Whately argued for divorce on grounds of desertion as well as adultery in books published in 1617 and 1624. Whately was brought before the Court of High Commission, and promptly reverted to the Anglican doctrine of the indissolubility of marriage (Haller, 1941–2:267–8). Even between the liberals there was considerable sectarianism on this issue. Milton, of course, encountered a good deal of controversy, and was denounced by his fellow-Puritans for his divorce pamphlets (Hill, 1977:131–2). And at the very beginning of the debate an interesting piece of sleight of hand shows how delicate the whole issue must have been. In 1541 Miles Coverdale's translation of Bullinger's treatise on marriage was published as *The Christen State of Matrimonye*. Primarily a plea for marriage as a union of minds, and a corresponding repudiation of the Catholic doctrine of celibacy as a way of perfection, this included a chapter recommending divorce not only for adultery but also for 'lyke and greater occasions' (Bullinger, 1541: sig. Kvi). *The Christen State of Matrimonye* was remarkably popular. Three new editions appeared within five years, and two more before the end of the century. Meanwhile, in 1542 there appeared *The Golden Boke of Christen Matrimonye* 'newly set forth in English by Theodore Basille'. 'Theodore Basille' was Thomas Becon, and *The Golden Boke* was actually Coverdale's translation of Bullinger again with four chapters silently erased, including the one on divorce.

The contest for the meaning of marriage cannot be isolated from the political struggles which characterize the century between the Reformation and the Revolution. Both sides make explicit the parallel between the family and the state, marriage and the monarchy. 'A householde is as it were a little commonwealth' (Dod and Cleaver, 1612:13). 'A familie, is a naturall and simple society of certaine persons, having mutuall relation one to another, under the private government of one' (Perkins, 1618:669). At one extreme Milton argues for liberty within marriage as directly analogous to liberty in the commonwealth:

> He who marries, intends as little to conspire his own ruine, as he that swears allegiance: and as a whole people is in proportion to an ill government, so is one man to an ill mariage. If they against any authority, covnant, or statute, may by the soveraign edict of charity, save not only their lives, but honest liberties from unworthy bondage, as well may he against any private covnant, which hee never enter'd to his mischief, redeem himself from unsupportable disturbances to honest peace, and just contentment.
>
> (Milton, 1959:229)

And if this position was not made explicit in the radical treatises before 1642, nonetheless it was identified by Anglican orthodoxy as implicit in the Puritan arguments. According to Bunny, divorce can lead only to 'disorder' (Bunny, 1610:161). Marriage cannot be dissolved at will any more than can the bond between master and servant, parent and child, 'the prince and the subject'. And for this reason, 'the more heed should bee taken, that no such gap should be opened to any, as wherby the looser sort, when they should get their desire in this, should cast about to obtaine the like in other things also of greater consequence' (ibid., p.52). Dove, whose name entirely belies his political position, argues strenuously that,

> As when a servant runneth from his master the chaine of bondage doth pursue him, and bring him backe againe to his maister, so when a woman leaveth her husband, the lawe of matrimony is as a chaine to draw her back againe to her husband.
>
> (Dove, 1601:33)

The libertines who believe in divorce pervert the scriptures for their own licentious ends, 'Even as others will proove rebellion and high treason out of the scriptures, that the people are above their King' (ibid., p.51). The parallel between domestic patriarchy and absolute monarchy is a commonplace of the seventeenth century, and reaches its most notorious formulation, of course, in Robert Filmer's *Patriarcha*.

Alice Arden, held in the chain of bondage which is marriage, in a period when liberty is glimpsed but not authorized, is caught up in a struggle larger than her chroniclers recognize. But it may be the political significance of Arden's assassination which causes Holinshed to identify Alice Arden's crime as marking the border between private and public, pamphlet and history.

5.4 The new family

There is an indication in *Arden of Faversham* that in opting for Mosby in place of Arden, a freely chosen sexuality based on concord in place of the constraints of the institution of permanent marriage, Alice Arden may be committing herself to a form of power more deadly still, and less visible. Mosby's individualism is precisely that:

> Yet Mistress Arden lives; but she's myself,
> And holy church rites makes us two but one.
> But what for that I may not trust you, Alice?

You have supplanted Arden for my sake
And will extirpen me to plant another.
'Tis fearful sleeping in a serpent's bed,
And I will cleanly rid my hands of her.
But here she comes, and I must flatter her ...

(VIII. 37–44)

The episode could be read as an allegory of the transition to
the liberal-humanist family, itself a mechanism of regulation
more far-reaching but less visible than the repressive ecclesiastical courts. Arden's absolute rights over Alice are clear, and
his threats are directed not against his wife but against the
man who means to rob him of her, for which he

Shall on the bed which he thinks to defile
See his disseevered joints and sinews torn
Whilst on the planchers pants his weary body,
Smeared in the channels of his lustful blood.

(I. 40–3)

This overt power and violence give way in Mosby's version
of marriage to distrust and surveillance veiled by flattery; in
an individualist society of 'equals' absolutist modes of control
are replaced by reciprocal fear between partners within the
social body. Further, flattery and death are the metaphorical
destiny of the wife in the new family. Her standing improves
(though always in subjection to her husband) but at the cost
of new and more insidious forms of control.

Liberal marriage, founded on consent, is 'appointed by God
himselfe, to be the fountaine and seminary of all sorts and
kinds of life, in the commonwealth and in the church' (Perkins,
1618:671). To this end the family becomes quite explicitly
an ideological apparatus, 'a schoole wherein the first principles
and grounds of government and subjection are learned:
whereby men are fitted to greater matters in church or
commonwealth' (Haller, 1941–2:246). In Puritan definitions

of marriage and the family as 'the fountain and seminary of good subjects' (Milton, 1959:447), it is made very clear that 'the holy and righteous government thereof, is a direct meane for the good ordering both of church and commonwealth; yea that the lawes thereof beeing rightly informed, and religiously observed, are availeable to prepare and dispose men to the keeping of order in other governments' (Perkins, 1618: Epistle Dedicatory). To ensure that the family becomes an adequate model and source of good government, the treatises recommend family prayers, grace before meals, keeping the sabbath, the education of the children and the servants, and the inculcation of the fundamental principles of law and order. The family, separated from the public realm of politics, none the less becomes a microcosm of it and, by practice and by precept, a training ground for the ready acceptance for the power relations established in the social body:

> For this first societie is as it were the schoole, wherein are taught and learned the principles of authoritie and subjection. And looke as the superiour that faileth in his charge, will proove uncapable of publike imployment, so the inferiour, who is not framed to a course of oeconomicall subjection, wil hardly undergoe the yoake of civill obedience.
>
> (ibid.)

The liberalism of the Reformers implies a constant scrutiny of marriage for fitness of mind and disposition, since harmony and concord are the precondition of a realm of hearth and home regulated from within. Vigilantly protected from sedition, and isolated from public and political affairs, the family is held in place in the social body as a model of the proper distribution of authority and submission, and thus the fountain and seminary of good subjects.

Read as an event which troubled the politics of the state, Alice Arden's crime was a defiance of absolutism and, in common with the constant reproblematization of such crimes in the period, as well as the great numbers of divorces established in the sixteenth century without recourse to the civil or ecclesiastical authorities, it constitutes evidence of the instability of central control at the time. It is this which accounts for the repeated attempts to define and redefine the crime, and which explains why it was so important and so impossible to furnish it with a final meaning. The assassination of Arden is never justified, but it is variously identified as a part of God's providential plan, as a tragedy, as the effect of social and enonomic change, or as an act of unauthorized heroism, a noble transgression of an absolute law. The representations of the crime are (sometimes contradictory, never neutral) contributions to a discursive struggle for the meaning of resistance to absolutism.

Read as an episode which troubled the politics of gender, Alice Aden's crime throws into relief a corresponding instability in the meaning of the family. The divorce debate, reaching a crisis in the 1590s, the decade which also produced three plays about women murdering their husbands, is the site of a discursive contest between distinct meanings of marriage. Offering a promise of freedom from the 'chain' (recurring metaphor for absolutism) of marriage, the liberal position on divorce leads in reality to a new mode of control, no longer centralized and overt, but internalized and invisible. The new family of the seventeenth century, still under 'the government of one', remains a place in which power is exercised privately in the interests of public order. Alice Arden's bid for freedom, as the play implies, would have led, had it succeeded, to a new form of subjection, both for the woman within the family and for the family within the state. No text of the 1590s could formulate this point in these terms. Indeed, the explicit identification of the family as a mechanism of social control probably has its tentative beginnings in the nineteenth century. None the less, Mosby's threat that he will subject Alice to surveillance, flattery and death indicates a glimpse in this text of an issue which is more complex than the simple opposition between authority and freedom, control and consent.

Women are defined by their difference from men, and the central place of this difference has been the reproductive process. Alice Arden's crime drew attention to the problem of Alice Arden's sexuality, and of the institution which had failed to hold it in place. For this reason too it was both important and impossible to furnish it with a final explanation. To defy the meaning of marriage is to reopen the question of the implications of sexual difference and thus the meaning of what it is to be a woman. Perhaps ultimately this above all was Alice Arden's crime.

6

SILENCE AND SPEECH

6.1 An uncertain place

The subject of liberal humanism claims to be the unified, autonomous author of his or her own choices (moral, electoral and consumer), and the source and origin of speech. Women in Britain for most of the sixteenth and seventeenth centuries were not fully any of these things. Able to speak, to take up a subject-position in discourse, to identify with the 'I' of utterance and the uttering 'I' which always exceeds it, they were none the less enjoined to silence, discouraged from any form of speech which was not an act of submission to the authority of their fathers or husbands. Permitted to break their silence in order to acquiesce in the utterances of others, women were denied any single place from which to speak for themselves. A discursive instability in the texts about women has the effect of withholding from women readers any single position which they can identify as theirs. And at the same time a corresponding instability is evident in the utterances attributed to women: they speak with equal conviction from incompatible subject-positions, displaying a discontinuity of being, an 'inconstancy' which is seen as characteristically feminine. Legally the position of women was inherently discontinuous, their rights fluctuating with their marital status. From the discourses defining power relations in the state women were simply absent; in the definitions of power relations within the family their position was inconsistent and to some degree contradictory. While the autonomous subject of liberalism was in the making, women had no single or stable place from which to define themselves as independent beings. In this sense they both were and were not subjects.

Within the framework of a contest between absolutism and an emerging liberal humanism, and with no determinate subject-position for women, a clearly delineated feminism arguing for the 'equality' or the 'rights' of women is unthinkable. This does not imply that voices were not raised, including women's voices, on behalf of women, but in the general crisis of the period we can hardly expect to find a consistent, united women's liberation movement. What we do find, however, is a series of contests for the place of women in the family and in society, which may in turn be understood as struggles to install women as subjects. In the course of these struggles women found a number of forms of resistance which we should not now be anxious to identify as feminist. Alice Arden's crime was one of these forms; witchcraft and inspired prophesying were others. Murderous or demonic, whores and saints, women were placed at the margins of the social body, while at the same time, in the new model of marriage they were uneasily, silently at the heart of the private realm which was its microcosm and its centre.

In about 1635 John Souch painted Sir Thomas Aston at the deathbed of his wife (see opposite). The dead Lady Aston, her face as white as the bedlinen which surrounds it, lies beside an empty cradle draped with black and surmounted by a skull. Sir Thomas stands facing the spectator. He has one hand on the skull and the other on a cross-staff, inscribed in Latin, 'the earth can be measured; grief is immeasurable'. He and his 3-year-old son are both in black. Sir Thomas, the cradle and the bed are at a slight angle to the spectator, with the effect that Sir Thomas appears at first glance to be leaning backwards a little. But in another visual plane, and on a different scale so that she is about the same size as her little boy, Lady Aston appears again in the picture, in the bottom

Sir Thomas Aston at the Deathbed of his Wife (c. 1635) by John Souch of Chester, reproduced by kind permission of the Manchester City Art Galleries

The Saltonstall Family (c. 1636–7) by David des Granges, reproduced by kind permission of the Tate Gallery, London

right-hand corner. She is alive, smiling very slightly, leaning her head on her hand, and in black.

What is the 'moment' of this picture? If we read it from the point of view of Sir Thomas, who commissioned it, and who stands in single, authoritative substantiality at the centre of its dominant visual field, the moment is that of his wife's death in childbirth, and another perspective presents the wife he remembers as she was in life. But this reading, which makes sense of the picture, defines Lady Aston in relation to her husband, shows her as she is reflected in his consciousness, now alive, now dead. She has no independent being, no fixed and single place on the canvas which matches the solid presence of her mourning husband. She too wears black. For her own death? For the child who was to have filled the empty cradle? For the grief of her husband and son? Or because the introduction of any other colour into this sombre representation of her husband's mourning would endow Lady Aston with a substantiality of her own, an independent life, a claim on our attention which would threaten the reading that locates Sir Thomas as in every sense the *subject* of the picture?

If Lady Aston's place is unfixed, the two wives of Sir Richard Saltonstall render the woman's place uncertain in a different way. In this painting of about the same period or a year or two later, Sir Richard leads two young children, the boy, still in petticoats, holding the hand of a younger girl, to the bedside of their dying mother (see opposite). Lady Saltonstall's hand reaches out to her husband's as he holds back the bed-curtain. Beside the bed, but facing away from it beyond Sir Richard and out of the canvas, sits the second Lady Saltonstall with her newborn son in swaddling clothes. The composition forms two groups, overlapping but distinct. A line of linked or outstretched hands joins the children, Sir Richard and their mother, and forms a horizontal unity. A separate composition-line connects a semicircular group consisting of the children, Sir Richard, their stepmother and the baby on her lap. But this group is physically separated by the dying figure in the bed. The first group excludes the second Lady Saltonstall.

The effect of this organization of the pictorial space is to close off the possibility of reading the painting as a celebration of polygamy. The two wives occupy distinct moments, 'complete' the family in different and not interchangeable ways. Independent of the other wife, each woman depends for her place in the picture on her relationship to Sir Richard, who stands at the centre of whichever composition-line the eye chooses to follow. But the simultaneous presence of both wives on the same canvas attributes to the place of each a certain precariousness in contrast to the solid figure of Sir Richard. Each is present in the meaning of the picture only at the expense of the other. The eye can eliminate either of the women without disrupting the coherence of the image. Indeed, in order to produce the painting's two distinct illusionist moments, it might be argued, it is necessary to eliminate first one woman and then the other. How are we to make sense of this precariousness, the instability which seems to define a woman's place in this period?

Legally the position of women was – and had been for centuries – clearly defined and equally unstable. Alan Macfarlane, eager to correct the erroneous impression that women had no rights at all in the Middle Ages and the Renaissance, points out that in the private sphere they had a good many. An unmarried woman who was of age was entitled to hold land, make a contract or a will, sue or be sued. The same held for widows, who were entitled normally to inherit a third of their husband's estate (and sometimes more) (Macfarlane, 1978:81, 131 ff.). But a key word here is 'unmarried'. This was the condition of women's legal and economic independence.[8] On marriage they surrendered these rights to their husbands (who by contrast had nothing to lose and much to gain from marriage), to recover them, or perhaps to enjoy them for the first time, as widows. T.E. in *The Lawes Resolutions of Womens Rights* ('The Womans Lawyer'), printed in 1632, draws attention to the paradox that widows mourn their husbands when in reality widowhood is the gateway to freedom (T.E., 1632:231–2).

In relation to property married women were thus like children, not legally recognized. On the other hand, unlike children, in criminal or capital matters wives were required to answer without their husbands, and, like Alice Arden, they would be burned for petty treason for the murder of a husband to whom they owed obedience, while husbands who murdered their wives were hanged. Thus, while men became legally both capable and accountable when they reached the age of majority, and stayed that way, women became capable while and only while they had no husbands, but were always accountable. Their relationship to the law in its entirety was paradoxical at best, and unfixed in that it was dependent on their relationship to men.

Meanwhile, unless in the exceptional case of a woman as sovereign of the realm, women exercised no legal rights as members of the social body. In these circumstances it is disingenuous (though not factually inaccurate) of Macfarlane to claim that 'the unmarried woman is equal to a man, owning property in her own name, inheriting estates' (Macfarlane, 1978:133). T.E.'s 'Woman's Lawyer', a handbook to the law as it related to women, gave a clearer picture when, in addition to detailing women's property rights and criminal accountability, it declared, 'Women have no voyse in Parliament, they make no lawes, they consent to none, they abrogate none. All of them are understood either married or to be married' (T.E., 1632:6).

Neither quite recognized as adults, nor quite equated with children, women posed a problem of identity which unsettled the law. T.E. raises an interesting problem about the proprieties implied by hierarchy. If it is treason for a servant to murder a master, is the murder of a mistress by a servant treason or only murder? The authorities, it seems, disagreed (ibid., p.208).

A similar problem concerning the symmetry between masters and mistresses repeatedly unsettled the political discourse of the sixteenth and seventeenth centuries. Mistresses command the women servants in the household and thus occupy a position of authority. In Canon LIX of 1604 one possible implication of this is evident. Masters and mistresses are placed symmetrically in the sentence, and both terms define positions of authority: 'all fathers, mothers, masters, and mistresses, shall cause their children, servants, and apprentices, which have not learned the catechism, to come to the church, at the time appointed' (Schochet, 1975:75). But when Humphrey Brailsford in *The Poor Mans Help* (1689) offers a synopsis of the accumulated conventional meanings of the fifth commandment ('Honour thy father and thy mother'), the position offered to his women readers is not quite so clearly defined: 'These words, father and mother, include all superiours, as well as a civil parent (the king and his magistrates, a master, a mistress, *or an husband*' (my italics, Schochet, 1975:80). The household, always 'under the government of one', contains an authoritative mistress who is also a subjected wife. Brailsford's juxtaposition of mistress and husband draws attention to the unfixed character of the woman's position. Once the distinction between public and private, state and family, is established, the position offered to a man is clear, single and non-contradictory: he is subordinate to the state and in control in his household. But the woman's position, unfixed in relation to the state, is also unfixed in the family. As Brailsford goes on, a hint of unease is evident in the relegation of the mistress to a parenthesis:

And I must have from my natural father, maintenance, education, instruction, correcting and blessing: from my king, justice, reforming abuses in religions, encouragement to the good, punishment to the bad: from my husband, love, direction, maintenance and protection: from my master (or mistress) instruction, food, correction, wages.

(Schochet, 1975:81)

But if mistresses call the resources of punctuation into play in this way, mothers unsettle the discourse to the point where the price of coherence is their repeated elimination. Paradoxically, however, this undermines the central guarantee of patriarchalism (the commitment to 'the government of one' in the state as in the family), since the political case rests finally on the biblical authority of the fifth commandment. The problem is how to reconcile the absolute power of the father with the biblical injunction: on the one hand, 'To *fathers* within their private families Nature hath given a supreme power' (my italics, Hooker, 1888, 1:242); on the other, 'Honour thy father *and thy mother*' (my italics, Exodus 20:12). In the conventional understanding of the power relations authorized by the fifth commandment, children owe obedience to both parents equally, but at the same time one parent owes obedience to the other. In other words, the wife is aligned with the children, the mother with the father. These subject-positions, offered to the same woman, cannot be held simultaneously without contradiction. Nor is it simply a question of a three-level hierarchy, a chain of command, where the husband gives orders to the wife, who in turn instructs the children. On the contrary, it is clear that the children owe obedience direct to the father. The hierarchy has two levels and the woman belongs firmly to neither.

Occasionally she is aligned clearly and unequivocally with the lower level. The following quotation from Robert Sanderson's critique of Hobbes, a series of rhetorical questions about who made the social contract, is probably an extreme case, placing women in a list of figures incapable of free choice and thus below the order of subjectivity:

> Had women, and children, and madmen, and fools, the freedom of suffrage, as well as men of age and fortunes, and understanding? ... Was the wifes interest towards making up the bargain equal with that of her husband?

Clearly the correct answer is 'no', but the second part of the same question comes as a surprise: 'and the childs with that of his parents?' (Schochet, 1975:185).

What is evident here as elsewhere is that both writer and reader are understood to be men. By that I do not mean to imply that in practice women did not or could not read Sanderson and his colleagues, but that in so far as the political discourse in question circulates among men it appears perfectly coherent. The terms 'husband', 'father' and 'master' are consistent with each other (they all designate positions of authority), and differentiated from each other (they define different sets of subordinates, specifically 'wife', 'child' and 'servants'). But the equivalent terms for women, 'wife', 'mother', 'mistress', are mutually incompatible. A woman reader trying to find a single, stable subject-position for herself within this discourse faces unanswerable questions: what is her relationship to her husband? subordinate, as a wife? or equal, as a parent? what is her relationship to her children? one of authority, as a parent, or one of equality in obedience to the governor of the household? The coherence defined by the masculine terms is threatened each time the feminine terms are placed alongside them. One solution is to discard all reference to women.

But this challenges the legitimacy of absolutism itself, since the patriarchalist argument that the state, like the family, needs an absolute governor derives its authority from the will of God, expressed in particular in the fifth commandment which includes mothers. A silent slide, in consequence, between 'parents' and 'men' was extremely common. In *The King's Book, A Necessary Doctrine and Erudition for any Christian Man* (1543), which is the statement, as its title implies, of acceptable Christian belief as authorized by both Convocation and Henry VIII, the exposition of the fifth commandment implicitly makes clear the nature of the problem. If 'honour' really means 'obey', as patriarchalism requires, and wives undertake to obey their husbands, then mothers are anomalous and consequently disappear, at least sporadically:

> In this commandment, by these words *father and mother*, is
> understand not only the natural father and mother which
> did carnally beget us, and brought us up, but also princes
> and all other governors, rulers, and pastors, under whom
> we be nourished and brought up, ordered and guided.
>
> And by this word *honour*, in this commandment, is not
> only meant a reverence and lowliness in words and outward
> gesture, which children and inferiors ought to exhibit unto
> their parents and superiors, but also a prompt and a ready
> obedience to their lawful commandments, a regard to their
> words. . . . This is the very honour and duty which not only
> the children do owe unto their parents, but also all subjects
> and inferiors to their heads and rulers.
>
> And that children owe this duty to their fathers, it
> appeareth in many places of scripture.
>
> (Lloyd, 1825:311–12)

Since most of the places of scripture reinstate mothers, the
rest of the discussion oscillates unpredictably between parents
and fathers, and this becomes common practice in the rest of
this century and the next. Thus, for instance, in the equally
authoritative *God and the King*, published by order of James I
in 1615, and reprinted by Charles II in 1663, we find the
following formulation: 'the fifth commandment, *Honour thy
father and thy mother*: where, as we are required to honour
fathers of private families, so much more the father of our
countrey' (Schochet, 1969:434). And in 1641 when Richard
Brathwait defines the power relations in the family in *The
Turtles Triumph*, a discussion of marriage which brings together
the fruits of his *English Gentleman* and *English Gentlewoman*,
he reaches for the conventional analogy with the state, which
turns out to permit no place at all for the wife:

> As every family is a private soveraignty, so ought there to

bee a disposition, order, or apt symmetry in every member
of that family. The members are ministers unto the head:
so are children and servants to the master of the house.

(Brathwait, 1641a:23)

The recurrent disappearance of mothers from interpretations
of the fifth commandment is one of the main planks of Locke's
liberal attack on the concept of the patriarchalist state: the
term is,

> *parents*, which, in common speech, I think, signifies *mother*
> as well as *father*, or if *parents* here signifies only *father*, 'tis
> the first time I ever yet knew it to do so, and by such an
> use of words, one may say anything.

(Locke, 1967, I:63)

But the axe Locke is grinding here concerns the state primarily.
He concludes that there is a distinction between the family
(where absolutism is acceptable) and the commonwealth
(where it is not), so that his reinstatement of mothers comes
to seem something of a debating point, particularly when we
find that he has the familiar difficulty with the relationship
between wives and mistresses: 'Let us therefore consider a
master of a family with all these subordinate relations of wife,
children, servants and slaves, united under the domestick rule
of a family.' The father's power is not unlimited, 'and none
too but what a *mistress of a family* may have as well as he'
(Locke, 1967, II: 86). Perhaps she may, but not coherently
while she is also a wife.

Late seventeenth-century liberalism retains most of the
unease about women which places them as simultaneously
present in and absent from the discourse of patriarchalism.
Thus it is primarily men who are born free as they are born
rational. Guy Miege in 1691 reproduces all the familiar
uncertainties about gender: 'Now 'tis plain, the law of nature
has put no difference (or subordination) amongst men, except
it be that of children to their parents, or of wives to their

husbands. So that, with relation to the law of nature, all men are born free' (Schochet, 1969:423–4). But there were attempts to find a place for women. Locke's *Two Treatises of Government* detach the 'honour' of the commandment from obedience, and make an effort to resolve the anomaly of woman's place in the family by defining a distinct sphere of obligation and authority for the wife (II, 82). This was by no means the first text to try to solve the problem in this way. Dod and Cleaver, whose popular manual of instruction for families, *A Godlie Forme of Householde Government* (1598), had run to at least seven editions by 1630, reproduce the common discursive unease about mothers, mistresses and wives, but grapple with the consequent contradictions by creating separate responsibilities for husbands and wives as 'governors' within the family. As regards their area of primary concern, the godly conduct of the household, their effort, it must be said, is not overwhelmingly successful. The husband's responsibilities occupy twenty-nine pages, and the wife's, with some repetition, rather less than two. In essence, the wife's responsibilities are to provide a visible model of submission, and not to get in the way, unless her husband is absent, when she carries out his will on his behalf:

> The wife also, which is a fellow-helper, hath some things belonging to her to further godlinesse in her familie: as for example, in her selfe to give example to her household of all readie submission to all good and Christian orders, to order her houshold affaires so carefully that no exercise of religion be hindred, or put out of place, at such time as they should be done: in her husbands absence: to see good orders observed as he hath appoynted: to watch over the manners and behaviour of such as be in her house, and to help her husband in spying out evils that are breeding, that by his wisedome they may be prevented or cured.
>
> (Dod and Cleaver, 1612:59–60)

In other words, the attempt to find a place of authority for the wife results in a renewed insistence on her submission. She is subsumed under the will of her husband: the orders, the organization of religious affairs and the wisdom are all his. Men are to command, servants and children are to obey, but a woman is to govern and not to govern, present as example or surrogate, but absent from the place where decisions are made.

In the family as in the state women had no single, unified, fixed position from which to speak. Possessed of immortal souls and of eminently visible bodies, parents and mistresses but also wives, they were only inconsistently identified as subjects in the discourses about them which circulated predominantly among men. In consequence, during the sixteenth century and much of the seventeenth the speech attributed to women themselves tended to be radically discontinuous, inaudible or scandalous.

6.2 Discursive discontinuity

One of the critical puzzles presented by Webster's *The White Devil* (1612) is how to reconcile the different positions from which Vittoria speaks. John Russell Brown identifies the problem in these terms:

> there are only four scenes of any length in which she appears and her mood, or tone, is very different in each of them. For an actress this presents a great difficulty, for there is no build-up of presentation; each of Vittoria's scenes starts on a new note, with little or no preparation in earlier scenes.
>
> (*The White Devil*, p.xlviii)

On the basis of a comparison between the first two of these scenes it is possible to state the problem more strongly still: the text makes no apparent effort to establish any continuity whatever between the Vittoria of 1.ii, the scene of her seduction by (or of?) Bracciano, and the Vittoria who eloquently defends herself against the charge that she is Bracciano's whore in the arraignment scene (III.ii). The oxymoron of the title (since white is the colour of innocence as well as of beauty, and Renaissance devils are conventionally black) is recapitulated in reverse in these consecutive appearances of the central female figure in the play.

The seduction is conducted entirely in the vocabulary of lust and money, with no hint of romantic love, and the cynical evaluation offered to the audience is confirmed by the sardonic comments of Flamineo:

> *Bracciano.* What value is this jewel?
> *Vittoria.* 'Tis the ornament
> Of a weak fortune.
> *Bracciano.* In sooth I'll have it; nay I will but change
> My jewel for your jewel.
> *Flamineo.* Excellent,
> His jewel for her jewel, – well put in duke.
> *Bracciano.* Nay let me see you wear it.
> *Vittoria.* Here sir.
> *Bracciano.* Nay lower, you shall wear my jewel lower.
> *Flamineo.* That's better – she must wear his jewel lower.
> (*The White Devil*, I. ii. 221–8)

Vittoria interrupts these exchanges to recount to Bracciano a dream which is a parable of murder. Again Flamineo's commentary makes sure the audience has taken the point: 'Excellent devil./She hath taught him in a dream/To make away his duchess and her husband' (I. ii. 256–8). At Bracciano's instigation, Flamineo breaks the neck of Vittoria's husband as he is about to jump a vaulting-horse; the duchess, Isabella, dies kissing a poisoned picture of Bracciano.

At her arraignment Vittoria progressively enlists the sympathy of the audience and of the commentators within the fiction, in this case the foreign ambassadors. She refuses to be tried in Latin, and then insists on plain English in place of the lawyer's inkhorn terms:

, will not have my accusation clouded
In a strange tongue: all this assembly
Shall hear what you can charge me with.

(III. ii. 18–20)

She points out, rightly, that Monticelso is both prosecution
and judge (l.225 ff.), and when he proceeds to sentence her
in the absence of any evidence at all, she insists that he has
'ravish'd justice' (l.274). In a series of spirited answers she
wins each round of the debate, and concludes:

Sum up my faults I pray, and you shall find
That beauty and gay clothes, a merry heart,
And a good stomach to a feast, are all,
All the poor crimes that you can charge me with.

(III. ii. 207–10)

Condemned to imprisonment in a house of penitent whores,
Vittoria insists, 'My mind shall make it honester to me/Than
the Pope's palace' (III. ii. 290–1). No Christian Stoic poet of
the period could have spoken better, or more plausibly.

Of course it would be possible to perform this scene with a
good deal of ironic business which would establish for the
audience its continuity with the seduction scene, so that
Vittoria's plausibility is precisely what identifies her as both
white and devilish. But the irony is not written into the text,
as it is in the case of Richard III, for instance, or Iago (another
white devil by contrast with his black victim). The problem
for the audience is not what Vittoria has done. That has been
established in I. ii. The question is rather what she *is*. (The
other two scenes in which she is central do not help to resolve
this problem.)

I am not here in quest of a novelistic 'character' for Vittoria,
a palpable life beyond the text, or even within it. What is at
issue is simply dramatic (or narrative) consistency. In a
morality play, where there are no human characters at all
unless we count the generalized protagonist, vices are

162

consistently vicious, virtues virtuous. In Webster's play, which could easily be read as a morality transformed into a play of social types, Bracciano is consistently 'quite lost', as he says at his first appearance (I. ii. 3), until he sees the devil come for him on his deathbed; Flamineo consistently facilitates evil, and manages, like Richard III, to evade the maze of conscience when he glimpses it (v. iv. 121); and Francisco, like so many other revengers, is portrayed as a good man impelled to evil by circumstances. Only Vittoria seems to have no place, intelligible to the audience as single and continuous, from which to speak, to be recognized.

There is, however, a minor instance of a parallel to Vittoria's discursive mobility in the case of Isabella, Bracciano's wife. The shift in discourse is not so striking because it is more clearly motivated in the text. None the less, it is evident that Isabella too speaks with equal plausibility from antithetical positions. Isabella is presented as a figure of wifely patience and reconciliation: 'all my wrongs/Are freely pardoned' (II. i. 12–13); 'these arms/Shall charm his poison' (II. i. 16–17). She pleads with her brother for mercy for her husband, and with her husband for affection:

> Nay my dear lord I will not have you angry, –
> Doth not my absence from you two months
> Merit one kiss?
>
> (II. i. 155–7)

When Bracciano repudiates their marriage-vow she takes public responsibility for their separation for the sake of peace between her husband and her brother. In the speech that follows a verbal violence which far exceeds Vittoria's is attributed, with no distancing interventions, to the saintly figure of Isabella, who longs

> To dig the strumpet's eyes out, let her lie
> Some twenty months a-dying, to cut off
> Her nose and lips, pull out her rotten teeth,

Preserve her flesh like mummia, for trophies
Of my just anger.

(II. i. 246–50)

A more recent play, concerned with consistency of character
and speech as expressive of an inner essence, a fixed
subjectivity, would show Isabella stumbling here, unable to
speak the words with fluency. But in the seventeenth-century
text there is no such hesitation. Isabella moves in a few lines
from the love and entreaty proper to a wife to an invective
which prompts Francisco to reproach her for unwomanly
excess: 'Look upon other women, with what patience/They
suffer these slight wrongs' (II. i. 240–1). The dramatic irony
resides in this comment and in the context of Isabella's
speeches, not in the speeches themselves.

There is nothing that quite matches this discursive mobility
in the fragmented subject of the morality plays, or in the
subject which is seen to be in process in its capacity for
succumbing to temptation and sudden repentance (Macbeth,
Angelo, Bertram). What is striking about Vittoria and Isabella
is that they take up subject-positions from which to speak
and to become agents of events, but these subject-positions
are radically discontinuous. What is also striking is that they
are women.

6.3 A question of patience

In *The White Devil* Bracciano says, 'Woman to man/Is either
a god or a wolf' (IV. ii. 91–2). 'To man' is important: in a
society where the circulation of discourses is controlled by
men the definition of women is inevitably patriarchal and
reductive. To what extent this definition is shared by women
themselves it is always difficult to say. There is no space
outside discourse from which women may silently intuit an
alternative definition, but it is worth noting that *The Tragedy
of Mariam* (1603–4?), the one play of the early seventeenth

century which we know to have been written by a woman, sharply problematizes patriarchal absolutism and women's speech. It is always possible to interrogate the dominant definitions, especially when these are themselves full of uncertainties, even though no coherent alternative may emerge from the process.

Bracciano's observation is additionally useful, however, in drawing attention to the way in which plays of this period tend to include contrasted female stereotypes, one saintly, submissive, faithful, forgiving and silent, and the other predatory, dominating, usually lustful, destructive and voluble. The contrast between the devilish Vittoria and the patient Isabella is to some degree reproduced in, for instance, the contrast between Goneril and Regan on the one hand and Cordelia on the other, Lady Macbeth and Lady Macduff, Cleopatra and Octavia, or Beatrice-Joanna and Isabella, at the centre of the main plot and sub-plot respectively in *The Changeling*. As Marilyn French points out, female sexuality, kept under male control, guarantees masculine supremacy over nature and over time, ensuring the stability of the family and the legitimacy of heirs. Women's sexuality unleashed is seen as able to destroy all control, undermining the institutions of society by threatening their continuity (French, 1982). Stereotypes define what the social body endorses and what it wants to exclude.

But the construction of stereotypes cannot ensure permanent stability, not only because the world always exceeds the stereotypical, but also in so far as the stereotypes themselves are inevitably subject to internal contradictions and so are perpetually precarious. This is the case with the type of the faithful, forgiving and silent woman, which probably finds its purest formulation in this period in the figure of patient Griselda. Like Isabella in *The White Devil*, Griselda is a wife who is infinitely patient in the multiple senses of the word: suffering, enduring, passive, submissive and uncomplaining. The story of a woman whose husband takes her children away, seems to have them murdered, sends her home to the humble cottage from which he took her, and then commands her to prepare a banquet for his new bride, can have appealed only, one would suppose, to the most vehemently misogynistic audience. That her 'reward' for enduring all this without protest is her reinstatement and reconciliation with her husband and her children, who have not been murdered after all but have been brought up by someone else, implies that for a woman an eventual place in the bosom of the (aristocratic) family is worth a lifetime of torment.

The first extant version of the Griselda narrative occurs in Boccaccio's *Decameron* (x. 10). The story was subsequently retold by Giovanni Sercambi and by Petrarch, then in two French versions, and by Chaucer in *The Clerk's Tale*. These medieval versions tend to introduce elements which to some degree mitigate the misogyny of the story. In Boccaccio's narrative, for instance, the stress is on the 'monstrous folly' of the husband, Gualtieri, who was lucky that in spite of his behaviour things turned out so well for him (Griffith, 1931:7). Petrarch's account places marginally less emphasis on Gualtieri's cruelty, but this version ends with a clear statement that Griselda does not constitute an example specifically for women to follow: on the contrary, the story is an allegory of the way human beings should behave when God puts their patience to the test (Bryan and Dempster, 1941:330). In *The Clerk's Tale*, as in *The Canterbury Tales* in general, no clear single position for the audience is signalled. Whether or not it is useful to talk in terms of a 'marriage-debate' in *The Canterbury Tales*, there is no doubt that the Clerk's tale of feminine submissiveness is offered in explicit contrast to the Wife of Bath's plea for female sovereignty, and there is no single narrative voice to authorize either.

The Renaissance versions, however, of which there are a good many, are on the whole less critical of Walter, less willing to treat the story as an allegory of the Christian life, and more emphatic that Griselda offers an example for women.

According to the title page, John Phillip's *Play of Patient Grissell* (1558–61) shows 'the good example of her pacience towards her husband'. *The Ancient, True and Admirable History of Patient Grisel* (1619) displays, rather more pragmatically, 'How Maides, By Her Example, In Their Good Behaviour, May Marrie Rich Husbands'. It also claims to tell a story 'in which is exemplified the true obedience and noble behaviour of vertuous women towards their husbands' (Collier, 1842:3). And *The Pleasant and Sweet History of Patient Grissell*, printed in 1630 or 1631, offers 'a patterne for all vertuous women' (Deloney, 1912:493), and concludes with the following exhortation:

> Thus you may see by this history, you that are women, the great good which commeth by patience and humility, for had this vertuous woman bin of a churlish and crabbed disposition, she had lost that great estate which she had, besides the happy love of a worthy and loving husband: therefore, ye women, as you are helpers for men, and were so created for that use, give no distaste to your loving husbands.
>
> (p. 495)

But there is a paradox for partriarchy in the narrative which only the 1630 version picks up explicitly. The story is about a woman, and its closure depends on her virtue: the final feast is a celebration of its heroine's victory. The 1630 version is therefore careful to make clear that Grissel is an exception among women: 'and men likewise, be not bitter to your wives, for the world hath not many Grissels' (ibid.).

This paradox leads to a more serious problem, which may help to account for the repeated re-telling of the story in the sixteenth and early seventeenth centuries in a series of attempts to resolve the difficulties it presents. Marriage as the story defines it is entirely absolutist, but the moral superiority of the wife calls into question the justice of this absolutism. It is the fact that Grissell submits absolutely which causes the courtiers in Phillip's play to exclaim, 'I have not seene hir like since the time of my creasion'; 'I never knew hir like in all my life daies' (*The Play of Patient Grissell*, ll.1990, 1995). In Dekker's play (*c.*1599), the sub-plot concerns a shrewish Welsh wife who is neither patient nor uncomplaining, and therefore merits taming. Gwalter solemnly explains to her husband that Grissil's luminous example demonstrates how important it is to curb a wife when she is young, before she shows signs of needing a bridle (*Patient Grissil*, v. ii. 238–51). In the 1619 version Gualter states his conditions when he offers his hand: Grisel must not repine at his pleasure or contradict his demands; as soldiers must obey without dispute, 'so must vertuous wives dutifully consent without reproofe, or the least contraction of a brow' (Collier, 1842:12). Grisel obeys all this perfectly. Like the model wife in Dod and Cleaver, she is visible only as a model of invisibility: in consequence, 'all his subjects resolved to obedience from her good example' (p.15).

But the justification of the absolutist definition of marriage is the frailty of women. Like Eve, they are patently more subject to the wiles of the devil. They are spiritually weaker, more evidently in need of guidance. Formed of Adam's rib to be a help meet for him, a woman cannot expect to participate in the superior wisdom and virtue of her husband. As the domestic conduct books laboriously reiterate, invoking the authority of St Paul, for these reasons the man is necessarily and naturally the head of the woman. Griselda, however, is temptation-proof, while Walter, with no grounds for his trial of her virtue, cannot easily be seen as her moral superior. How then can his power to torment her be seen as morally just? In offering a model of absolutist marriage the story challenges the very foundations of marital absolutism.

None of the texts explicitly poses the problem in these terms. Deloney's ballad version (1593?) manages to evade the question by motivating the testing. In the early versions Walter invents the story of the people's envy at Griselda's elevation. In the ballad this envy is presented as real, and the trials are devised in order to display the heroine's own acceptance of the Marquess's sovereign will and thus to disgrace her detractors (Deloney, 1912:346–50). It might be questioned whether such absolute sovereignty could not find simpler ways of dealing with popular discontent, but the story has its own coherence.

Phillip's play, the first of the extant sixteenth-century versions, is also in a sense the most contradictory. In order to avoid sacrificing the basis of the husband's right to rule, his superior moral virtue, the play isolates the impulse to test Grissell in the allegorical figure of Politic Persuasion. Politic Persuasion is defined on the title page as the Vice, and he displays most of the characteristics of the conventional morality Vice: he talks nonsense, tells lies, leads people astray and destroys social harmony. But he cannot be identified, as the Vice so often can, with the hero's predisposition to sin and so to bring about his own damnation. On the contrary, Politic Persuasion has no interest in damning Gautier: he simply hates Grissell for her virtue, and loves 'inconvenience', 'confusion', 'mischife' (*The Play of Patient Grissell*, ll.896–900). It is entirely at the suggestion of Politic Persuasion that Gautier begins the testing process, and the play shows Gautier himself faltering when he is compelled to recognize his own brutality and Grissell's virtues which, despite her humble origins, 'yeld such equall dome' (l.1575: entitle her to equal judgement, equality?) that further trials cannot be justified. Politic Persuasion, however, spurs him on with the encouragement, 'it is time now to playe the man' (l.1583), and 'Let your countenance be sterne, like a gentillman looke byg' (l.1586).

Marital absolutism, in other words, is here identified with the Vice, who is introduced into the play precisely in an effort to preserve its conventional moral justification. Politic Persuasion seems to personify a temporary derangement of the hero which disappears at the end of the story as a condition of closure. The concept of the infinite redeemability of men is most familiar from Shakespeare's 'problem comedies', *Measure for Measure* and *All's Well that Ends Well*, where Angelo and Bertram are evidently to be understood as husbands worth winning once they have repented of their earlier errors. (It is hard to think of female parallels in the period: women's innocence, once lost, is gone for ever.) But the presence of Politic Persuasion, and the attribution to him of responsibility for Grissell's suffering, is evidence that the play is struggling with the problem of how to justify the gap between power and virtue. The introduction of the Vice permits the play to externalize to some degree Gautier's tyranny and so to preserve the conventional justification of patriarchy: men are in control because they are wiser and better. At the same time, however, in so far as Gautier consents to Persuasion he is clearly implicated in his own actions, and the problem the story presents is not solved.

The 1619 version, the most explicitly misogynist of the texts, also concedes that the Marquess's course was 'dangerous' (Collier, 1842:24). He ought to have been appeased by his wife's evident patience. The people are on her side; Gualter's continued torture is 'wilfulness' (p.26). In addition, the narrative shows Grisel playing a part in the Marquess's political life, mediating in controversies with his nobles and urging peace in disputes with foreign princes (p.15). In conjunction with the narrator's constant vituper-ation against women's desire for liberty ('oh, hellish device of the divell', p.33) and the invective against the 'filthinesse' of seeing 'a woman so presumptuous as to take an account of her husbands actions and businesse' (p.32), this simply reduces the text to ideological incoherence.

Only Dekker's dramatic version, where there is no Vice and the envy of the people is an invention of the Marquess, foregrounds the contradiction starkly. The brutality of the story is not softened in any way; Grissil does not utter a word of protest, and after the reconciliation she remains silent (what could she say?). The play thus leaves the audience to confront the problem of the moral duty to submit to an immoral power, and to ponder the question whether there is any proper limit to the silent endurance of patriarchal tyranny.

The subsumption of the wife's will under her husband's provides no position from which she is able to protest. Phillip's play takes this point to its logical conclusion. Grissell's anguish is at the centre of the drama, but it is defined obliquely since she is forbidden by the project of the play to speak of it. All the pleading is allotted to a Nurse, who dwells on the horror of the events, while Grissell silently displays her patience.

A wife's right to speak, to subjectivity, to a position from which to protest, is among the central questions of Elizabeth Cary's play, *The Tragedy of Mariam* (1603–4?). *The Tragedy of Mariam, the Faire Queene of Jewry* centres on the marital relations between Mariam and Herod, and explores the limits of a dutiful wife's right to resist a tyrannical husband. Herod's crimes are considerably in excess even of Walter's. He has divorced his first wife, murdered Mariam's brother and grandfather, and given instructions that Mariam shall be killed as soon as news is delivered of his own death. The play begins with the news. Mariam's long opening speech dramatizes in Senecan (or French classical) manner her fluctuations of mood as she responds to Herod's supposed death. She has long wished to be free of him; rage and scorn have put her love to flight; by restraining her he has taught her to long for liberty. But she has never loved another, and now his death recalls her former love for him. Surely his crimes forbid her to mourn for him? And yet he loved her; and so,

> Why now me thinkes the love I bare him then,
> When virgin freedome left me unrestraind:
> Doth to my heart begin to creepe agen.

> (ll.73–5)

Throughout the first half of the play all the characters except Mariam rejoice at the news of Herod's death. Exactly half way through the play it is revealed that the news was false. This releases Mariam's abhorrence and fear all over again:

> When I his death beleev'd, compassion wrought,
> And was the stickler twixt my heart and him:
> But now that curtaine's drawn from off my thought,
> Hate doth appeare againe with visage grim:
> And paints the face of Herod in my heart,
> In horred colours with detested looke
>
> (ll.1158–63)

Her fear prompts her to use her sexuality to appease him, but she has forsworn his bed. He 'loves' her, but she refuses to capitalize on that:

> I know I could inchaine him with a smile:
> And lead him captive with a gentle word,
> I scorne my looke should ever man beguile,
> Or other speech, then meaning to afford.
>
> (ll.1166–9)

Her innocence is her hope and her defence.

Mariam is a subject: she speaks from a definite position, even when this is one of inner conflict. The play makes clear that *she* (that is, the subjectivity which precedes and undergoes the conflict) is attempting to reconcile contrary values, and that her goal is what the twentieth century might call the preservation of her integrity. Meaning and speech, she says, are to be unified, and meaning is located in a consciousness united with the utterance which is its outward expression. The play finds for its heroine a specified place in a modern world where language is transparent to subjectivity.

But the play makes it equally and repeatedly clear that it is Mariam's speech which puts her in danger. Sohemus cautiously steers a course between sympathy and disapproval:

Poor guiltles Queene. Oh that my wish might place
A little temper now about thy heart:
Unbridled speech is Mariams worst disgrace,
And will indanger her without desart.

(ll.1184–7)

The contradictions – 'guiltles', 'disgrace', 'without desart' –
are symptomatic of the play's consistent unease about its
heroine's right to speak. The Chorus comments in detail on
Mariam's failure to 'bare her selfe of power as well as will'
(l.1222), but the position of the Chorus at this point is
puzzling. The issue again is women's speech in marriage:

When to their husbands they themselves do bind,
Doe they not wholy give themselves away?
Or give they but their body not their mind,
Reserving that though best, for others pray?
  No sure, their thoughts no more can be their owne,
  And therefore should to none but one be knowne.

(ll.1237–42)

The argument appears to be that women give their minds to
their husbands and their thoughts should therefore not be
made known to outsiders. The Chorus concludes, 'Now
Mariam had, (but that to this she bent)/Beene free from feare,
as well as innocent' (ll.1253–4). But the play as a whole
makes clear that what brings about Mariam's death is not
her openness with other people but her spoken defiance of
Herod himself. It is because she has *not* given her mind to a
tyrant (because she is a unified, autonomous subject) that
Mariam remains innocent and meets her death with heroism.
Her refusal to flatter and to seduce her husband is the source
of her tragedy: 'I cannot frame disguise, nor never taught/My
face a looke dissenting from my thought' (ll.1407–8). Perhaps,
then, the 'none but one' of line 1242 should be read as the
speaker herself? Mariam is in danger because she speaks her
thoughts to Herod. Perhaps she would be wiser to keep them

to herself, precisely because in marriage they are no longer her own? At this moment the transparency of the text falters as it confronts its own theorization of its challenge to marital absolutism, and the Chorus evades the full implication of the play's identification of a wife as a subject. If speech is the expression of a subjectivity, and if women as subjects are individuals (undivided) only on the basis of the unity of thought and speech, can speech be given away in marriage? If so, marriage is the surrender of subjectivity, a retreat from the place the play has defined for its heroine into a condition where thought is forbidden, a state of unconsciousness, non-being.

However we read the Chorus here there are difficulties. What is clear, however, is that the play as a whole seems to oscillate between endorsement and disapproval of Mariam's defiance. In bringing into uneasy conjunction classical heroism and Elizabethan absolutist marriage, the text foregrounds the difficulty in the period of being both a liberal-humanist subject and a wife. Griselda does not speak, and is rewarded: Mariam speaks – and dies.

Unresolved contradictions issue in tragedy. The play glimpses the possibility of a militant feminism which might have resolved Mariam's difficulty, but it evades the implications of this too. Salome, who is in love with Silleus, wants to initiate a bill which will make divorce available to women, as it already is in Judaea to men:

> Why should such priviledge to man be given?
> Or given to them, why bard from women then?
> Are men then we in greater grace with Heaven?
> Or cannot women hate as well as men?
> Ile be the custome-breaker: and beginne
> To shewe my sexe the way to freedomes doore.
>
> (ll. 315–20)

But the play admits no sympathy with this position. Salome is a wicked woman, spiritual sister of Vittoria and Lady

Macbeth. Mariam quite explicitly loves no one other than Herod; she does not consider the possibility of divorce. Constabarus gives the play's verdict on Salome's proposal: 'Are Hebrew women now transformed to men? ... suffer this, and then/Let all the world be topsie turved quite' (ll.435–8).

Divorce initiated by women, equality of the sexes ... such concepts would indeed have brought about a world turned upside-down. What is significant, however, is that in a play written by a woman these possibilities should be so sharply formulated, even if only to be equally sharply repudiated. Elizabeth Cary's play, exploring the problem of a woman's right to speak, was a closet drama clearly not offered for performance – or certainly not for performance on the public stage. There is some evidence that she was reluctant to publish it (*The Tragedy of Mariam*, p.xvii). Certainly the circumstances of its publication ten years after it was probably written are unknown. The author is declared on the title page to be a lady, but her name is withheld, though the dedication contains enough clues to enable her identity to be fairly easily discovered. Women are entitled to speak and forbidden to speak, anxious to write and reluctant to be known to write. Ironically, there may be a sense in which the conditions of the production of this text re-enact the contradictions it so eloquently defines. The play's absence not only from the literary canon but from most histories of drama, and the lack of an accessible modern edition, indicate that at least some of these conditions may still obtain in the twentieth century.

Heywood 's *A Woman Killed with Kindness* (1603) offers a final example of a play which problematizes a woman's place in an absolutist marriage. The play opens with two contrasting definitions of the relations between husband and wife. Frankford and Anne are newly married. Sir Francis Acton salutes the bride:

> A perfect wife already, meek and patient.
> How strangely the word 'husband' fits your mouth,

Not marry'd three hours since, sister. 'Tis good;
You that begin betimes thus, must needs prove
Pliant and duteous in your husband's love.

(I. 37–41)

'A perfect wife', 'meek and patient', 'pliant and duteous': these
are the key terms of the Griselda story. Sir Charles Mountford,
however, compliments Frankford in a vocabulary which
conflicts strikingly with this, evoking the emerging liberal
definition of marriage:

You both adorn each other, and your hands
Methinks are matches. There's equality
In this fair combination; you are both scholars,
Both young, both being descended nobly.
There's music in this sympathy, it carries
Consort and expectation of much joy.

(I. 65–70)

The play makes no comment on the clash of values here
defined, and it is the absolutist meaning which appears to
determine the plot. Anne, without apparently taking any
initiative in the proceedings, verbal or otherwise, is seduced
by Wendoll. Frankford, his vengeful arm withheld by a maid
who is a clear descendant of an angel of mercy or a morality
virtue (XIII. 68–9), resists the impulse to violence, and instead
banishes Anne from his house, separating her from their
children. Repentant, remorseful, driven out of the family
which is now the source of her identity, Anne Frankford
refuses food and so starves herself to death. She makes no
protest at her treatment: 'He cannot be so base as to forgive
me,/Nor I so shameless to accept his pardon' (XIII. 139–40).
Her only deliberate action in the play is a negative one: she
takes her punishment on herself by letting herself die. Her
identity lost, she wastes away.

But in spite of the absolutism of the story, the liberal values
of Sir Charles Mountford's speech are perhaps not wholly

suppressed. Frankford's 'kindness' is either divine or brutal. The text tends to emphasize the second element:

> I'll not martyr thee
> Nor mark thee for a strumpet, but with usage
> Of more humility torment thy soul,
> And kill thee even with kindness.
>
> (XIII. 153–6)

Anne's 'torment' is pitiful: even the surly Nicholas weeps. But above all, the devices by which Frankford acquires his evidence of Anne's infidelity – the forged letter to himself, the false keys to the door of his own house, the silent ascent to his chamber – all evoke the comic cuckold rather than an authoritative source of good government in the household, and as in the case of Walter in the Griselda story, they draw attention to the gap between moral standing and power. The absolute right of one human being to require another's death in payment for an injury must be predicated on a radical inequality. Frankford's absurdity, in conjunction with the oxymoron of the title, which is reiterated in the final line of the play, invites the audience to a certain unease at such absolutism.

In the last scene of the play Frankford forgives the dying Anne, emblematically reinstating her in her place in the family:

> My wife, the mother to my pretty babes,
> Both those lost names I do restore thee back,
> And with this kiss I wed thee once again.
>
> (XVII. 115–17)

The episode evokes the reinstatement of Griselda, but the reconciliation with Anne, who has sinned, is conditional on her death, the ultimate silence. *A Woman Killed with Kindness* confronts the problem that the domestic conduct books evade, the question of what happens when an absolutist marriage fails to conform to the model. What the play reveals in the process is that the stability of the family requires the subjugation of women to the point where they must be willing to efface themselves finally in order to preserve it. The questions concerning domestic power and justice which the play so explicitly raises are dissolved in death, and the family is emblematically restored by the self-elimination of the offending wife.

6.4 The demonization of eloquence

If Griselda speaks it is only to acquiesce in the will of her husband. Anne Frankford laments but does not protest. According to Thomas Gataker in 1624, 'A meeke and a quiet spirit, in a woman especially, is a thing, saith Saint Peter, much set by in Gods sight' (Halkett, 1970:40). This spirit manifested itself in an equally quiet voice. Cordelia's voice was 'ever soft,/Gentle, and low – an excellent thing in woman' (*King Lear*, v. iii. 272–3). Octavia, Antony's forgiving, reconciling wife, has a low voice (*Antony and Cleopatra*, III. iii. 13).

St Paul had made it clear that women should not speak in church: if there was anything they wanted to know they should ask their husbands at home (I Cor. 14:34–5). This principle was easily extended to other areas. The creation of a domestic realm which was the special province of the woman progressively circumscribed the topics as well as the place of her speech. Brathwait in *The English Gentlewoman*, which first appeared in 1631, discusses in some detail the question whether and where it is proper for women to speak. Young women should keep silence in the company of men or their elders. And he advises his women readers, in cases where they may speak without immodesty: 'make choyce of such arguments as may best improve your knowledge in houshold affaires, and other private employments'. Public issues are not appropriate topics for women: 'to discourse of state-matters, will not become your auditory: nor to dispute of high points of divinity.... Women, as they are to be no speakers in the Church, so neither are they to be disputers of controversies of the Church.' But it is almost certainly best to say nothing at all: 'Silence in a woman is a moving rhetoricke, winning most, when in words it wooeth least.... More shall wee see fall into sinne by speech then silence' (Brathwait, 1641a:319–20). Dod and Cleaver in *A Godlie Forme of Householde Government* confirm this: 'Silence is a gravitie, when she abstaineth and holdeth her peace from speaking when it doth not become her to speake' (Dod and Cleaver, 1612:95).

A Godlie Forme of Householde Government experiences a good deal of uncertainty about exactly how patriarchal it means to be. Bullinger's *The Christen State of Matrimonye*, translated by Coverdale in 1541 and widely read in the sixteenth century, is quite radical in its treatment of women, and is scrupulously non-sexist when it comes to discuss how a man or woman who intends to marry should make a sound choice. When Dod and Cleaver reproduce whole passages of Coverdale's translation of *The Christen State*, as they commonly do (without acknowledgement, of course), they also appropriate the non-sexist nouns and pronouns. Their own interpolations, however, are much more patriarchal. Thus when they discuss a list of signs of godliness in a potential partner they consider men and women indifferently until they reach the third sign on the list. At this point the text reasserts by a feminine pronoun the obvious fact that in practice it is men who choose: 'The third signe is, her talke or speech, or rather her silence'. The next sentence comes from *The Christen State*: 'For a man or womans talking, is the mirror or messenger of the minde, in the which it may commonly be seene without, in what case the man or woman is within'. Speech is expressive of subjectivity. Almost at once, however, the Dod and Cleaver text snatches back what it has so dangerously given, the possibility that women's speech should define them as subjects. The next sentence is not from *The Christen State*:

'Now silence is the best ornament of a woman, and therefore the law was given to the man, rather then to the woman, to shew that he should be the teacher, and she the hearer; and therefore shee is commanded to learne of her husband. I Corinthians, 14, 34–35' (Dod and Cleaver, 1612:104).

Coriolanus addresses his wife as 'My gracious silence' (*Coriolanus*, II. i. 166), thus contrasting her with his militaristic and voluble mother whose eloquence is the cause of his destruction. As women writers acknowledged in their practice in the seventeenth century as well as in the nineteenth, to speak may be to adopt the voice of a man. Elizabeth I, who spoke powerfully, did so most famously to deny her femininity: 'I know I have the body of a weak and feeble woman, but I have the heart and stomach of a king'. (The women rulers of Europe presented a problem for sixteenth-century patriarchy, but one which could be resolved by perceiving them as holders of a male office, 'princes', and thus only secondarily women in the eyes of the state (Maclean, 1980:61–3).) In *The White Devil* Vittoria, speaking in her own defence, but not wanting to lose the appeal of her femininity, identifies a contradiction:

> Humbly thus,
> Thus low, to the most worthy and respected
> Lieger ambassadors, my modesty
> And womanhood I tender; but withal
> So entangled in a cursed accusation
> That my defence of force like Perseus,
> Must personate masculine virtue.
>
> (III. ii. 130–36)

To 'personate' (impersonate) is 'to speak with the voice of'; 'virtue' (virtù) is strength as well as virtue. Vittoria exceeds the bounds of the feminine. (To his credit, the English ambassador seems to like the effect: 'She hath a brave spirit', l.140.)

Domestic absolutism requires that women be able to speak

in order to acquiesce, but it withholds the right to use that ability to protest or to make demands. To speak from a place of independence, from an autonomous position, to be, in other words, a subject, is to personate masculine virtue. In the play *Lingua, or the Combat of the Tongue and the Five Senses for Superiority* (1607) Lingua (the tongue), dressed in a crimson gown with white accessories, is identified as a woman, 'an idle, prating dame' (1. i) who sows dissension and employs deceit in her effort to become a sixth sense, *equal* to the other five. Her polyglot eloquence elicits nothing but general revulsion, however, and she is finally imprisoned in the house of Gustus (taste) where thirty tall watchmen are to prevent her from wagging abroad. *Lingua* had been reprinted five times by 1657.

To speak in order to complain was a punishable offence – for women. From the sixteenth century onwards scolds were led through the streets in the scold's bridle, an instrument with an iron framework to enclose the head and a metal gag or bit which restrained the tongue. Alternatively they were judicially humiliated by being publicly ducked (or cucked) in water several times for speaking out of turn – to protest, for instance, against injury (Spargo, 1944). It might be supposed that the young wife had a case in the ballad, 'The Cucking of a Scold'. She was outraged when the constable urinated against her wall.

> She cal'd him beastly knave,
> And filthy Jacke for this,
> And said that every cuckold now
> Against her wall must pisse:
> And in most raging sort,
> She rail'd at him so long,
> He made a vow he would revenge
> This most outragious wrong.
>
> (Rollins, 1922:74)

It was the woman who was punished, hung about with neats'

tongues and duly cucked to the delight of the community. The earliest recorded instance of the practice of cucking a scold is 1542, and the evidence is that it went on well into the seventeenth century (Spargo, 1944:33–9). Scolds were by definition women. There was no equivalent crime for men.

In the world turned upside-down of the 1640s and 1650s women began to prophesy or to speak with tongues, and were regarded as saints (Smith, 1979; Berg and Berry, 1981). Commonly permitted to preach, speak and vote within the separatist sects, women began to be audible outside them too in the affairs of the family and the state, in spite of continued condemnation by orthodoxy (Thomas, 1958). They laid claim to religious equality and rights as citizens, presenting petitions and organizing demonstrations (Higgins, 1973). Elizabeth Lilburne and others, delivering a petition to parliament in May 1649, insisted that they were sure of their 'creation in the image of God, and of an interest in Christ equal unto men, as also of a proportionable share in the freedoms of this commonwealth'. 'Have we not,' they continued, 'an equal interest with the men of this nation in those liberties and securities contained in the *Petition of Right*, and other good laws of the land?' A right to salvation was one thing; to claim an interest and a voice in law and politics was quite another, and was evidently too much for the House of Commons, which promptly instructed them to return to their proper place:

> The House sent them this answer by the Sergeant: 'That the matter they petitioned about was of an higher concernment than they understood, that the House gave an answer to their husbands, and therefore desired them to go home, and look after their own business, and meddle with their huswifery'.
>
> (Hampton, 1984:215–16)

Evidently meaning and subjectivity were primarily the possession of men, and women who spoke were seen to be transgressing the system of differences which defined the natural order.

'Woman to man/Is either a god or a wolf.' The image of a wolf evokes a ravening predator trafficking by night to steal the sheep from the fold. Women of this kind, repositories of the dark mystery of female sexuality, steal men out of the family and destroy the fundamental institutions of society. Beyond the control of law, they are outlawed by the social body, pushed to the margins of speech, and yet spoken of more volubly than their patient sisters. These personators of masculine virtue recur in the plays of the period as eloquent and deadly. Beatrice-Joanna in *The Changeling* wishes she had been created a man, able to choose her own partner: 'Oh, 'tis the soul of freedom!' (II. ii. 109). Seizing the liberty to which she is not entitled, she persuades De Flores to murder the man her father has chosen for her to marry, and triumphs in her own ingenuity: 'So wisdom by degrees works out her freedom' (III. iv. 13). Lady Macbeth repudiates her sex and taunts her husband with his unmanly cowardice. Her eloquence makes him a regicide. Her predecessor, Shakespeare's Joan of Arc, La Pucelle of 1 *King Henry VI*, puts heart into the enemy by her rhetoric. Vittoria persuades Bracciano to murder his wife. Cleopatra insists on fighting in the battle of Actium:

> A charge we bear i'th'war,
> And, as the president of my kingdom, will
> Appear there for a man. Speak not against it;
> I will not stay behind.
>
> (*Antony and Cleopatra*, III. vii. 16–19)

Predictably, these creatures who speak with voices which are not their own are unfixed, inconstant, unable to personate masculine virtue through to the end. Lady Macbeth sleepwalks, compelled to utter what she may not speak by day, and so betrays the truth. La Pucelle, deserted by her familiars, frantically asserts her innocence and then her pregnancy to escape the death she deserves. Beatrice-Joanna overestimates her own wisdom: De Flores, servant, Vice, man, deflowerer and therefore master, progressively takes control. Cleopatra flees from the battle of Actium and Antony loses the war.

Paradoxically, however, these figures are also in a sense heroic, and to this extent the plays offer their audiences no single, unified position from which to judge the heroines who refuse the place of silent subjection allotted to women. Cleopatra finally repudiates the instability of the feminine as she becomes agent of her own destiny, the absolute subject of suicide:

> My resolution's plac'd, and I have nothing
> Of woman in me. Now from head to foot
> I am marble-constant; now the fleeting moon
> No planet is of mine.
>
> (Antony and Cleopatra, v. ii. 236–9)

The final visual image of Cleopatra in the play is of the queen in her robes of state, steadfast, imperious; and of 'a lass unparallel'd' (v. ii. 314), her crown awry, the asp at her breast, perhaps evoking the medieval emblem of lechery, a young woman whose breast and genitals are devoured by serpents. A woman, at once whore and mother ('The stroke of death is as a lover's pinch', l.293; 'Dost thou not see my baby at my breast?', l.307), who simultaneously refuses the feminine, the figure of Cleopatra is thus plural, contradictory, an emblem which can be read as justifying either patriarchy on the one hand or an emergent feminism on the other, or perhaps as an icon of the contest between the two.

Presented as transgressing the system of differences which gives meaning to social relations, these dramatic heroines are defined as extra-human, demonic. Beatrice-Joanna is a 'changeling', not only shifting, changeable, but also super-natural, a child left by fairies. (The word occurs, for instance, in Reginald Scot's late sixteenth-century list of uncanny products of the imagination: 'witches, urchens, elves, hags, fairies, satyrs ... nymphes, changlings ... the hell waine, the fierdrake, the puckle' (Scot, 1930:86).) Vittoria is a white devil. La Pucelle is a witch. Cleopatra is enchanting (I. ii. 125), cunning (I. ii. 141), a serpent (I. v. 25), a fairy (IV. viii. 12), a witch (IV. xii. 47) and a gipsy (I. i. 10; IV. xii. 28), not only an Egyptian but, then as now, wandering and alien, beyond the margins of the social body (*OED*, 1). Lady Macbeth is explicitly aligned with the witches. She continues the work they begin. The witches are at the borders of what is female (*Macbeth*, I. iii. 45–7); Lady Macbeth invokes spirits to unsex her (I. v. 37ff.).

In this sense these figures are placed outside and beyond the system of differences which defines and delimits men and women. The demonization of women who subvert the meaning of femininity is contradictory in its implications. It places them beyond meaning, beyond the limits of what is intelligible. At the same time it endows them with a (supernatural) power which it is precisely the project of patriarchy to deny. On the stage such figures are seen as simultaneously dazzling and dangerous; off the stage their less dazzling but equally dangerous sisters were systematically eliminated. The English witchcraze, the demonization of women who were seen as voluble, unwomanly and possessed of an unauthorized power, is coterminous with the crisis in the definition of women and the meaning of the family. Witchcraft was first made a statutory offence in 1542 and the last statute against witchcraft was repealed in 1736 (Thomas, 1973:525). The main period for executions was 1559–1675; thereafter convictions became very rare (ibid., p.540). Within this period there were peaks in the 1580s and 1590s, when the divorce debate was also reaching a climax, and in 1645–7, when women were claiming an unprecedented voice in the affairs of church and state.

Of the witches executed in England, 93 per cent were women (Larner, 1981:89). James I was easily able to explain this: women are morally frailer, as the example of Eve demonstrates (James I, 1966:43–4). John Stearne, an associate of Matthew Hopkins, the witchfinder of the 1640s, also pointed out that women are more impatient, and being injured, more malicious in seeking revenge (Stearne, 1648:11). But witches were also women who failed to conform to the patriarchal ideal of femininity (Larner, 1981:102). They might have beards (*Macbeth*, I. iii. 45–7; Thomas, 1973:678). They were often ugly. Elizabeth Sawyer in *The Witch of Edmonton*, who conforms closely to the stereotype of the witch as it appears in the pamphlets which regaled the public with details of witch trials and confessions, describes herself as 'like a bow buckl'd and bent together' (II. i. 4). Elizabeth Sowtherns (Old Demdike) was about eighty and blind (Potts, 1613, sig. B IV, B 3r). Her associate, Anne Whittle, 'was a very old withered spent and decreped creature, her sight almost gone' (ibid., sig. D 2r). But Old Demdike's daughter, Elizabeth Device, was more repellent than either:

> This odious witch was branded with a preposterous marke in nature, even from her birth, which was her left eye, standing lower then the other; the one looking downe, the other looking up, so strangely deformed, as the best that were present in that honorable assembly, and great audience, did affirme, they had not often seene the like.
>
> (ibid., sig. G Ir)

Witches were, as their appearance tended to demonstrate, 'unwomanly'. Joan Flower, already given to oaths and imprecations, was so distressed when her daughter lost her job that 'she grew past all shame and womanhood' and began to practise witchcraft against the children of the former employers (Rosen, 1969:372). She was executed in 1619. Early in the 1590s Judith Phillips was arraigned and punished as a 'cunning' and 'unwomanly' confidence trickster. Though she was married, Judith Phillips made her own living by various forms of fortune-telling and magic. The pamphlet *The Bridling, Sadling and Ryding, of a rich Churle in Hampshire*

186

(1595) has a picture of her riding on the back of the man she has defrauded (ibid., p.215).[9] Joan Vaughan (or Varnham) began the struggle that led to her execution for witchcraft in 1612 by performing something unspecified 'either in speech or gesture so unfitting and unseeming the nature of womanhood that it displeased the most that were there present' (ibid., p.345). As Christina Larner points out, other women were as readily offended as men, because women who conformed to the requirements of patriarchy felt threatened by its repudiation (Larner, 1981:102). Joan Vaughan on this occasion gave especial offence to the 'virtuous and godly' Mistress Belcher, 'who was so moved with her bold and impudent demeanour that she could not contain herself, but suddenly rose up and struck her' (Rosen, 1969:345). The subsequent misadventures of Mistress Belcher and her brother led inevitably to Joan's conviction and death.

Witches were also voluble. According to Larner's account of the characteristics of Scottish witches, 'the essential individual personality trait does seem to have been that of a ready, sharp and angry tongue.... The richness of language attributed to witches is considerable' (Larner, 1981:97). Elizabeth Sawyer blamed her 'bad tongue' (*The Witch of Edmonton*, II. i. 11). It was offered in evidence against Joan Pechey that she was frequently heard 'vehemently speaking' when she was alone in the house (Rosen, 1969:111). Elizabeth Device was totally unable to remain silent in court, but exclaimed and cried out constantly, so that when her 9-year-old daughter appeared against her and it was evident that nothing would keep her mother quiet, the judge ordered the defendant to be taken away (Potts, 1613: sig. F 4v-G 1r). In much the same way Elizabeth Sawyer, according to Henry Goodcole's prose account, confirmed the court's worst suspicions, uttering,

in the hearing of the judge, jury, and all good people that stood by, many most fearfull imprecations for destruction against her selfe then to happen, as heretofore she had wished and indeavoured to happen on divers of her neighbours.

And the text concludes primly, 'Thus God did wonderfully overtake her in her own wickednesse, to make her tongue to be the meanes of her owne destruction, which had destroyed many before' (Goodcole, 1621: sig. B 1r).

These women, at the extreme edges of the social body, old, poor and often beggars, show themselves to be as discursively mobile as Vittoria and Isabella, or as, in a different way, La Pucelle or Beatrice-Joanna. Vehement denial turns readily to detailed confession, and often back again. It is almost as if, allotted a subject-position in a familiar discourse, they seize it eagerly and sometimes eloquently. Alice Samuel of Warboys is in some respects the most striking instance.

In 1589 Alice Samuel was alleged by the Throckmorton children to be causing their fits by witchcraft. Her first reaction was silence: 'The old woman, hearing this, sat still and gave never a word, yet looked very ruefully, as afterwards was remembered by them that saw her' (Rosen, 1969:242). Two years later, when the fits and the accusations showed no sign of remission, the Throckmortons sent for Alice. She did her best to avoid interrogation, but when Lady Cromwell snatched off Alice's kerchief and cut a lock of her hair, Alice spoke: ' "Madam, why do you use me thus? I never did you any harm as yet." These words were afterwards remembered' (p.254). There was no safety in silence, but speech too was dangerous. Each was a signifying practice. Lady Cromwell died a little over a year later, remembering Alice's ominous 'as yet' on her deathbed.

In 1590 Pickering, uncle of the Throckmorton chldren, took it upon himself with two other Cambridge scholars to interrogate Alice. This time she responded like any scold:

she was very loud in her answers and impatient, not suffering any to speak but herself. One of them desired her

to keep the woman's virtue and be more silent; she answered
that she was 'born in a mill, begot in a kill, she must have
her will', she could speak no softlier.

The greatest part of her speech was railing words against
Master Throckmorton and his children, saying that he did
misuse her in suffering his children so to play the wantons
in accusing of her and bringing her name into question.

(p.255)

The Throckmortons then moved her into their house and
compelled her to predict the children's fits. When she
reluctantly did so her predictions were borne out by events.
But she consistently denied that she was a witch. Finally,
under instructions from Throckmorton, she repeated after
him commands to the spirits that they should leave the
children. The children instantly recovered, and Alice at once
fell to her knees saying, 'Good master, forgive me ... I have
been the cause of all this trouble to your children ... I have
forsaken my maker and given my soul to the Devil' (p.274).
Having adopted the discursive position Throckmorton had
literally constructed for her, Alice wept all day, and all the
following day, when she was the theme of the sermon and
was required to confess publicly in church.

Allowed to return to her cottage and her husband, she at
once withdrew her confession. The following day, threatened
with being brought before the Bishop of Lincoln if she
remained obdurate, she confessed again. When her husband,
John, learned that she had confessed once more, he moved
to hit her, but was restrained by those present. She was then
taken to Lincoln anyway – and there she confessed again. At
her trial she claimed to be with child, and stated that the
man who had given her her familiars was the father. Since
she was about eighty this caused much laughter. She denied
the killing of Lady Cromwell in court, but confessed it on the
scaffold.

It is easy to attribute these shifts of Alice Samuel – from

silence to scolding and from confession to denial – to a combination of panic and senility. But there is another – or a more specific – way of interpreting her behaviour. Enjoined to silence, women have no position from which to define their own being. Alice eventually adopts whatever position is allotted to her, even if this means collaborating in her own conviction and execution. The Throckmortons can get her to confess; her husband can get her to revert to the woman's virtue of silence; on the scaffold when there is no longer anything to gain or lose she can be induced to confess what she has previously denied.

Alice, however, never took up a position in the discourse of witchcraft with such relish as Joan Prentice of Chelmsford, when in 1589 she confessed in elaborate detail to a relationship between herself and Satan in the form of a ferret (Rosen, 1969:186–8). Or as Elizabeth Bennett, who in 1582 gave a fluent and circumstantial account of her pursuit by two importunate spirits, Suckin and Lierd, until she finally succumbed to their threats (ibid., pp.121–5). Witches were assured of an audience. They were closely interrogated by examiners, and their statements were written down and scrutinized for hidden significances. They were questioned again in court, and what they said was often transcribed and published. Ursula Kemp, condemned at St Osyth in 1582, was visited in prison by a succession of her former neighbours, and the information she gave them was now sufficiently authoritative to be passed on to the magistrate (ibid., pp.137, 153). For women whose requests for a drink of ale or a gill of milk had frequently proved apparently inaudible, these experiences must have been remarkable.

The supreme opportunity to speak was the moment of execution. The requirement for confessions from the scaffold, so that the people could see how church and state combined to protect them from the enemies of God and society, paradoxically also offered women a place from which to speak in public with a hitherto unimagined authority which was not diminished by the fact that it was demonic. Mary Smith 'confessed openly at the place of execution, in the audience of multitudes of people gathered together (as is usual at such times) to be beholders of her death' (Roberts, 1616:60). Agnes Waterhouse proclaimed from the scaffold that she had been a witch for fifteen years 'and had done many abominable deed'. When the bystanders pressed her for details she readily supplied them (Rosen, 1969:81). Witches were women who broke silence and found an unauthorized voice, but the social body required that they paid a high price for the privilege of being heard.

To speak is to possess meaning, to have access to the language which defines, delimits and locates power. To speak is to become a subject. But for women to speak is to threaten the system of differences which gives meaning to patriarchy. In the twentieth century women are still in many ways at the margins of speech, even if, mercifully, the world now has even fewer Grissels than it had in the Renaissance. According to Dale Spender, in mixed conversations men still do most of the talking – and almost all the interrupting (Spender, 1980:41–51). In the Renaissance fear and condemnation of women's speech, in the identification of female eloquence as a transgression, and in the resistance of women to that identification, we can see made explicit contradictions and contests which have contributed to the making of both the patriarchy and the feminism of the present.

7
FINDING A PLACE

7.1 Women as subjects

In the absolutist version of marriage women are objects of exchange and the guarantee of dynastic continuity; in the liberal version they are autonomous subjects freely exercising their power to choose a husband and becoming partners in the affective family which is the seminary of good citizens. Such liberalism was rare but not unthinkable in the pre-revolutionary period, and in the drama it is possible to see the new concepts emerging. It is also possible to see, in the period before liberalism becomes synonymous with common sense, explorations of some of the flaws in that ideal, some of the limitations of the liberal concept of marriage.

Women as subjects find a place – in the home, in the bosom of the family. This, of course, is precisely where they were before, but this time the place is (to varying degrees) chosen – on the basis of romantic love. The degree of choice is one of the areas of uncertainty in the texts of the period. The Duchess of Malfi, who takes the initiative and woos Antonio, is rare in the seventeenth century. Indeed, even in the twentieth century the Duchess's behaviour has seemed so scandalous that the majority of recent critical discussions of the play have taken it for granted that her 'wantonness' and 'wilfulness' in so challenging convention are to blame for the tragic events the play depicts. More commonly the plays, like the domestic conduct books, inadvertently betray an uneasy alliance between liberalism and patriarchy, showing women as free to choose to the extent that they are free to acquiesce. The position of the woman in the family is stabilized in a form which is now familiar as one of negotiator between the father and the children, an authoritative parent who nonetheless softens the discipline imposed by the father. 'Mothering' is thus differentiated from 'fathering' as a process of nurturing, caring, protecting.

The price women pay for finding a place is their exclusion from the political. With the installation of liberalism, the emphasis on the parallels between the family and the state decreases. After 1660 the family progressively becomes a privileged, private realm of retreat from a public world increasingly experienced as hostile and alien. Once the family is outside politics, the power relations within the family are excluded from political analysis. The position of women, at the centre of the family, is thus no concern of political theory. In consequence a new and more insidious form of patriarchy, a 'chosen' patriarchy, comes to rule there unchallenged.

Unchallenged, that is, except by women themselves. To have a place in discourse, even a domestic one, to have a subject-position from which to speak, however inadequate, is to be able to protest. In the late seventeenth century we also find an emerging feminism, a mode of resistance which offers an explicit analysis of women's oppression. The depoliticization of the family led to an incoherence in liberalism. As subjects, women began to be entitled to a place in a political discourse whose terms included 'freedom', 'rights', 'votes'; as wives they were not. Defined primarily as members of the family, indeed as its centre, women who were 'temporarily' outside its sheltering structure, as widows for instance, could acceptably earn a living, not simply by taking part in or carrying on the work of their husbands, but in their own right – as actresses and playwrights, for example. But such women were thereby part of the public, political world, and their existence threw into relief the fact that they were equal citizens with unequal rights.

The history of the installation of women as subjects is not one of steady and deliberate assaults on the territory of patriarchal absolutism. On the contrary, it is a story of startling and radical conceptual and discursive advances followed by hesitations, uncertainties and retreats. First, the advances. Early in the sixteenth century, before the campaign against popery began to entail a suspicion of all aspects of Italian culture, the circulation of humanist discourses in England produced new definitions of good government in the state and in the family. The humanist subject, rational author of his or her own choices, was to be persuaded rather than coerced, and a sound (and persuasive) education was probably enough to guarantee a rational and virtuous adult – of either sex. Medwall's humanist play, *Fulgens and Lucres* (*c*.1500) concerns Lucres's choice of a husband. One suitor is a patrician of dubious virtue and the other is a poor and virtuous scholar. Lucres's wise and worthy father, Fulgens, is proud of his daughter's judgement and discretion as well as of her beauty (ll.258ff.). When the suitors present themselves to him he at once refers them to Lucres. He is prepared to discuss their qualities with her, and to give her advice, but the decision is hers: 'I am not the man/That wyll take from her the liberte/Of her own choice' (ll.336–8). Lucres accepts this freedom and asks her father for his counsel. But the text makes it clear that her choice is unconstrained, and at the same time prudent and rational. She defines the terms of the debate between her suitors, reprimands them if they threaten to exceed the bounds of propriety, weighs her father's advice judiciously, and finally makes the proper decision – in favour of poverty with virtue. The play thus affirms marriage as the location of liberal and affective values rather than as a guarantee of dynastic continuity.

More important, Lucres is seen as the author of meaning. The play is primarily, of course, a debate on the nature of true nobility and only secondarily a romantic comedy. Nobility, it concludes, is not a matter of birth but of virtue and of service to the state. But it is Lucres who authorizes this definition for a courtly audience which, presumably, at this date contained many who were not already fully persuaded of these humanist values. The figures identified as A and B, whose discussion opens and concludes the play, consider whether it has ended satisfactorily. A would have preferred another conclusion, but B puts him right:

> Ye, thou art a maister mery man! –
> Thou shall be wyse I wot nere whan.
> > Is not the question
>
> Of noblenes now fully defynde
> As it may be so by a womans mynde?
> > What woldyst thou have more?
>
> > > (ll.881–6)

Determined anti-feminists in the audience might take these words ironically, but B goes on to explain the moral of the play in a manner which contains no trace of irony, and we are therefore left with the remarkable possibility that the play offers 'a woman's mind' as the guarantee of meaning in an instance so central to the concerns of humanism as the definition of true nobility.

Fulgens and Lucres, as far as it is possible to judge, was distinctly radical in its own time. The dramatic descendants of Lucres are obviously Shakespeare's comic heroines, and most notably Portia, who speaks with wisdom and authority to resolve the legal and moral dilemmas defined in *The Merchant of Venice*. But the differences are instructive too. Portia, like the other heroines of Shakespeare's romantic comedies, is invested with authority by her auditors within the fiction on condition that she changes her clothes and speaks with the voice of a man. In Shakespearean comedy women literally 'personate masculine virtue', with the effect of bringing about reconciliation and integration, but it is on the grounds of their discursive and subjective discontinuity that they are presented as able to do so.[10] Moreover, Portia is not free to choose among her suitors, but is subject to the will of her father, whose binding wisdom is shown in the casket scenes to reach from beyond the grave. A century later than *Fulgens and Lucres*, *The Merchant of Venice* is none the less rather less radical in its treatment of women as subjects. The comparison offers an instance of the irregular and contradictory nature of textual history. *Fulgens and Lucres* presents its startling case with a freshness and clarity unblurred by subsequent decades of discursive uncertainty about women's subjectivity. *The Merchant of Venice*, on the other hand, reproduces some of the theoretical hesitation within which it is situated.

Another possible descendant of Lucres is the heroine of *Godly Queen Hester*, a play of uncertain date and unknown author, not printed until 1561 but conjecturally attributed by W. W. Greg to the second half of the 1520s (*Godly Queen Hester*, p.x). If Greg is right about the date, we are entitled to find here vestiges of the same humanism which informs the earlier text. The play follows fairly closely the biblical story of Esther, who persuaded her husband to put a stop to the persecution of the Jews by his minister, Haman. The title page presents Hester as a model for women of duty and humility and it is made quite clear that she owes her husband obedience, but it is Hester herself who argues the case for this position, and it is explicitly her eloquence which induces Assuerus to choose her as his queen.

When 'many maidens' are brought before him so that he may choose a wife, Assuerus admires their beauty but pays particular attention to those whose appearance suggests qualities of wisdom and constancy. Mardocheus proffers Hester as pure, meek, demure, but also 'In learninge and litterature, profoundely seene,/In wisdome, eke semblant to Saba the Quene' – and thus fit to be the wife of a prince (ll.258–9).

The king at once determines to put to the test 'her lernynge and her language' (l.264), and asks her to tell him what virtues are appropriate to a queen. Hester replies that the king of course has control, but he might sometimes choose to listen to his queen, 'more for love than for awe' (l.277). If the king goes to war the queen must rule in his place: she must therefore share his virtues (ll.282–93). There is nothing in Hester's definition of the qualities of a wife which conflicts with the most absolutist pronouncements of the domestic conduct books of a later period; what is remarkable is that it is her fluency and her wisdom which identify her as the right person to be queen. What is even more remarkable is that the pronouns in the king's reply are plural:

> Then I doute not, but the wysdome of us two
> Knytte both to gether in parfytte charyte
> All thynges in thys realme shall cumpas so,
> By truth and justice, law and equitye,
> That we shall quenche all vice and deformitie.
>
> (ll.296–300)

Hester promptly urges Assuerus to ensure that the poor of the realm are better fed: they are too weak with hunger to be able to serve him adequately (ll.304–26). When the persecution of her people begins, Hester's excellent case on their behalf ensures the king's protection and Aman is hanged.

Here again it is evidently possible in the sixteenth century to conceive of a woman as a unified, rational being, the virtuous author of her own eloquence. In the later drama perhaps only Paulina in *The Winter's Tale* is shown as a woman who equally consistently and effectively propels a king towards the good.

Nearly a hundred years after the conjectural date of *Godly Queen Hester*, *The Duchess of Malfi* (1613–14) stands as a perfect fable of emergent liberalism. The text valorizes women's equality to the point where the Duchess woos Antonio, repudiating the hierarchy of birth in favour of individual virtue; it also celebrates the family, identifying it as a private realm of warmth and fruitfulness separate from the turbulent world of politics, though vulnerable to it. Act III scene ii shows the Duchess alone with Antonio and Cariola (who as a loyal servant is a member of the seventeenth-century family). Their exchanges are intimate, affectionate and playful. Indeed, it is this spirit of play which causes Cariola and Antonio to steal out of the room while the Duchess brushes her hair, and which is brutally dissipated by the entry of Ferdinand, the personification of patriarchal absolutism.

In a ballad of 1630, ' 'Tis Not Otherwise: Or the Praise of a Married Life', a young man rejoices in the moral improvements and physical comforts marriage has brought him. The birth of a child intensifies his happiness:

> The babe doth grow, and quickly speaks,
>   this doth increase my joy,
> To heare it tattle, laugh, and squeake,
>   I smile and hug the boy:
> I watch it play with great delight,
>   and hush it when it cryes,
> And ever wish it in my sight,
>   then *'tis not otherwise.*
>
> (Rollins, 1922:360)

The ballad evokes the opening scene of domestic intimacy in *The Winter's Tale*, Lady Macduff's playful exchanges with her son (*Macbeth*, IV. ii), or Antonio's reluctant repudiation of the pleasures of the nuclear family:

> Say a man never marry, nor have children,
> What takes that from him? only the bare name
> Of being a father, or the weak delight
> To see the little wanton ride a-cock-horse
> Upon a painted stick, or hear him chatter
> Like a taught starling.
>
> (*The Duchess of Malfi*, I. i. 398–403)

These pleasures, the play makes clear, are to be Antonio's destiny after all. On the other hand, the first act of tyranny of Ferdinand and the Cardinal is to divide⁻ the family by divorcing the Duchess and Antonio and separating their children. The Duchess's final words to Cariola identify her as a nurturing, loving mother:

> I pray thee, look thou giv'st my little boy
> Some syrup for his cold, and let the girl
> Say her prayers, ere she sleep.
>
> (IV. ii. 203–5)

Motherhood, caring, the child-orientated, affective family unit: there is a direct line of descent from the new seventeenth-century definitions of familial relationships to the current representation of happy families in advertisements for margarine and breakfast cereals. What threatens the affective nuclear family is frequently an external tyranny, here the patriarchal absolutism of Ferdinand and the Cardinal, representatives of the family in its other meaning, whose behaviour – the divorce, the banishment, the imprisonment of the Duchess – identifies them with the newly differentiated public world of state power, law and politics. In this too the play anticipates the system of differences which gives meaning to the discourse of liberalism. The terms of the liberal analysis are a series of oppositions between the individual and society, private and public, family and state, in which the first is always understood to be threatened by the encroachment of the second. Moreover, it is the second which is 'political'. Politics is thus devalued by contrast with the true fulfilment available within the enclave of the family. Domestic relationships are defined as affective rather than political in a discourse which works to suppress recognition of the power relations which structure the family, and by this means liberalism opens a gap for the accommodation of an uncontested, because unidentified, patriarchy. In consequence the affective ideal which is so glowingly defined in *The Duchess of Malfi* collapses into the sad history of collaboration between liberalism and sexism which defines the western family from the seventeenth century to the present.

7.2 Advice and consent

The Duchess of Malfi marks one discursive limit of the sexual politics of the early seventeenth century. Other plays of the period which confront similar issues identify more sharply the problems which tended to impede the installation of women as subjects. Among these is the question of the freedom of choice of a marriage partner. Liberalism depends on consent and this in turn depends on the autonomy of the subject. My choices spring out of what *I am*, and only a speaker entitled to mean these words is truly free to make a deliberate decision. For most of the sixteenth and seventeenth centuries women have only a sporadic, precarious hold on such autonomy. *The Duchess of Malfi*, like *Fulgens and Lucres*, claims for its heroine the right to choose a husband. More commonly, however, such a right is seen as sharply conditional.

Freedom of choice and the miseries of enforced marriage are a constant and recurring concern in the period. There is some evidence of a debate about the extent of parental control in marriage, but it is a debate in which the two sides are not in practice very sharply polarized. On one side John Stockwood argues for parental choice in *A Bartholmew Fairing for Parentes* (1589), 'shewing that children are not to marie, without the consent of their parentes, in whose power and choise it lieth to provide wives and husbandes for their sonnes and daughters' (title page). But Stockwood insists that parents should not exercise compulsion (p.81), and he appeals to them to take on the responsibility of finding a suitable partner in a way consistent with the will of God (p.85). On the other side Daniel Rogers in *Matrimoniall Honour* (1642) proposes a number of ways in which children might go about persuading their parents to give their consent, including seeking the aid of the

Church and the magistrate, but he does not advocate open defiance (unless it is only the mother who objects, in which case the child may proceed with a clear conscience) (pp.80–1). But most of the popular discussions of the matter conclude that on the one hand children should not marry without parental consent, and on the other parents should not withhold consent without powerful and compelling reasons (Bullinger, 1541: sig. B ii v – D i v; Perkins, 1618:684–5; Brathwait, 1641b:21).

The domestic conduct books thus define an ideal and on the whole evade the problem of what happens when one of the parties refuses to conform to it. The plays, by contrast, since fiction depends on obstacles to the implementation of good sense, dwell in detail on the dangers and difficulties which ensue when parental choice fails to coincide with the wishes of the children. Renaissance comedy inherits this motif from Plautus and Terence, and here the sympathy of the audience is invariably invoked in favour of the children. In tragic treatments of the theme, too (*Romeo and Juliet*, *The Maid's Tragedy*, *The Witch of Edmonton*, *The Second Maiden's Tragedy*, for instance), the audience is usually invited to endorse young love as opposed to aged greed, obstinacy or hypocrisy.

But it is not always clear that the degree of freedom which is very nearly universally approved is allotted equally to men and women. Brathwait takes a very liberal line on freedom of choice in *The English Gentleman*, urging his readers in fairly strong terms to make the decision for themselves (p.145), but there is no equivalent passage in *The English Gentlewoman*, the companion volume addressed to women. The gender of the person making the choice oscillates wildly in the case of Dod and Cleaver (see above, pp.179–80). But at the beginning of the passage in question this text reveals its own patriarchal assumptions very clearly when it suddenly makes it apparent that 'everyone' is in fact male: 'everie one that intendeth to marrie, shoulde choose him a meet, fit, and honest mate: for

201

there lyeth much weight in the wise election, and choise of a wife' (Dod and Cleaver, 1612:99). In the drama too there is perhaps an assumption that freedom does not quite extend to women. It is not, for instance, self-evident that the audience is invited to sympathize with Beatrice-Joanna when she asserts her will against her father's in *The Changeling*, and she herself claims that freedom of choice is confined to men (II. ii. 107–13).

The classic dramatic treatment of the liberal case against parental compulsion is *The Miseries of Enforced Marriage* (1607). This play by George Wilkins was based, like *A Yorkshire Tragedy* (1608), on the Calverley murders, though in the Wilkins version murder is only threatened, and an unexpected happy ending produces general reconciliation and rejoicing. *The Miseries of Enforced Marriage* concerns William Scarborrow who at seventeen establishes a pre-contract of marriage with Clare Harcop. Subsequently his uncle and his guardian threaten to lay waste his property if he refuses to marry Katherine, his guardian's niece. Faced with ruin, William reluctantly agrees, protesting that the marriage makes him an adulterer and his children bastards. Clare kills herself when he writes to tell her he is married. William abandons Katherine and his children in his Yorkshire house, and pursues the career of a prodigal in London, in the company of Sir Francis Ilford. Ironically, William thus lays waste his own property, reducing his brothers and sister as well as his wife and children to poverty. The honest family butler invents a series of schemes to save them all, including a marriage between William's sister and the spendthrift Sir Francis Ilford. Finally William is prevailed upon to repent and is restored to his grateful wife and children. His guardian dies, recognizing the error of enforced marriage, and making William heir to twice his former wealth.

As even a bare summary of the plot suggests, there are oddly incompatible elements in the play. It is made very clear that the uncle and the guardian are villains, even though the law scandalously permits them to behave as they do. It is also clear that they mean well: ironically the object of the marriage they plan for William is to ensure that he settles down and does not squander his inheritance. The play, as the title indicates, demonstrates the evils of well-intentioned authoritarianism and constitutes a plea for freedom of choice. The happy ending, however, is predicated on the acquiescence of two women in the miseries of marriages chosen for them by others. Katherine exceeds even Griselda in the patience with which she submits to the marriage and subsequently to William's desertion and the impoverishment of the family. The marriage is arranged by her uncle and carried out at her first meeting with William. Similarly William's sister co-operates with the scheme to marry her to Ilford to save the Scarborrow fortunes. Deceived into believing that his wife is an heiress, Ilford curses and kicks her when she reveals the truth. She does not protest when he snatches the jewels she is wearing and then deserts her. The couple are reunited without explanation in the final scene, and she declares, 'heeres my husbands hand in mine,/And I rejoyce in him, and he in me' (*The Miseries of Enforced Marriage*, ll.2825–6).

Narrative closure is thus conditional on the submission of two women and the death of a third. William's 'repentance' might have presented more of a problem had Clare lived. Her convenient suicide makes way for the happy ending. While William's enforced marriage to a patient and obedient wife is defined as 'misery' because it is not freely chosen, not based on love, the sufferings of his wife and his sister, whose marriages are not freely chosen either, are simply dissipated in the promise of future happiness which attends William's repentance and return to the arms of his family. Love, which in men is a passion that cannot be constrained, is evidently in women the fruit of dutiful obedience to arrangements made on their behalf by others. At the centre of a play on the evils of enforced marriage, the exchange of women remains apparently unquestioned.

The sub-plot of *A Woman Killed with Kindness* raises, and fails to resolve, the problem of women as objects of exchange between men. Sir Charles Mountford, in prison for debt, is released by his mortal enemy, Sir Francis Acton, who pays the £500 he owes. Learning that the reason for this generous act is Sir Francis's desire for his sister, Sir Charles, still penniless, determines to pay off the debt of honour he has incurred in 'one rich gift' (x. 124). Susan, dressed like a bride, is to be presented to Sir Francis in place of the money. The sum is constantly reiterated in the discussion between Susan and her brother (xiv. 25, 38, 45, 70).

The play does not simply endorse this procedure. Susan pleads with Sir Charles to save her honour. He calls himself a 'barbarous outlaw', an 'uncivil kern' (xiv. 5), a ruffian (ll.8, 36), more like a stranger than a brother (ll.50–1). His 'cold heart shakes with shame' (l.49). None the less, he is adamant: 'O sister! only this one way,/With that rich jewel you my debts may pay' (ll.47–8). 'Shall I', he rhetorically asks,

> die in debt
> To Acton, my grand foe, and you still wear
> The precious jewel that he holds so dear?
>
> (ll.51–3)

To save her brother's honour Susan agrees to be handed over to Sir Francis, taking with her the knife which she will use to redeem her own.

In the course of the discussion between them Sir Charles makes what he himself identifies as a 'strange assertion': 'Thy honour and my soul are equal in my regard' (ll.60–1). He too will kill himself after the event (l.62). Brother and sister are thus presented in symmetrical terms, both losing their honour to Sir Francis, both subsequently to redeem it. Both will die by their own hands. The difference, of course, is that Sir Charles prevails on his sister to be the price of the redemption of his debt to another man. The problem is apparently dissolved when Sir Francis offers to make Susan his wife, but since this too has the effect of cancelling the debt, a parallel is drawn between marriage and prostitution on which the play makes no explicit comment. Susan merely 'yields to fate' (xiv. 148).

In *'Tis Pity She's a Whore*, printed in 1633, freedom of choice is problematized in a rather different way, with the effect of foregrounding the limits of liberalism itself as well as the vestiges of absolutism which remain within it. Florio explicitly rejects the mercenary motive that leads to enforced marriages. His daughter, Annabella, is to be free to choose for herself:

> As for worldly fortune,
> I am, I thank my stars, blessed with enough;
> My care is how to match her to her liking;
> I would not have her marry wealth, but love.
>
> (*'Tis Pity She's a Whore*, I. iii. 8–11)

Annabella chooses freely – and chooses her brother. The liberal concept of freedom of choice depends in practice on the silent exclusion of a whole range of freedoms.

When his daughter becomes pregnant Florio at once selects her a husband, and the weeping Annabella is formally betrothed to Soranzo in a ritual which shows clearly where the power to choose now resides:

> *Florio.* My Lord Soranzo, here
> Give me your hand; for that *I give you this.*
>
> (my italics, III. vii. 50–1)

Confronted by its own limits, liberalism readily falls back into the familiar pattern of enforced marriage.

Evidently love, in Florio's definition free and unconstrained, is in practice free only as long as it is confined to the objects defined as appropriate by the social body. As Ford's play makes clear, these objects do not include a brother or sister. We can easily increase the list of exclusions: parents, children, members of the same sex.... The identification of 'perversion' is one of the means by which the liberal valorization of freedom is prevented from offering any serious impediment to control by the social body of one of its central institutions.

7.3 Love and marriage

Women find a place in marriage, and the cement of liberal marriage is romantic love. True love is human happiness in its highest, most intense and most ideal form. Authorized by nature (birds do it), love is a harmony of souls and bodies which comes to constitute the proper foundation of family life. Love in this period is differentiated increasingly decisively from lust as having its origins in the mind, the very essence of the humanist subject. The imbrication of two minds, united and yet distinct, legitimates desire and sanctifies the conception of children. As an intimate, private relationship, love is the repudiation of the political, its antithesis.

In *The Duchess of Malfi* marriage is represented as a transcendent union based on romantic love:

> *Duchess.* Bless, heaven, this sacred Gordian, which let
> violence
> Never untwine.
> *Antonio.* And may our sweet affections, like the spheres,
> Be still in motion.
> *Duchess.* Quickening, and make
> The like soft music.
> *Antonio.* That we may imitate the loving palms,
> Blest emblem of a peaceful marriage,
> That ne'er bore fruit divided.
> *Duchess.* What can the church force more?
>
> (I. i. 480–8)

Love emulates both the divine (the music of the spheres) and nature (palm trees). It is the source of procreation (fruit). It springs from the subjectivities of the characters, and the institution of the church can only ratify a condition that they themselves have legitimately made indivisible. Love excludes the political: 'All discord, without this circumference,/Is only to be pitied' (I. i. 469–70).

It is in this period that love and marriage become indissolubly linked and love itself becomes fully moralized and spiritualized, not now as a neoplatonic rung on the ladder to the love of God, as it is in the cases of Dante's Beatrice or Petrarch's Laura, but as the wholly human ground of a lifetime of domestic concord. Since then fiction, lyric poetry, the cinema and pop music have so idealized romantic love, so celebrated its joy and naturalness, that it is an effort to remember that love once had other attributes. We need a genealogy of romantic love. In the meantime it is perhaps worth drawing attention, however briefly, to its moral ambiguity in Chaucer's *Troilus and Criseyde*, for instance, where the palinode condemns as worthless the passion celebrated in Book III. A similar ambiguity recurs in Sidney's *Astrophil and Stella* (1582?) where the hero repeatedly reproaches himself for desiring Stella instead of heaven on the one hand or worldly honour on the other. *Antony and Cleopatra*, which defines love in cosmic imagery, also identifies it as 'dotage'. In these instances love conflicts with duty. But with the development of the affective nuclear family, love and duty become synonymous. In Chaucer's *Knight's Tale* love is arbitrary, destructive, and also the height of folly. The absurdity of love as well as its delight is the source of much that is comic in Shakespearean comedy. But in the seventeenth century the capricious, arbitrary desires of an earlier period are progressively harnessed to a civilized and civilizing morality and, without losing any of their mystery, are arrested, fixed, domesticated. It is not until the nineteenth century that the love of a good woman develops its full redemptive power, but it is possible to identify the rudiments of this position in his guardian's plans for William Scarborrow.

True love is, of course, eternal. 'Love is not love/That alters when it alteration finds.' It is for this reason that true love properly issues in marriage, and this in turn ensures the stability of the family as a seminary of good subjects. But the course of its installation as the basis of the family does not run entirely smooth. One of the paradoxes of eternal love is that its tragic possibilities are also intensified. In *The Second Maiden's Tragedy* (1611) the Lady kills herself in order to perpetuate love even beyond the grave:

> His lust may part me from thee, but death, never;
> Thou canst not lose me there, for, dying thine,
> Thou dost enjoy me still. Kings cannot rob thee.

> (III. iii. 144–6)

The conceit here depends, of course, on the retention of the absolutist concept of women as objects, property to be possessed. A similar eternity of possession is implicit in the emblematic spectacle of Giovanni, in the final scene of *'Tis Pity She's a Whore*, keeping the spectators at bay as he holds Annabella's heart before him on a dagger.

Located in the first instance in the mind, true love also shows an unstable tendency to efface the sexuality it was its project to authorize. The identification of love with marriage, and of marriage with what is private, implies a sexuality which is whispered rather than proclaimed. Ultimately, moreover, the spiritualization of love leads to a sexual reticence within marriage itself. Love is differentiated from lust, but the two are yoked by violence together in the marriage bed. The precariousness of their unity issues in the scale of prostitution in the nineteenth century, 'corrected' by the idealization of the sexual in the twentieth. The sexual fix, the fixing of the sexual as a guarantee of moral and physical health, and the fixing of the sexes, a man and a woman (Heath, 1982), offers in our own time to save the family from the disintegration threatening it from the right (individualism) and from the left (feminism).

In *The Broken Heart*, printed in 1633, the spiritualization of love implies that if true minds are separated there is no solace in the union of bodies. Penthea, contracted to Orgilus, is married against her will to Bassanes. To endure a loveless marriage is to be 'buried in a bride-bed' (II. ii. 38). Orgilus withdraws to contemplate a transcendent, unalterable and curiously sexless passion. When he meets Penthea by accident, his declaration of love is entirely changeless, entirely pure:

> Time can never
> On the white table of unguilty faith
> Write counterfeit dishonour. Turn those eyes,
> The arrows of pure love, upon that fire
> Which once rose to a flame, perfumed with vows
> As sweetly scented as the incense smoking
> On Vesta's altars; virgin tears, like
> The holiest odours, sprinkled dews to feed 'em
> And to increase their fervour.
>
> (II. iii. 25–33)

A reference to the body in his next speech proves to be purely metaphorical (l.36) and 'intercourse' (l.39) had no sexual connotations before 1798 (*OED*). At the end of this episode there is some indication that Orgilus makes an unspecified physical overture, which is at once repulsed (ll.106–9), but the lovers do not seriously contemplate the possibility of adultery.

The separation of true minds is existential death. Eternally divided from the man she eternally loves, Penthea refuses food until life is extinguished. In revenge for her death Orgilus kills Ithocles, author of the enforced marriage, in the presence of Penthea's corpse, and then chooses for himself a mode of death which parallels hers, opening his veins so that the blood flows out of them. These bodies, visible on the stage, drained of being, constitute emblems of the immobilizing power of a romantic love which is at once unalterable and unable to be fulfilled because it implies a union beyond the mingling of bodies.

In the same play Calantha, who is betrothed to Ithocles,

simply ceases to live when she learns of his death. She arranges the disposition of the kingdom and places her mother's wedding ring on the finger of the dead man: 'Thus I new-marry him whose wife I am./Death shall not separate us' (v. iii. 66–7). Her death has no visible external cause: she dies of a broken heart. Love, life and marriage have become in effect synonymous, all three centred in the heart which breaks when the marriage-union is broken.

Meanwhile, by an odd loop of reasoning, spiritualized marriage becomes intelligible as an essential state of being which transcends the letter of the law. Romantic love, free and unconstrained, does not necessarily confine itself to couples who are legally at liberty to marry. When a legal marriage is loveless, and thus no marriage at all (cf. Milton, 1959:456; Halkett, 1970:8), the same force which stabilizes the institution of marriage can paradoxically be invoked to authorize and stabilize an adulterous union of minds and bodies. By the second half of the seventeenth century marriage has become a plural term, defining an affective relationship as readily as a legal one. Dryden's *All for Love* (1677) is an extraordinary instance of this redefinition of marriage.

The play is a rewriting for the Restoration stage of Shakespeare's *Antony and Cleopatra*, and the distance between the two texts is a measure of the transformation of love in the course of the seventeenth century. The relationship between Dryden's Antony and Cleopatra is oddly domestic. All the imagery which in the earlier text defines Cleopatra as demonic is silently erased; the emphasis on the physical nature of her sexuality is eliminated; and the discursive instability produced as she simultaneously embraces and refuses the feminine disappears. The lies, evasions and caprices which cause the catastrophe in 1607 are all attributed seventy years later to Alexas the eunuch. Dryden's Cleopatra is transparently honest, unable to sustain a deceit. As a place begins to be found for women, the uncertainty and instability defining women's sexuality is transferred to the forms of

sexuality which transgress the newly established system of
differences, modes of sexual deviance which seem not to have
elicited much interest in the earlier period. Alexas as a eunuch
is neither a man nor a woman, and is therefore unstable.

In the later version Cleopatra's love for Antony is eternal:
she never loved Caesar. The tragedy is that death threatens
not a precarious, arbitrary and dangerous sexual passion, but
a long and happy union open to destruction only by forces
outside itself:

> Think we have had a clear and glorious day,
> And heav'n did kindly to delay the storm
> Just till our close of ev'ning. Ten years' love,
> And not a moment lost, but all improved
> To th'utmost joys – what ages we have lived!
> And now to die each other's.
>
> (*All for Love*, v. 389–94)

In Shakespeare's play Antony's political obligations are
compelling. He is 'a third of the world' and the audience
glimpses some of the implications of the collapse of empire
which is the consequence of his 'dotage'. Antony's dismissal
of politics – 'Kingdoms are clay' (*Antony and Cleopatra*, I. i.
35) – is repudiated at his next appearance (I. ii. 112–14),
and this oscillation between love and politics structures the
play. Dryden's Antony also oscillates, but between personal
loyalties – to his friend, Ventidius, his wife, Octavia, and to
Cleopatra. The private is valorized at the expense of the public,
and political obligation is relegated, apparently without irony,
to the inferior status it still holds in the discourse of liberalism.
Ventidius urges Antony to go from Cleopatra.

> Go? Whither? Go from all that's excellent?
> Faith, honor, virtue, all good things forbid
> That I should go from her who sets my love
> Above the price of kingdoms. Give, you gods,
> Give to your boy, your Caesar,

> This rattle of a globe to play withal,
> This gewgaw world, and put him cheaply off;
> I'll not be pleased with less than Cleopatra.
> (*All for Love*, II. 439–46)

The play is subtitled, 'The World Well Lost'.

Moralized, tamed, unchanging, love is inseparable from the marriage of true minds. The project of the play, according to Dryden's Preface, was to present 'famous patterns of unlawful love', adultery 'founded on vice' (*All for Love*, pp.12, 13). But true love cannot be contrary to the spirit of the law, though it may contradict the letter. Sexual passion founded on vice is now by definition something quite different. Dryden's Cleopatra who represents 'faith, honor, virtue', is in effect if not in name married to Antony, and the text increasingly defines her position in these terms. 'Nature', she declares, 'meant me/A wife, a silly, harmless, household dove': it is fortune which has made her a mistress (IV. 91–4). Death will remove fortune's impediment:

> I have not loved a Roman not to know
> What should become his wife – his wife, my Charmion!
> For 'tis to that high title I aspire,
> And now I'll not die less. Let dull Octavia
> Survive, to mourn him dead; my nobler fate
> Shall knit our spousals with a tie too strong
> For Roman laws to break.
> (v. 412–18)

The conflicting claims of Octavia and Cleopatra are the claims of two wives. Octavia loves Antony too – but not enough. Her patience is not infinite and she is finally unable to forgive Antony for preferring Cleopatra (IV. 414–28). Her retreat is the triumph of true, transcendent conjugal love.

Love is a necessary ingredient of Restoration heroic drama, and here it is above all the civilizing power of love which is taken for granted. Virtuous heroes need the complementary love of a virtuous woman to tame their fiery courage, harness their restless energies and integrate them into civil society. Masculinity is strong and resolute: feminine tranquillity and moral sensibility soften the ruthlessness of the masculine world. A new set of stereotypes defines women as the opposite but indispensable sex. Gradually a space has been specified for women at the centre of the private realm of love and harmony which is marriage. The disruptive elements of female sexuality have been banished, along with the discursive instability which defined it, to find a place among whores, hysterics or sexual deviants: true love is moral, domestic, constant. Good women are partners in the formation of the affective family, where the absolutist ideal of patient submission has been transformed into active, forgiving, reconciling love. It is the constancy of good women which is the source of stability within the family. Men – like Antony – are necessarily caught up in public affairs; their wives guarantee them a still haven from a restless world. Women have become identified as the agents of conjugal love.

Thus, for instance, in Catherine Trotter's play, *The Fatal Friendship* (1698), the hero, after his second and bigamous marriage, turns back to his first wife for solace – and receives it. Gramont, married to Felicia in secret because of their poverty, finds that he is unable to ransom his friend, rescue his son from pirates or protect his wife from destitution. To save his family and his friend he bigamously marries the wealthy Lamira, but cannot bring himself to consummate his marriage. Appalled by what he has done and failed to do, he returns in desperation to Felicia:

> Her nature's calm, by no rough passions tossed,
> A harbour from this tempest, upon her gentle bosom
> All the disorders of my soul will cease,
> Or I despair ever to find my peace.

(III. i)

Shown as more patient than Octavia, but more active than

Griselda, Felicia induces Gramont not to kill himself but to live for her sake. He dies in another cause, but his death turns out to be the means of saving his family, since his wealthy father repents his former harshness and takes in the deserving Felicia, promising to ransom the child from the pirates. The family thus triumphs, preserved not by the wife's submission, as in the Griselda story, but by her active constancy.

Marriage is a partnership, but partnership does not ensure equality. On the contrary, when two oxen are yoked together, the bigger and stronger of them naturally bears a greater part of the burden (Speght, 1617:12). Thus, while the new meaning of marriage offers women a position as subjects, it does not fundamentally challenge patriarchy. Indeed it reinforces it to the extent that true love becomes the solvent of inequality, the source of women's pliability and the guarantee of marital concord. This is made explicit, though without any obvious element of irony, in *Women Beware Women* (1621?). Wives, Isabella proposes, are slaves whose subjection is made 'happy' by love:

> They do but buy their thraldoms, and bring great portions
> To men to keep 'em in subjection –
> As if a fearful prisoner should bribe
> The keeper to be good to him, yet lies in still,
> And glad of a good usage, a good look sometimes.
> By 'r Lady, no misery surmounts a woman's:
> Men buy their slaves, but women buy their masters.
> Yet honesty and love makes all this happy,
> And, next to angels', the most blest estate.
>
> (I. ii. 170–78)

Love makes slavery blessed. Patriarchal power relations have not changed very much in a marriage where the wife is 'to bee governed with love, not overruled by tyranny', as Robert Wilkinson put it in 1615 (Halkett, 1970:84). In a period just before the collaboration of liberalism and patriarchy had naturalized the affective nuclear family, Dod and Cleaver spelt out more clearly, in a passage where 'we', the writers and readers, are evidently men, the advantages for 'us' of this arrangement:

> And if wee have regarde unto commoditie and profite, there is nothing that giveth so much as doth a good wife, no not horses, oxen, servants or farmes: for a mans wife is the fellow and comforter of all cares and thoughts, and doe more faithful and true service unto him, then either maid-servant or man-servant, which doe serve men for feare, or else for wages: but thy wife will be led onely by love, and therefore she doth every thing better then all other.
>
> (1612:152–3)

The argument was evidently a common one. Bathsua Makin was to take it up rather sharply in her essay defending women's education: 'Had God intended women onely as a finer sort of cattle, he would not have made them reasonable' (Makin, 1673:23).

According to Dod and Cleaver, a woman's place is further up in the hierarchy of values than horses, oxen or servants, and she works harder than any of them – for love. A century later a similar point was made, though from an alternative perspective, by a woman. Mary Astell's *Some Reflections upon Marriage* first appeared anonymously in 1700 (though in many respects it might have been written at any time since then). By the third edition in 1706 it included a preface (an appendix in later editions) which acknowledged that the author was a woman. The voice in the body of the text, however, is ostensibly masculine. None the less, in the following extract the third person pronouns invite the reader to take up a position in relation to the argument which differs radically from that offered by Dod and Cleaver. The passage identifies what a husband wants from marriage:

> He wants one to manage his family, an house-keeper, one whose interest it will be not to wrong him, and in whom

therefore he can put greater confidence than in any he can hire for money. One who may breed his children, taking all the care and trouble of their education, to preserve his name and family. One whose beauty, wit, or good humour and agreeable conversation, will entertain him at home when he has been contradicted and disappointed abroad; who will do him that justice the ill-natur'd world denies him; that is, in any one's language but his own, sooth his pride and flatter his vanity, by having always so much good sense as to be on his side, to conclude him in the right, when others are so ignorant, or so rude, as to deny it. Who will not be blind to his merit nor contradict his will and pleasure, but make it her business, her very ambition to content him; whose softness and gentle compliance will calm his passions, to whom he may safely disclose his troublesome thoughts; and in her breast discharge his cares; whose duty, submission and observance, will heal those wounds other people's opposition or neglect have given him. In a word, one whom he can entirely govern, and consequently may form her to his will and liking, who must be his for life, and therefore cannot quit his service, let him treat her how he will.

(Astell, 1730:24–5)

Half way through the passage 'his' (the husband's) 'language' is differentiated from anyone else's, so that the reader is invited to reinterpret ironically all that has gone before. In consequence, when the final sentence offers a summary 'in a word', in a language shared by reader and writer, it is clear that the perspective that has been offered is feminine – and feminist.

7.4 Women's speaking justified

Some Reflections upon Marriage is a remarkable book. It never explicitly challenges male sovereignty in marriage but it subjects it to various kinds of irony. How can women fail to admire men? 'Have they not founded empires and overturn'd them? Do they not make laws and continually repeal and amend them? Their vast minds lay kingdoms waste' (Astell, 1730:36). It is not obvious that Swift belongs on the English syllabus if Astell does not. Not only have men displayed their eminence in developing the arts of gambling and deep drinking; in addition,

> Their subtlety in forming cabals and laying deep designs, their courage and conduct in breaking through all tyes, sacred and civil, to effect them, not only advances them to the post of honour, and keeps them securely in it for twenty or thirty years, but gets them a name, and conveys it down to posterity for some hundreds; and who would look any further?
>
> (Astell, 1730:53).

As in the previous passage, the irony works here because the argument is so close to the claims actually made on behalf of patriarchy.

Locke in *Two Treatises of Government* had conceded that women had rights (Locke, 1967, II: 82). But in his repudiation of the patriarchalist arguments of Filmer and others that the state needed a head in just the same way as a family did, he introduced a distinction between the modes of government in the family and the state. In transferring power from the sovereign to the social body, Locke saw no cause for altering the power of the husband over his wife. The husband, it was made clear in Locke's text, had 'to order the things of private concernment in his family, as proprietor of the goods and land there, and to have his will take place before that of his wife in all things of their common concernment'. But the husband's power was purely 'conjugal', and 'not a political power of life and death over her' (Locke, 1967, I: 48). Patriarchalism was a justification of absolute power in the family and in the state. In its insistence on the parallel between the two, patriarchalism included the family within the political. By breaking down the analogy between family and state, microcosm and macrocosm, Locke effectively removed the family from the sphere of politics – and consequently depoliticized the relationships within it. Astell challenges the logic of this position. 'If absolute sovereignty be not necessary in a state, how comes it to be so in a family? Or if in a family why not in a state; since no reason can be alledged for the one that will not hold more strongly for the other?... For if arbitrary power is evil in it self, and an improper method of governing rational and free agents, it ought not to be practis'd anywhere.' And more tersely, 'If *all men are born free*, how is it that all women are born slaves?' (Astell, 1730:66).

Some Reflections also makes explicit the contradiction implicit in the Griselda story. The only real inequalities are inequalities of virtue; the surest sign of a noble mind is the ability to bear unjust treatment with equanimity; in this world it may be necessary sometimes to offer obedience 'for order's sake' to those who do not otherwise deserve it; however in these circumstances the victims 'cannot but have an inward sense of their own real superiority' (Astell, 1730:32–3).

Like Bathsua Makin's *Essay to Revive the Antient Education of Gentlewomen*, *Some Reflections* begins to acknowledge the social construction of the subject. Perhaps it is impossible to put the feminist case without making this fundamental break with liberal-humanist common sense. In Makin's version,

Custom, when it is inveterate, hath a mighty influence: it hath the force of nature it self. The barbarous custom to breed women low, is grown general amongst us, and hath prevailed so far, that it is verily believed (especially amongst a sort of debauched sots) that women are not endued with such reason, as men; nor capable of improvement by education, as they are.

(Makin, 1673:3)

218

As Mary Astell rather more laconically puts it, 'Sense is a portion that God himself has been pleased to distribute to both sexes with an impartial hand, but learning is what men have engross'd to themselves' (Astell, 1730:69).

It is evident in these texts, and others like Margaret Fell's *Womens Speaking Justified* (1666), that women had found a voice. There were, of course, earlier instances of women's writing in defence of women, but they are notably less radical, and the pseudonyms often make it difficult to be sure that the authors were not male pamphleteers eager to increase their incomes by writing replies to the anti-feminist tracts they themselves had produced. Constantia Munda and Esther Sowernam, both of whom replied in 1617 to Joseph Swetnam's *The Arraignment of Lewde, Idle, Froward, and Unconstant Women* (1615), may well come into this category. Their pamphlets consist largely of invective. Mary Tattlewell and Joane Hit-Him-Home, authors of *The Womens Sharpe Revenge* (1640) may in practice have been John Taylor. Jane Anger's *Protection for Women* (1589) is a more serious contribution to the debate, arguing that men insist on women's inferiority because they know that in reality women are generally wiser and more moral. When women reprove men with good counsel, men resent it. And Rachel Speght in *A Mouzell for Melastomus* (1617), the first of the replies to Swetnam, puts a good deal of stress on the concept of women as companions, sharing their husbands' burdens. 'Marriage is a merri-age, and this worlds Paradise, where there is mutuall love ... a joyfull union and conjunction, with such a creature as God hath made meete for man, for none was meete till she was made' (Speght, 1617:14).[11] But the distance between this position and Astell's is readily apparent.

What fills the space between them is the installation of women as subjects through the redefinition of the family. Loving partners, specialists in domesticity, nurturing, caring mothers, they progressively became autonomous, unified, knowing authors of their own choices. As subjects women were entitled to make a living – to become actresses on the Restoration stage, or even writers, like Aphra Behn who, not without a struggle, became a successful professional dramatist. In fiction too they are shown as entitled to speak without transgression. Behn herself rewrote *The Miseries of Enforced Marriage* as a Restoration comedy and *The Town Fop; or, Sir Timothy Tawdrey* (1676) shows women taking action to alleviate the miseries their counterparts had accepted patiently in the earlier play. While Clare Harcop killed herself on learning that William was married, Celinda, her equivalent in the later play, is seen dressed as a boy defending her lover in a fight at his wedding feast. Katherine, William's wife, waited and pleaded for his return to her: Diana, having failed to seduce the disguised Celinda in revenge, prevails on her uncle to arrange a divorce. William's sister marries Ilford to save the family: Phillis marries Sir Timothy Tawdrey to save her honour and secure a happy ending. Enforced marriage is not indissoluble, because it is not based on love, and women are not purely objects of exchange but agents of their own destinies.

The transformation is less startling when we remember that while *Miseries* is written largely in the mode of tragedy, *The Town Fop* is consistently and confidently comic, and the comic tradition since Medwall, or at least since Shakespeare, had permitted the presentation of women who were to some degree self-determining without being demonic. None the less, in conjunction with the decline of the witchcraze on the one hand, and the rise of a recognizable feminism on the other, it is possible to read this text as marking a change in the discursive position of women.

It is hardly necessary to point out, of course, that the installation of women as subjects was not the end of our problems. Liberalism does not guarantee equality. People may be equal by nature, but excellence, age, virtue, birth or other distinguishing characteristics [gender, for instance] may justify inequalities (Locke, 1967, II: 54). To have a subject-position, however, is to occupy a place in discourse, to be able to speak – though it does not guarantee an audience. To be a subject is to be able to claim rights, to protest, and to be capable, therefore, of devising a mode of resistance more sharply focused than prophesying, witchcraft or murder. It is to be in a position to identify and analyse the nature of women's oppression.

The position allotted to women, the position of the subject in liberal humanism, is one in which unity, autonomy and choice are always imaginary. The gap between the 'I' of utterance and the uttering 'I', between the subject which speaks and the subject which is only represented – symbolized – in the symbolic order, is the location of a desire which cannot be satisfied. And the gap thus produced is the place of a resistance which it is the task of liberal humanism to depoliticize, privatize, psychologize or, in psychoanalysis and sexology, specifically to sexualize. Women as subjects find a position in the discourses about them and addressed to them, and are consequently able to speak. But their speech is predicated on an absence which a feminism that refuses the liberal-humanist modes of self-fulfilment is able to appropriate for politics. The installation of women as subjects is the production of a space in which to problematize the liberal-humanist alliance with patriarchy, to formulate a sexual politics, to begin the struggle for change.

8

CONCLUSION:
CHANGING THE PRESENT

The period of struggle for and against the construction of the liberal-humanist subject has been presented within the literary institution as a golden world of happily hierarchic social relations, and of a rich culture, oral in origin and still, even in its written forms, resonating with the expressive rhythms of speech. If they concurred in nothing else, T. S. Eliot, F. R. Leavis and E. M. W. Tillyard joined forces to produce between them this account of the period of great literature before the Revolution of the 1640s. Their narrative, repressing (as bad art, or boring) many of the texts I have cited, shows inequality as natural, conducive to harmony, thrilling. On an alternative reading, however, the period was one of enforced silence, and of intense and violent conflict, producing an order which still bears the marks of the conflict and the violence, and perhaps of the silence too. This reading foregrounds the resistance which culminated in revolution, and points to the continued failure of liberal humanism to deliver the promised equality of access to power.

At moments of crisis twentieth-century Britain tends to turn to Shakespeare for reassurance. In 1984 the film *The Dresser* displayed British talent to international audiences in a nostalgic portrait of the grand tradition of Shakespearean acting. *The Dresser* explicitly dramatized the parallel use of Shakespeare as propaganda during the Second World War, and might serve to remind us of the film of *Henry V*, Olivier's *tour de force* in this mode, made in 1944. *Henry V* opens in the Globe Theatre. In the 1980s the Globe is being reconstructed close to its original location to the highest possible standards of (conjectural) accuracy.[12]

The twentieth-century identification of the age of gold with the Renaissance was in part a reaction against Victorianism. In the nineteenth century the vanished world of magic and mystery, of humanity and chivalry, was medieval. This construction of lost Utopias, like its counterpart, the Whig interpretation of history, is characteristic of liberal humanism. The use of the past for nostalgic myth-making on the one hand, or the affirmation of progress on the other, has the advantage of deflecting resistance, but it is symptomatic, none the less, of a deep anxiety about the present. Sharing the anxiety about the present, I have tried instead to read history in its difference. The present is neither the culmination of the past nor its antithesis. There are no golden worlds, lost or newly found.

The history of the subject in the sixteenth and seventeenth centuries indicates, however, that there are radical discontinuities. On this reading the past affirms the possibility (the inevitability?) of change. It demonstrates that subjectivity as liberal humanism defines it is not natural, inevitable or eternal; on the contrary, it is produced and reproduced in and by a specific social order and in the interests of specific power-relations. In addition, it is apparent that discourses fail to control the definitions they propose, to arrest the play of meaning precisely where it threatens their deployment. Women disrupt the discourses designed to contain them; tyranny and resistance to tyranny trouble the case for absolutism. Enjoined to silence, women find unauthorized forms of speech; subjects execute the monarch – and become subjects in another (but not altogether distinct) sense.

Sovereignty, even in liberal humanism, produces resistance as the condition of its meaning, its difference, its visibility.

Subjects, in consequence, exceed the space allotted to them, 'work by themselves' to challenge as well as to confirm the existing order. Because liberal humanism cannot guarantee the unity, the knowledge and the freedom it proclaims as its project, its history since the late seventeenth century is one of struggle. The subject, however defined, addressed, enticed, enlisted, does not finally stay in place. Meaning, the condition of subjectivity, is a location of change.

The future implications of change, its direction and the interests it serves are questions for us to resolve. The pressure to do so is increasingly urgent.

NOTES

1 Frances Yates identified the cosmic meanings of the Globe and attributed them to the influence of the Vitruvian account of ancient Roman theatre (Yates, 1969). John Orrell is unconvinced by the case for Vitruvius, but is willing to see the Globe as a Theatre of the World, adducing the additional evidence that the stage was built to face the midsummer sunrise (Orrell, 1983: 157).

2 For an important alternative reading of this episode, which is not incompatible with mine, see Barker and Hulme, 1985.

3 The Ghost in *Hamlet* may be a borderline case: the audience does not know for certain that Claudius is guilty until the prayer scene (III. iii). But here the enigma stressed by the text is not whether the Ghost's story is accurate, but the moral status of the Ghost's instructions to Hamlet, and this is not, I think, resolved by the play as a whole.

4 For an argument to substantiate in detail this reading of the 'To be or not to be' speech, see Belsey, 1979.

5 See e.g. Emmison, 1970 and Weiner, 1975. Weiner gives no instances at all. Emmison lists 131 cases of murder brought before the Essex county courts in the Elizabethan period. In three of these (or possibly two, if the case of the Great Wakering woman mentioned on p.149 is the same as the one listed on p.150) women were charged with poisoning their husbands. In each case the woman was acquitted, which implies (since acquittals, except in cases of employers murdering their servants, are rare) that the evidence must have been very slender.

6 Surprisingly, there were only two instances of women protesting

that they were similarly frightened of their husbands, and one of these had already been subject to marital violence.

7 The Cromwellian Marriage Act of 1653 placed the whole matter in the hands of the civil magistrates, but gave no indication of the possible grounds for divorce. This legislation was not re-enacted after the Restoration (Powell, 1917:99–100).

8 There is evidence that in certain trades married women were legally treated as if they were single, but this was a matter of local custom (Clark, 1982:151–3).

9 Phyllis riding Aristotle recurs in stories and paintings all over Europe as a type of the unruly woman. The drawing of Judith Phillips bears a considerable resemblance to Hans Baldung Grien's woodcut of Phyllis and Aristotle, though Judith and her victim are fully dressed. See Davis, 1975:135–6 and Plate 11.

10 For a discussion of the disruption of sexual difference in the comedies, see Belsey, 1985.

11 The pamphlets from the period before the Revolution have been reprinted in modern spelling (Shepherd, 1985).

12 The ideological implications of the invocation of an Elizabethan golden age are discussed by Simon Barker, 1984.

BIBLIOGRAPHY

Abbreviations

Alexander William Shakespeare, *The Complete Works*, ed. Peter Alexander, London, Collins, 1951.

Dodsley R. Dodsley, *Old Plays*, ed. W. C. Hazlitt, London, Reeves & Turner, 1874.

EETS Early English Text Society.

Macro *The Macro Plays*, ed. Mark Eccles, EETS 262, London, Oxford University Press, 1969.

MSR Malone Society Reprints.

S and S *English Morality Plays and Moral Interludes*, ed. Edgar T. Schell and J. D. Schuchter, New York, Holt, Rinehart & Winston, 1969.

Editions of plays cited, listed by title

All for Love (1677), John Dryden, ed. David M. Vieth, London, Edward Arnold, 1972.

All's Well that Ends Well (1603–4), William Shakespeare, Alexander.

Antonio's Revenge (c.1600), John Marston, ed. W. Reavley Gair, Manchester, Manchester University Press, 1978.

Antony and Cleopatra (1607–8), William Shakespeare, Alexander.

Apius and Virginia (1567?), R. B., *Tudor Interludes*, ed. Peter Happé, Harmondsworth, Penguin, 1972.

Arden of Faversham (c.1590), ed. M. L. Wine, London, Methuen, 1973.

The Broken Heart (printed 1633), John Ford, ed. T. J. B. Spencer, Manchester, Manchester University Press, 1980.

Bussy d'Ambois (1603–4), George Chapman, *The Plays of George Chapman*, ed. T. M. Parrot, New York, Russell & Russell, 1961, vol.1.

The Cardinal (1641), James Shirley, *Jacobean and Caroline Tragedies*, ed. Robert G. Lawrence, London, Dent, 1975.

The Castle of Perseverance (c.1400–25), Macro.

The Changeling (1624), Thomas Middleton and William Rowley, ed. N. W. Bawcutt, London, Methuen, 1958.

The Conquest of Granada (1670–1), John Dryden, *The Works of John Dryden* vol.11, ed. John Loftis and David Stuart Rhodes, Berkeley, University of California Press, 1978.

Coriolanus (1608?), William Shakespeare, Alexander.

The Disobedient Child (1560s), Thomas Ingelend, Dodsley, vol.2.

Doctor Faustus (1592?), Christopher Marlowe, *The Complete Works*, ed. Fredson Bowers, Cambridge, Cambridge University Press, 1973, vol.2.

The Duchess of Malfi (1613–14), John Webster, ed. John Russell Brown, London, Methuen, 1964.

Enough is as Good as a Feast (c.1560), W. Wager, ed. R. Mark Benbow, London, Edward Arnold, 1968.

Everyman (c.1500), S and S.

The Fatal Friendship (1698), Catherine Trotter, *The Female Wits*, ed. Fidelis Morgan, London, Virago, 1981.

Fulgens and Lucres (c.1500), Henry Medwall, *The Plays of Henry Medwall*, ed. Alan H. Nelson, Cambridge, D. S. Brewer, 1980.

The Glass of Government (1575), George Gascoigne, *The Works of George Gascoigne*, vol.2, ed. J. W. Cunliffe, Cambridge, Cambridge University Press, 1910.

Godly Queen Hester (printed 1561), *Materialien zur Kunde des alteren englischen Dramas*, vol.5, ed. W. W. Greg, Louvain, A. Uystpruyst, 1904.

Hamlet (1601), William Shakespeare, Alexander.

Julius Caesar (1599), William Shakespeare, Alexander.

King Henry V (1599), William Shakespeare, Alexander.

1 King Henry VI (1590–1), William Shakespeare, Alexander.

3 King Henry VI (1590–1), William Shakespeare, Alexander.

King Lear (1605), William Shakespeare, Alexander.

King Richard II (1595–7), William Shakespeare, Alexander.

King Richard III (1591), William Shakespeare, Alexander.

The Life and Death of Doctor Faustus (1697), William Mountfort, London, 1697.

Lingua: or the Combat of the Tongue and the Five Senses for Superiority (1607), Dodsley, vol.9.

Love Triumphant, or Nature Will Prevail (1694), John Dryden, London, 1694.

Lusty Juventus (c.1550), R. Wever, *Four Tudor Interludes*, ed. J. A. B. Somerset, London, Athlone Press, 1974.

Macbeth (1606), William Shakespeare, Alexander.

The Maid's Tragedy (1610–11), Francis Beaumont and John Fletcher, ed. Howard B. Norland, London, Edward Arnold, 1968.

Mankind (1471?), Macro.

The Marriage Between Wit and Wisdom (1579), Francis Merbury?, *English Moral Interludes*, ed. Glynne Wickham, London, Dent, 1976.

The Marriage of Wit and Science (c.1569), ed. Arthur Brown, Oxford, MSR, 1961.

Measure for Measure (1604), William Shakespeare, Alexander.

The Merchant of Venice (1596–8), William Shakespeare, Alexander.

The Miseries of Enforced Marriage (1607), George Wilkins, ed. Glenn H. Blayney, Oxford, MSR, 1964.

Mustapha (1594–1609), Fulke Greville, *Poems and Dramas*, ed. Geoffrey Bullough, Edinburgh, Oliver & Boyd, 1939, vol.2.

Nature (*c.*1490–1500), Henry Medwall, *The Plays of Henry Medwall*, ed. Alan H. Nelson, Cambridge, D. S. Brewer, 1980.

The Nature of the Four Elements (*c.*1520), John Rastell, *Three Rastell Plays*, ed. Richard Axton, Cambridge, D. S. Brewer, 1979.

Nice Wanton (*c.*1550), *English Moral Interludes*, ed. Glynne Wickham, London, Dent, 1976

Othello (1604?), William Shakespeare, Alexander.

Patient Grissil (*c.*1599), Thomas Dekker (with Chettle and Haughton), *The Dramatic Works of Thomas Dekker*, vol. 1, ed. Fredson Bowers, Cambridge, Cambridge University Press, 1953.

Philaster (1609?), Francis Beaumont and John Fletcher, ed. Andrew Gurr, London, Methuen, 1969.

The Play of Patient Grissell (1558–61), John Phillip, ed. R. B. McKerrow and W. W. Greg, Oxford, MSR, 1909.

Respublica (1553), S and S.

The Revenge of Bussy d'Ambois (*c.*1611), George Chapman, *The Plays of George Chapman*, ed. T. M. Parrott, New York, Russell & Russell, 1961, vol.1.

The Revenger's Tragedy (1607), Cyril Tourneur, ed. R. A. Foakes, London, Methuen, 1966.

Romeo and Juliet (1594–6), William Shakespeare, Alexander.

The Second Maiden's Tragedy (1611), ed. Anne Lancashire, Manchester, Manchester University Press, 1978.

Sejanus his Fall (1603), Ben Jonson, *Ben Jonson*, vol.4, ed. C. H. Herford and Percy Simpson, Oxford, Oxford University Press, 1932.

The Siege of Rhodes (1656), William Davenant, London, 1656.

Sir John van Olden Barnevelt (1619), John Fletcher and Philip Massinger?, *A Collection of Old English Plays*, vol.2, ed. A. H. Bullen, London, Wyman & Sons, 1882–5.

The Spanish Tragedy (*c.*1590), Thomas Kyd, ed. Philip Edwards, London, Methuen, 1959.

1 Tamburlaine (1587), Christopher Marlowe, *The Complete*

Works, ed. Fredson Bowers, Cambridge, Cambridge University Press, 1973, vol.1.

The Tempest (1611), William Shakespeare, Alexander.

The Tide Tarrieth No Man (1576), George Wapull, S and S.

'Tis Pity She's a Whore (c.1630?), John Ford, ed. Derek Roper, London, Methuen, 1975.

Titus Andronicus (1590?), William Shakespeare, Alexander.

The Town Fop; or, Sir Timothy Tawdrey (1676), Aphra Behn, *Works*, ed. Montague Summers, New York, Phaeton Press, 1967, vol.3.

The Tragedy of Mariam (1603–4?), Elizabeth Cary, ed. W. W. Greg, Oxford, MSR, 1914.

The Trial of Treasure (1567), Dodsley, vol.3.

Troilus and Cressida, or Truth Found Too Late (1679), John Dryden, London, 1679.

Venice Preserved (1682), Thomas Otway, ed. Malcolm Kelsall, London, Edward Arnold, 1969.

A Warning for Fair Women (c.1590), ed. Charles Dale Cannon, The Hague, Mouton, 1975.

The White Devil (1612), John Webster, ed. John Russell Brown, London, Methuen, 1966.

The Winter's Tale (1611), William Shakespeare, Alexander.

Wisdom (c.1460), Macro.

Wit and Science (early 1530s), John Redford, *Tudor Interludes*, ed. Peter Happé, Harmondsworth, Penguin, 1972.

The Witch of Edmonton (1621), Thomas Dekker (with Ford and Rowley), *The Dramatic Works of Thomas Dekker*, vol.3, ed. Fredson Bowers, Cambridge, Cambridge University Press, 1958.

A Woman Killed with Kindness (1603), Thomas Heywood, ed. R. W. Van Fossen, London, Methuen, 1961.

Women Beware Women (1621?), ed. J. R. Mulryne, London, Methuen, 1975.

The World and the Child (1500–22), S and S.

A Yorkshire Tragedy (1608), ed. Sylvia Feldman, Oxford, MSR, 1973.

Other works cited or consulted

Aarslef, Hans (1982), *From Locke to Saussure: Essays on the Study of Language and Intellectual History*, London, Athlone Press.

Adams, H. H. (1943), *English Domestic or Homiletic Tragedy, 1575–1642*, New York, Columbia University Press.

Althusser, Louis (1969), *For Marx*, tr. Ben Brewster, Harmondsworth, Penguin.

— (1971), *Lenin and Philosophy and Other Essays*, tr. Ben Brewster, London, New Left Books.

Anderson, Alan and Gordon, Raymond (1978), 'Witchcraft and the status of women', *British Journal of Sociology*, 29, 171–84.

Anderson, Perry (1979), *Lineages of the Absolutist State*, London, Verso.

Anger, Jane (1589), *Jane Anger her Protection for Women*, London.

Ariès, Philippe (1973), *Centuries of Childhood*, Harmondsworth, Penguin.

Astell, Mary (1694), *A Serious Proposal to the Ladies for the Advancement of their True and Greatest Interest*, London.

— (1730), *Some Reflections upon Marriage*, Dublin.

Bacon, Francis (1960), *The New Organon*, ed. Fulton H. Anderson, New York, Bobbs-Merrill.

Barker, Francis (1984), *The Tremulous Private Body*, London, Methuen.

— and Hulme, Peter (1985), 'Nymphs and reapers heavily vanish: the discursive con-texts of *The Tempest*', in Drakakis, John (ed.), *Alternative Shakespeares*, London, Methuen.

— *et al.* (eds) (1981), *1642: Literature and Power in the Seventeenth Century*, Colchester, University of Essex.

Barker, Simon (1984) 'Images of the sixteenth and seventeenth centuries as a history of the present', in Francis Barker *et* al. (eds), *Confronting the Crisis: War, Politics and Culture in the Eighties*, Colchester, University of Essex.

Barrett, Michele and McIntosh, Mary (1982), *The Anti-Social Family*, London, Verso.

Becon, Thomas (1542), *The Golden Boke of Christen Matrimonye*, London.

Belsey, Catherine (1979), 'The case of Hamlet's conscience', *Studies in Philology*, 76, 127–48.

— (1985), 'Disrupting sexual difference: meaning and gender in the comedies', in Drakakis, John (ed.), *Alternative Shakespeares*, London, Methuen.

Benjamin, Walter (1977), *The Origins of German Tragic Drama*, tr. John Osborne, London, New Left Books.

Berg, Christine and Berry, Philippa (1981), 'Spiritual whoredom: an essay on female prophets in the seventeenth century', in Barker, Francis *et al.* (eds), *1642: Literature and Power in the Seventeenth Century*, Colchester, University of Essex.

Bevington, David M. (1962), *From 'Mankind' to Marlowe*, Cambridge, Mass., Harvard University Press.

Blayney, Glenn H. (1956), 'Wardship in English drama (1600–1650)', *Studies in Philology*, 53, 470–84.

— (1959), 'Enforcement of marriage in English drama (1600–1650)', *Philological Quarterly*, 38, 459–72.

Bossy, John (1975), 'The social history of confession in the age of the Reformation', *Transactions of the Royal Historical Society*, 5th series, 25, 21–38.

Brathwait, Richard (1641a), *The English Gentleman; and the English Gentlewoman; Both in One Volume Couched*, London.

— (1641b), *The Turtles Triumph*, London.

Bricker, Charles and Tooley, R. V. (1969), *A History of Cartography*, London, Thames & Hudson.

Bryan, W. F. and Dempster, Germaine (1941), *Sources and Analogues of Chaucer's Canterbury Tales*, Chicago, University of Chicago Press.

Bryson, Norman (1983), *Vision and Painting: the Logic of the Gaze*, London, Macmillan.

Bullinger, Henry (1541), *The Christen State of Matrimonye*, tr. Miles Coverdale, London.

Bunny, Edmund (1610), *Of Divorce for Adulterie and Marrying Againe*, Oxford.

Butler, Martin (1984), 'Royal slaves? The Stuart court and the theatres', *Renaissance Drama Newsletter*, Supplement 2, University of Warwick.

Caxton, William (1913), *The Mirror of the World*, ed. Oliver H. Prior, EETS, extra series 110, London, Oxford University Press.

Chaucer, Geoffrey (1957), *Works*, ed. F. N. Robinson, London, Oxford University Press.

Clark, Alice (1982), *Working Life of Women in the Seventeenth Century*, London, Routledge & Kegan Paul.

Cohen, Murray (1977), *Sensible Words, Linguistic Practice in England 1640–1785*, Baltimore and London, Johns Hopkins University Press.

Collier, J. P. (ed.) (1842), *The History of Patient Grisel. Two Early Tracts in Black-letter*, London, Percy Society.

Corrie, G. E. (ed.) (1850), *Certain Sermons Appointed to be Read in Churches*, Cambridge and London, Cambridge University Press and John W. Parker.

Cotton, Nancy (1980), *Women Playwrights in England c.1363–1750*, London and Toronto, Associated University Presses.

Coward, Rosalind (1983), *Patriarchal Precedents*, London, Routledge & Kegan Paul.

— (1984), *Female Desire: Women's Sexuality Today*, London, Granada.

Davies, Kathleen M. (1977), 'The sacred condition of equality: how original were Puritan doctrines of marriage?', *Social History*, 5, 563–80.

Davis, Natalie Zemon (1975), 'Women on top', *Society and Culture in Early Modern France*, London, Duckworth.

Delany, Paul (1969), *British Autobiography in the Seventeenth Century*, London, Routledge & Kegan Paul.

Deloney, Thomas (1912), *Works*, ed. F. O. Mann, Oxford, Oxford University Press.

Descartes, René (1968), *Discourse on Method and the Meditations*, tr. F. E. Sutcliffe, Harmondsworth, Penguin.

Dod, John and Cleaver, Robert (1612), *A Godlie Forme of Householde Government*, London.

Dollimore, Jonathan (1984), *Radical Tragedy: Religion, Ideology and Power in the Drama of Shakespeare and his Contemporaries*, Brighton, Harvester.

Donaldson, Ian (1982), *The Rapes of Lucretia: a Myth and its Transformations*, London, Oxford Unversity Press.

Donzelot, Jacques (1980), *The Policing of Families*, tr. Robert Hurley, London, Hutchinson.

Dove, John (1601), *Of Divorcement*, London.

Dryden, John (1978), *Works*, vol.11, ed. John Loftis and David Stuart Rhodes, Berkeley, University of California Press.

Duby, George (1978), *Medieval Marriage*, Baltimore and London, Johns Hopkins University Press.

Dusinberre, Juliet (1975), *Shakespeare and the Nature of Women*, London, Macmillan.

E., T. (1632), *The Lawes Resolutions of Womens Rights*, London.

Easlea, Brian (1980), *Witch-hunting, Magic and the New Philosophy*, Brighton, Harvester.

Easthope, Antony (1983), *Poetry as Discourse*, London, Methuen.

Ebsworth, J. W. (ed.) (1895), *The Roxburghe Ballads*, vol.8, Hertford, The Ballad Society.

Eisenstein, Elizabeth L. (1979), *The Printing Press as an Agent of Change*, 2 vols, Cambridge, Cambridge University Press.

Ellrodt, Robert (1975), 'Self-consciousness in Montaigne and Shakespeare', *Shakespeare Survey*, 28, 37–50.

Emmison, F. G. (1970), *Elizabethan Life: Disorder*, Chelmsford, Essex County Council.

— (1973), *Elizabethan Life: Morals and the Church Courts*, Chelmsford, Essex County Council.

Engels, Friedrich (1972), *The Origin of the Family, Private Property and the State*, London, Lawrence & Wishart.

Fell, Margaret (1666), *Womens Speaking Justified*, London.

Filmer, Robert (1949), *Patriarcha and Other Political Works of Sir Robert Filmer*, ed. Peter Laslett, Oxford, Blackwell.

Foucault, Michel (1970), *The Order of Things*, London, Tavistock.

— (1978), *I, Pierre Rivière ...*, Harmondsworth, Penguin.

— (1979a), *Discipline and Punish: the Birth of the Prison*, tr. Alan Sheridan, Harmondsworth, Penguin.

— (1979b), *The History of Sexuality*, vol.1, tr. Robert Hurley, London, Allen Lane.

Fraser, Antonia (1984), *The Weaker Vessel: Woman's Lot in Seventeenth-Century England*, London, Weidenfeld & Nicolson.

French, Marilyn (1982), *Shakespeare's Division of Experience*, London, Cape.

Furnivall, F. J. and Pollard, A. W. (eds) (1904), *The Macro Plays*, EETS extra series 91, London, Oxford University Press.

Gardner, Helen (ed.) (1972), *The New Oxford Book of English Verse*, Oxford, Oxford University Press.

George, Margaret (1973), 'From "goodwife" to "mistress"', *Science and Society*, 37, 152–77.

Gildersleeve, Virginia Crocheron (1961), *Government Regulation of the Elizabethan Drama*, New York, Burt Franklin.

Goldberg, Jonathan (1983), *James I and the Politics of Literature*, Baltimore and London, Johns Hopkins University Press.

Golding, Arthur (1573), *A Briefe Discourse of the Murther of G. Saunders*, London.

Goodcole, Henry (1621), *The Wonderfull Discoverie of Elizabeth Sawyer a Witch*, London.

Green, André (1979), *The Tragic Effect*, tr. Alan Sheridan, Cambridge, Cambridge University Press.

Greenblatt, Stephen (1980), *Renaissance Self-Fashioning: from More to Shakespeare*, Chicago, University of Chicago Press.

— (1981), 'Invisible bullets: Renaissance authority and its subversion', *Glyph 8*, Baltimore and London, Johns Hopkins University Press, 40–61.

Griffith, Dudley D. (1931), *The Origin of the Griselda Story*, Seattle, Washington University Press.

Guattari, Felix (1984) *Molecular Revolution*, tr. Rosemary Sheed, Harmondsworth, Penguin.

Gurr, Andrew (1970), *The Shakespearean Stage, 1574–1642*, Cambridge, Cambridge University Press.

Hagstrum, Jean H. (1980), *Sex and Sensibility: Ideal and Erotic Love from Milton to Mozart*, Chicago, University of Chicago Press.

Halkett, John (1970), *Milton and the Idea of Matrimony*, New Haven, Yale University Press.

Haller, William and Malleville (1941–2), 'The Puritan art of love', *Huntington Library Quarterly*, 5, 235–72.

Hallett, Charles A. and Elaine S. (1980), *The Revenger's Madness*, Lincoln, University of Nebraska Press.

Hamilton, Roberta (1978), *The Liberation of Women: a Study of Patriarchy and Capitalism*, London, Allen & Unwin.

Hampton, Christopher (1984), *A Radical Reader: the Struggle for Change in England, 1381–1914*, Harmondsworth, Penguin.

Hattaway, Michael (1982), *Elizabethan Popular Theatre: Plays in Performance*, London, Routledge & Kegan Paul.

Heath, Stephen (1976), 'Narrative space', *Screen* 17, no.3, 68–112.

— (1982), *The Sexual Fix*, London, Macmillan.

Heinemann, Margot (1980), *Puritanism and Theatre*, Cambridge, Cambridge University Press.

Heywood, Thomas (1612), *An Apology for Actors*, London.

Higgins, Patricia (1973), 'The reactions of women, with special reference to women petitioners', in Manning, Brian (ed.), *Politics, Religion and the English Civil War*, London, Edward Arnold, 177–222.

Hill, Christopher (1964), *Society and Puritanism in Pre-Revolutionary England*, London, Secker & Warburg.

— (1975), *The World Turned Upside Down*, Harmondsworth, Penguin.

— (1977), *Milton and the English Revolution*, London, Faber & Faber.

Hirst, Paul and Woolley, Penny (1982), *Social Relations and Human Attributes*, London, Tavistock.

Hobbes, Thomas (1968), *Leviathan*, ed. C. B. Macpherson, Harmondsworth, Penguin.

Hobsbawm, Eric (1965), 'The crisis of the seventeenth century', in Aston, T. (ed.), *Crisis in Europe, 1560–1660*, London, Routledge & Kegan Paul.

Hodgson Phyllis (ed.) (1982), *The Cloud of Unknowing and Related Treatises*, Salzburg, University of Salzburg.

Holdsworth, W. S. (1924), *A History of English Law*, vol. 4, London, Methuen, 17 vols, 1922–72.

Hooker, Richard (1888), *Works*, ed. J. Keble, Oxford, Oxford University Press, 3 vols.

Hopkins, Matthew (1647), *The Discovery of Witches*, London.

Howard, G. E. (1904), *A History of Matrimonial Institutions*, Chicago, University of Chicago Press, 3 vols.

Howell, Wilbur Samuel (1961), *Logic and Rhetoric in England 1500–1700*, New York, Russell & Russell.

Howson, John (1606), *Uxore Dismissa*, Oxford.

Hume, Robert D. (1976), *The Development of English Drama in the Late Seventeenth Century*, Oxford, Oxford University Press.

Hunter, G. K. (1978), *Dramatic Identities and Cultural Tradition*, Liverpool, Liverpool University Press.

James I (1965), *Political Works*, ed. Charles Howard McIlwain, New York, Russell & Russell.

— (1966), *Daemonologie*, Edinburgh, Edinburgh University Press.

Jardine, Lisa (1983), *Still Harping on Daughters: Women and Drama in the Age of Shakespeare*, Brighton, Harvester.

Jordanova, L. J. (1981), 'The history of the family', in

Cambridge Women's Studies Group (ed.), *Women in Society*, London, Virago, 41–54.

Lacan, Jacques (1979), *The Four Fundamental Concepts of Psychoanalysis*, tr. Alan Sheridan, Harmondsworth, Penguin.

— (1982) 'Desire and the interpretation of desire in *Hamlet*', in Felman, Shoshana (ed.), *Literature and Psychoanalysis*, Baltimore and London, Johns Hopkins University Press, 11–52.

Larner, Christina (1981), *Enemies of God*, London, Chatto.

Laslett, Peter (1977), *Family Life and Illicit Love in Earlier Generations*, Cambridge, Cambridge University Press.

Leavis, F. R. (1962), *The Common Pursuit*, Harmondsworth, Penguin.

Lenman, Bruce and Parker, Geoffrey (1980), 'The state, the community and the criminal law in early modern Europe', in Gatrell, V. A. C., Lenman, Bruce and Parker, Geoffrey (eds), *Crime and the Law: the Social History of Crime in Western Europe Since 1500*, London, Europa Publications, 11–48 .

Levine, David (1977), *Family Formation in an Age of Nascent Capitalism*, New York, Academic Press.

Lewis, C. S. (1936), *The Allegory of Love*, Oxford, Oxford University Press.

Little, David (1970), *Religion, Order and Law: a Study in Pre-Revolutionary England*, Oxford, Blackwell.

Lloyd, Charles (1825), *Formularies of Faith*, Oxford, Oxford University Press.

Locke, John (1967), *Two Treatises of Government*, ed. Peter Laslett, Cambridge, Cambridge University Press.

— (1975), *An Essay Concerning Human Understanding*, ed. Peter H. Nidditch, Oxford, Oxford University Press.

Lockyer, Roger (ed.) (1959), *The Trial of Charles I*, London, Folio Society.

Macfarlane, Alan (1978), *The Origins of English Individualism*, Oxford, Blackwell.

McGregor, O. R. (1957), *Divorce in England*, London, Heinemann.

Maclean, Ian (1980), *The Renaissance Notion of Woman*, Cambridge, Cambridge University Press.

Makin, Bathsua, (1673), *An Essay to Revive the Antient Education of Gentlewomen*, London.

Manning, Brian (1978), *The English People and the English Revolution*, Harmondsworth, Penguin.

Marshburn, Joseph H. (1949), ' "A Cruell Murder Donne in Kent" and its literary manifestations', *Studies in Philology*, 46, 131–40.

Marvell, Andrew (1972), *The Complete Poems*, ed. Elizabeth Story Donno, Harmondsworth, Penguin.

Maus, Katharine Eisamen (1982), 'Arcadia lost: politics and revision in the Restoration *Tempest*', *Renaissance Drama*, 13, 189–209.

Milton, John (1959), *The Complete Prose Works*, vol.2, ed. Ernest Sirluck, London, Oxford University Press.

— (1962), *The Complete Prose Works*, vol.3, ed. Merritt Y. Hughes, New Haven and London, Yale University Press.

— (1968), *Poems*, ed. John Carey and Alastair Fowler, London, Longman.

Moretti, Franco (1983), *Signs Taken for Wonders: Essays in the Sociology of Literary Forms*, London, Verso.

Muir, Kenneth (ed.) (1962), *Macbeth*, London, Methuen.

Mullaney, Steven (1980), 'Lying like truth: riddle, representation and treason in Renaissance England', *English Literary History*, 47, 32–47.

Munda, Constantia (1617), *The Worming of a Mad Dogge*, London.

Orgel, Stephen (1975), *The Illusion of Power: Political Theater in the English Renaissance*, London, University of California Press.

— and Strong, Roy, (1973), *Inigo Jones: the Theatre of the Stuart Court*, London, Sotheby Parke Bernet, 2 vols.

Orrell, John (1983), *The Quest for Shakespeare's Globe*, Cambridge, Cambridge University Press.

Pêcheux, Michel (1982), *Language, Semantics and Ideology: Stating the Obvious*, tr. Hans Nagpal, London, Macmillan.

Perkins, William (1618), *Christian Oeconomie*, tr. Thomas Pickering, *Works*, vol.3, Cambridge.

Pevsner, Nikolaus (1962), *North-East Norfolk and Norwich (The Buildings of England)*, Harmondsworth, Penguin.

Potter, Lois (1980), 'The plays and the playwrights', in Sanders, Norman *et al.* (eds), *The Revels History of Drama in English*, vol.2, 1500–76, London, Methuen.

Potts, Thomas (1613), *The Wonderfull Discoverie of Witches in the Countie of Lancaster*, London.

Powell, C. L. (1917), *English Domestic Relations 1487–1653*, New York, Columbia University Press.

Power, Eileen (1975), *Medieval Women*, Cambridge, Cambridge University Press.

Prall, Stuart E. (1966), *The Agitation for Law Reform During the Puritan Revolution*, The Hague, Martinus Nijhoff.

Rainolds, John (1609), *A Defence of the Judgment of the Reformed Churches*, London.

Reiss, Timothy J. (1982), *The Discourse of Modernism*, Ithaca and London, Cornell University Press.

Roberts, Alexander (1616), *A Treatise of Witchcraft*, London.

Rogers, Daniel (1642), *Matrimoniall Honour*, London.

Rollins, Hyder E. (ed.) (1920), *Old English Ballads 1553–1625*, Cambridge, Cambridge University Press.

— (1922), *A Pepysian Garland*, Cambridge, Cambridge University Press.

Rosen, Barbara (ed.) (1969), *Witchcraft*, London, Edward Arnold.

Rudwin, Maximilian (1931), *The Devil in Legend and Literature*, Chicago, Open Court.

Ryan, Michael (1982), *Marxism and Deconstruction: A Critical Articulation*, Baltimore and London, Johns Hopkins University Press.

Sarsby, Jacqueline (1983), *Romantic Love and Society*, Harmondsworth, Penguin.

Schochet, Gordon J. (1969), 'Patriarchalism, politics and mass attitudes in Stuart England', *Historical Journal*, 12, 413–41.

— (1975), *Patriarchalism in Political Thought*, Oxford, Blackwell.

Scot, Reginald (1930), *The Discoverie of Witchcraft*, ed. Montague Summers, London, John Rodker.

Sheehan, Michael M. (1971), 'The formation and stability of marriage in fourteenth-century England: evidence of an Ely register', *Medieval Studies*, 33, 228–63.

Shepherd, Simon (1981), *Amazons and Warrior Women: Varieties of Feminism in Seventeenth-Century Drama*, Brighton, Harvester.

— (ed.) (1985), *The Women's Sharpe Revenge*, London, Fourth Estate.

Sidney, Philip (1962), *Poems*, ed. W. A. Ringler, Oxford, Oxford University Press.

Sinfield, Alan (1983), *Literature in Protestant England, 1560–1660*, London, Croom Helm.

— (in press), 'Power and ideology: an outline theory and Sidney's *Arcadia*', *English Literary History*.

Skinner, Quentin (1978), *The Foundations of Modern Political Thought*, Cambridge, Cambridge University Press, 2 vols.

Smith, C. F., (1979), 'Jane Lead: mysticism and the woman cloathed with the sun', in Gilbert, Sandra M. and Gubar, Susan (eds), *Shakespeare's Sisters: Feminist Essays on Women Poets*, Bloomington, Indiana University Press, 3–18.

Smith, Henry (1591), *A Preparative to Marriage*, London.

Southern, Richard (1957), *The Medieval Theatre in the Round*, London, Faber & Faber.

— (1976), 'Theatres and scenery', in Loftis, John *et al.* (ed.), *The Revels History of Drama in English*, vol.5, 1660–1750, London, Methuen.

Sowernam, Esther (1617), *Esther Hath Hang'd Haman*, London.

Spargo, J. W. (1944), *Juridical Folklore in England Illustrated by the Cucking-Stool*, Durham, North Carolina, Duke University Press.

Speght, Rachel (1617), *A Mouzell for Melastomus*, London.

Spencer, Christopher (ed.) (1965), *Five Restoration Adaptations of Shakespeare*, Urbana, University of Illinois Press.

Spender, Dale (1980), *Man Made Language*, London, Routledge & Kegan Paul.

Spenser, Edmund (1980), *The Faerie Queene*, ed. A. C. Hamilton, London, Longman.

Spivack, Bernard (1958), *Shakespeare and the Allegory of Evil*, New York, Columbia University Press.

Stearne, John (1648), *A Confirmation and Discovery of Witch Craft*, London.

Stockwood, John (1589), *A Bartholmew Fairing for Parentes*, London.

Stone, Lawrence (1972), *The Causes of the English Revolution 1592–1642*, London, Routledge & Kegan Paul.

— (1979), *The Family, Sex and Marriage in England, 1500–1800*, Harmondsworth, Penguin.

Stroup, Thomas Bradley (1965), *Microcosmos: the Shape of the Elizabethan Play*, Lexington, University of Kentucky Press.

Swetnam, Joseph (1615), *The Arraignment of Lewde, Idle, Froward and Unconstant Women*, London.

Tattlewell, Mary and Hit-Him-Home, Joane (1640), *The Womens Sharpe Revenge*, London.

Taylor, John (1630), 'The unnaturall father', *Works*, London.

Thomas, Keith (1958) 'Women and the civil war sects', *Past and Present*, 13, 42–62.

— (1959), 'The double standard', *Journal of the History of Ideas*, 20, 195–216.

— (1973), *Religion and the Decline of Magic*, Harmondsworth, Penguin.

Tyndale, William (1528), *The Obedience of a Christen Man*, Marlborow, Hesse.

Ullman, Walter (1967), *The Individual and Society in the Middle Ages*, London, Methuen.

Walzer, Michael (1965), *The Revolution of the Saints*, Cambridge, Mass., Harvard University Press.

Warner, Marina (1983), *Joan of Arc, the Image of Female Heroism*, Harmondsworth, Penguin.

Weimann, Robert (1978), *Shakespeare and the Popular Tradition in the Theater*, Baltimore, Johns Hopkins University Press.

Weiner, C. S. (1975), 'Sex roles and crimes in late Elizabethan Hertfordshire', *Journal of Social History*, 8, 38–60.

Westman, B. H. (1974), 'The peasant family and crime in fourteenth-century England', *Journal of British Studies*, 13, 1–18.

Weston, C. C. and Greenberg, J. R. (1981), *Subjects and Sovereigns: the Grand Controversy over Legal Sovereignty in Stuart England*, Cambridge, Cambridge University Press.

White, R. S. (1982), *Innocent Victims: Poetic Injustice in Shakespearean Tragedy*, Newcastle upon Tyne, Tyneside Free Press.

Wickham, Glynne (1959), *Early English Stages, 1300–1660*, vol.1, 1300–1576, London, Routledge & Kegan Paul.

— (1963), *Early English Stages, 1300–1660*, vol.2 (i), 1576–1660, London, Routledge & Kegan Paul.

— (1972), *Early English Stages, 1300–1660*, vol.2 (ii), 1576–1660, London, Routledge & Kegan Paul.

Williams, Raymond (1981), *Culture*, London, Fontana.

Wilson, Thomas (1551), *The Rule of Reason*, London.

Wright, Louis B. (1935), *Middle-Class Culture in Elizabethan England*, Ithaca, Cornell University Press.

Yates, Frances A. (1969), *Theatre of the World*, London, Routledge & Kegan Paul.

— (1975), *Astraea, the Imperial Theme in the Sixteenth Century*, London, Routledge & Kegan Paul.

INDEX

Plays are listed by their titles and other texts normally by their authors or editors.

difference 6, 58, 223;
discontinuity of 4, 83; and
fiction 5, 6, 10; learned 5;
and liberal humanism 34,
52–3; of marriage 138–48,
214; play of 223; plurality of
5, 6, 28–33, 53, 184; in
process 6, 224; and salvation
60–4; subject as origin of 42;
and truth 56, 72–3;
uncertainty of 29–33
Measure for Measure 100, 170
Merchant of Venice, The 195–6
Miege, Guy 158–9
Mill, John Stuart 8
Milton, John 34–5, 119; on
marriage and divorce 140–3,
146, 210
*Miseries of Enforced Marriage,
The* 202–3, 220
morality plays 15, 16, 26, 32,
36–9, 43, 47–8, 58, 62, 88,
91, 162, 164
Moretti, Franco 100
motherhood 199, 219
Muir, Kenneth 26
Munda, Constantia 219
Munday, Antony 136
Mustapha 106–9

Nature 17
Nature of the Four Elements, The
63, 66–7, 69
New Right 8
Nice Wanton 70

Olivier, Laurence 223
Orgel, Stephen 24, 25, 26
Orrell, John 28, 225
Othello 48–9, 123, 162

Page, Mistress 136
Page of Plymouth 137–8
Parker, Henry 118
patience 95, 113–14, 116, 140,
163, 175–6, 183, 212, 213;
patient Griselda 165–71,
174, 176, 177, 178, 191,
203, 214, 218
Patient Grissil 168
patriarchalism 99–100, 143–4,
155, 156, 158, 193, 217–18
patriarchy 164–5, 167, 171,
179, 184, 185, 187, 191,
199, 201; defiance of 134;
and femininity 186; and
liberalism 193, 200, 214,
221; and monarchy 144; *see
also* absolutism, love
Paul, St 32, 59, 65, 72, 168,
178
Pepys, Samuel 81
Perkins, William 110, 143, 145,
146, 201
Petition of Right 182
Petrarch 166, 207
Philaster 89–90
Phillips, Judith 186, 226
Pinter, Harold 52
Plato 64
Plautus 201
Play of Patient Grissell, The 167–
9
*Pleasant and Sweet History of
Patient Grissell, The* 167
Pollard, A. W. 19
Potter, Lois 30
Potts, Thomas 186, 187
Powell, C. L. 139, 226
Poynant, John 139